Perspectives On America
Volume 1

Readings in United States History to 1877

Edited by
John A. Trickel
Richland College

AMERICAN HERITAGE ■ CUSTOM PUBLISHING
A Division of Forbes Inc.
60 Fifth Avenue
New York, New York 10011

D1361610

This Thing Called History by Linda Clark Goodrich. Reprinted by permission.

"The Jamestown Fiasco" is from *American Slavery, American Freedom: The Ordeal of Colonial Virginia* by Edmund S. Morgan. Copyright © 1975 by W. W. Norton & Company, Inc. Reprinted by permission of W. W. Norton & Company, Inc.

Pentecost in the Backwoods by Bernard A. Weisberger, Copyright © 1959 Bernard A. Weisberger.

"The Nature of Southern Separatism" from *The Impending Crisis* by David M. Potter. Completed and edited by Don E. Fehrenbacher. Copyright © 1976 by the Estate of David M. Potter. Reprinted by permission of HarperCollins Publishers, Inc.

Copyright © 1997 by John A. Trickel.

Reprinted 1998.

CIP Data is available.
Printed in the United States of America
10 9 8 7 6 5 4 3 2

ISBN 0-8281-0996-6

CONTENTS

ACKNOWLEDGMENTS

Like all projects, this finished work is the product of many people. I want to thank Marianne Dombroski, Acquisitions Editor, and Christopher Cimino, National Sales Director, for their many helpful suggestions. To Heather Hurabiell goes sincere gratitude for following up on those myriad details that all such projects require. I want to thank my students for their feedback and suggestions as to what articles they found interesting and useful. No acknowledgement would be complete without mentioning the love of my family—so to Rita, Erik and Brooke, my love and gratitude to you.

John A. Trickel
Richland College

NOTES FROM THE EDITOR

The formulation of any book of historical readings is fraught with traps. Are the articles scholarly and accurate? Can students read, understand and enjoy the material? How can the articles be best organized? What are the best sources for finding appropriate entries? In the following pages, the editor made conscious decisions to provide the reader with a wide variety of historical perspectives. The interests of historians is so varied and broad that to limit offerings to diplomatic, political, social or military approaches would be deceiving. Thus, what has been brought together is an eclectic collection sampling many of the interests of modern writers. The book contains traditional political and biographical entries, as well as, economic, social, environmental and military topics. The hope is that each provide an interesting insight to the reader.

The sources for such writings are numerous. Books, monographs, and historical journals are a few of the most common. For this collection, the editor relied heavily on the many distinguished authors who have contributed to *American Heritage Magazine*, supplemented with chapters from two outstanding recent books. In all cases an attempt was made to balance scholarship, clarity of writing, and general interest. If the reader is able to find enjoyment and an occasional surprise, much of the intent of this work will be achieved.

For those of you using this book as part of a history class, the following comments might help. The editor hoped to stimulate your imagination and interest, so begin by just reading and enjoying the flow of the narrative. When you have finished, try to formulate a general statement that sums up the main focus of the article. Create a short list of the major lines of development of the article. Once these tasks are completed the reader can better appreciate the intentions and insights the writer offers.

Enjoy the book!

John A. Trickel, Ed.D.
Professor of History
Richland College

THIS THING CALLED HISTORY?

Linda C. Goodrich

Although almost everyone has had history classes, frequently it is confused with chronology or genealogy. Linda C. Goodrich gives her perspective on the discipline of history and why it is important to understand its nature and lessons.

There is a line in a popular song from many years ago that said: "Love, like youth, is wasted on the young." Obviously this was said by someone older, perhaps someone longing for the vitality of youth and yet mindful of how heedless youth often is of the complexities of our world. The study of history is hardly something that is (or should be) the sole province of those older, but history instructors often remark on how differently older students approach the study of history when compared to their youthful counteparts. Why might this be so?

After many years of reflection on this, I have probably given as many answers as I have gone through stages of my own life. One could rightly conclude that such answers vary with one's experiences, whether born of age, friends, upbringing, education or any of the multitude of other aspects of our experience. Generalization is difficult. But some tentative threads emerge from my own thoughts about it.

History is, when all is said and done, an art. This will strike many as odd, especially if they are accustomed to thinking of history as simply "the past." Years of drill on dates, battles and kings may have so numbed them to the point that history seems a long litany of undisputed facts. Alas, there are no twelve-step programs to help those who have been so victimized, no systematic means by which to bring them to the richness of viewing the lives of the millions who went before us and whose toil, whose bravery, and whose vision constructed that thinveneeroforderthatwecallcivilization.

To be fair to those who labored long to bring an understanding of history to each new generation, let us agree that one cannot think historically without accurate data, accurate at least to the degree that we can establish such. Newspapers are replete with stories about the appalling ignorance of many of our citizens regarding our shared past, stories which show students unable to identify the century in which, for instance, the Civil War occurred. If we are to think about our common social existence with any degree of sophisitication, we must be well-grounded in at least the fundamentals of that existence. Yet, even if we grant that there is much more to history than simply facts, what is there about history that might justify terming it an art?

Consider the situation faced by historians of two very different periods, ancient history and contemporary times. In the case of the former, there are so few records that remain with which to construct a history of those times. Ancient historians must go far beyond the scant number of texts that are available and utilize the findings of archaeologists, linguists, physical and cultural anthropologists, literary scholars, and a host of others in order to come to a fuller understanding of their subjects. Arriving at a nuanced understanding of ancient life, of its glories, its challenges or its legacy, requires careful speculative investigation of available sources. If the shield of Heracles spoken of in Homer's Iliad refers to the growing of grain, can we assume that settled agricultural communities were common? Ancient historians must mine carefully and fully the resources available, asking critical and skeptical questions of each source as they go. If their work is done well, the result is artful indeed.

Historians of contemporary times (the twentieth century) face a very different situation. Lack of information is hardly a concern for most, as mountains of records confront them. The question then is not what can be found but what is to be included? Regardless of how much a historian attempts to be objective in presenting what happened, his or her personal beliefs and values will inevitably color the choice of subject, the evidence selected, the way the information is presented, and, of course, the conclusions drawn from the episode studied.

Some critics of history point to the bias of historians and thus discount the entire endeavor. Is history, as Napoleon charged, a fable agreed upon? In some sense, yes. A generation ago, Frances Fitzgerald's work, America Revised, looked at the high school history texts that were used from the turn of the century until that time. What emerged were very different pictures of our country, at one time emphasizing the clash of ideas and values and at another stressing the essential continuity of our past. One might reasonably ask if the same country was being studied by all these texts. But there is an important idea here: by and large, the same fundamentals were available to the many historians studied, yet the conclusions these historians drew were very different. Why is this important? Let me attempt to answer that by pointing briefly to the experiences of those who lived through one of the tragic experiments of humankind, twentieth century communism. In The Book of Laughter and Forgetting, Milan Kundera says the following:

"The first step in liquidating a people is to erase its memory. Destroy its books, its culture, its history, then have somebody write new books, manufacture a new culture, invent a new history. Before long the nation will begin to forget what it is and what it was. The world around it will forget even faster."

We would expect tyrants to seek physical control and domination, but why would they bother with something as seemingly inconsequential as history? One answer was given by Stephen Spender who saw in history the means by which the living memories of the past were carried forward into the future. What we have been, what are our common stories and understandings, how we see ourselves—this is the stuff of history. We study the past to know the present. Two millenia ago, Cicero said that to be ignorant of history is to be forever a child. If you will think but a minute on that, the truth of it will become obvious. The children you know look upon the world before them as a "given," and they understandably assume that it has probably always been as they see it now. They have no sense of the living web of cause and effect that is our world. They cannot know of the struggles of people, great or common, to build something of permanence for us to use and enjoy. They must age before they can understand the words of Newton who humbly acknowledged: "If I have seen further than others it is by standing on the shoulders of giants." The study of history is your opportunity to stand on the shoulders of giants, to pay homage to the many who labored before you to improve the world they found. Among them are saints and sinners, seers and scoundrels. It is a rich tapestry of human life in which the continuing questions that beset all times are answered in sometimes unique and engaging ways by those who went before. In *The Tempest* Shakespeare said, "We are such stuff as dreams are made on, and our little life is rounded with a sleep." We are also such stuff as history is made on, and those who find life about them interesting understand its richness better by learning how it came to be.

EVERYTHING YOU NEED TO KNOW ABOUT COLUMBUS

Gloria Deák

*The controversy and fascination over the extraordinary voyages of Christopher Colum-
bus have again peaked as the five hundredth anniversary passed of that epic first voyage. In the following article Gloria Deák assesses the questions surrounding that
momentous effort. The after shocks of which would forever change the flora and fauna
of the "new world."*

Did Columbus discover the New World?

No. But how pleased he would have been to learn that he is often credited with discovering
two vast, far-flung continents whose size and variety he could scarcely have begun to imagine.
Those continents had been populated for millennia by a mix of peoples whose cultures were
as diverse as their lands. They may have migrated from northeastern Asia more than fifteen
thousand years ago. When they came is still a matter of warring scholarship, but those natives
were the discoverers of the New World.

Columbus met only a small number of them after he had successfully navigated the
Ocean Sea, as the Atlantic was then known. His disclosure of their existence baffled Renaissance Europe but eventually led to knowledge of an entire new hemisphere. The Genoese
mariner made the announcement of his triumphant crossing in a letter addressed to his Spanish patrons, King Ferdinand and Queen Isabella. He declared that he had "found very many
islands filled with people without number, and of them all I have taken possession for their
Highnesses, by proclamation and with the royal standard displayed, and nobody objected."
This arrogant usurpation was wholly in line with Europe's determination to expand its ordained and Christian world.

There are claims that other explorers crossed the Ocean Sea long before Columbus. St.
Brendan and the Irish are credited with the earliest voyages, dating from the opening phase of
the Middle Ages in the seventh century. The Vikings touched base in the far northern lands
during the eleventh century, as did Bristol seamen four centuries later. But it was not until
Columbus's extraordinary feat of navigation in 1492 that the presence of a New World was revealed to the wonderment of the Old.

Of course, the term *New World* is thoroughly Eurocentric. But it's convenient, it's here to
stay, and we shall use it.

What exactly did he do in 1492?

He sailed west from the Canary Islands following an ocean route he had mapped and survived a thirty-three-day trip to make landfall in a new world on October 12.

For years people had scoffed at the idea of a westward route to the Indies. The success of
Columbus's trip was due as much to his passionate belief in what he was doing as to his enlightened decision to sail west-southwest from the Canary Islands along the twenty-eighth
parallel, thus avoiding the treacherous counter winds of higher latitudes. Had he invoked the
words of the great Italian poet as he embarked? Dante had written in *The Divine Comedy,*
"And turning our stern towards the morning we made wings of our oars for our wild flight,
bearing always to the south-west." It is doubtful that Columbus's ships would have survived a
more northerly crossing.

Was Columbus the first to believe the earth was round?

Not at all. Every educated man in his day believed it was a sphere, and every European
university taught the concept in geography classes. There were, of course, some who clung to
the ancient biblical notions that the earth was a flat disk with Jerusalem in the center and that
one could fall off the edge. But seamen like Columbus knew better from practical experience:
They saw that mountains appeared on the horizon before the land came into view and that
the hulls of departing ships disappeared before the masts.

The controversial issue in Columbus's day was not the earth's shape but its size. This had
enormous implications for the explorer's ambitious plans. Geographers projected widely diver-
gent calculations, but they shared a common belief that the earth was much smaller than it is,
some gauging it at two-thirds of its actual circumference. In the third century B.C. Eratosthenes
had come quite close to an accurate guess at the world's true belt size of twenty-four thousand
miles. Among those who inspired Columbus were Marinus of Tyre and Ptolemy, both of the second century A.D., and Pierre d'Ailly and Paolo dal Pozzo Toscanelli, geographers of his own century. Columbus shared with the last two a firm belief that the Ocean Sea was navigable.

Toscanelli's concepts were particularly appealing because the Florentine not only had put
forward low figures for the width of the ocean on a world chart but, as early as 1474, had
urged the Portuguese king to consider a voyage westward to Cathay (China). When Columbus subsequently used Toscanelli's chart to substantiate his claim that he could cross the
Ocean Sea, he further reduced its low mileage estimates.

Where did he think he was going?

He hoped to reach the Indies. That was the geographic term then in use for the eastern
stretches of Asia, which included the fabled land of Cathay, the island of Cipangu (Japan),
Burma, India, Indonesia, and the Moluccas.

A route to the Indies had for some time been the goal of Portuguese princes who
sought a nautical path to trade in Oriental silks and spices. Convinced the way lay eastward
via the southern coast of Africa, they staunchly backed the repeated attempts of their navi-
gators to find it. Columbus was aware of these forays but stubbornly held to his view that
the most direct route to the Indies lay not eastward but westward, by the Ocean Sea. He expected he might pass some islands along the way, but he had no idea he would come upon
new continents.

What were his ships like?

Columbus sailed with a diminutive fleet of three-masted vessels: the *Niña*, the *Pinta*, and
the *Santa María*. The *Niña* and the *Pinta*, classed as caravels, measured at about sixty tons

each—that is, they could carry sixty Spanish tuns, a liquid measure, of wine. Lightly constructed, caravels were known for their speed. The *Santa María* was classed as a *nao* (a Spanish word for ship) and estimated at about ninety tons. This somewhat larger vessel was round and chunky, less graceful-looking than the caravels, and definitely less maneuverable.

Columbus was proud of his ships, as well he might be, since all three made it on a blind journey to a phantom destination. Still, he did have his troubles with them. On the third day out, the rudder of the *Pinta* jumped. He wrote in his diary that it was repaired off the Canary Islands "with great labor and diligence of the Admiral." There, too, the *Niña,* which was lateen-rigged (outfitted with triangular sails hung at a forty-five- to sixty-degree angle to the deck), had to be fitted with square sails on yards parallel to the deck. Lateens could sail closer to the wind, but square-rigged vessels were easier to maneuver.

The *Santa María* was Columbus's flagship, but the *Niña* became his favorite (*Niña* was a nickname; the craft's true name was the *Santa Clara*). The *Santa María* ran aground in the New World, and Columbus came home aboard the *Niña.* Measured against today's transoceanic vessels, Renaissance ships were pitifully small. Their average length of seventy to one hundred feet would be dwarfed by the nearly one thousand sleek feet of the *Queen Elizabeth 2.*

If people were already living there, why did they call it the New World?

The phrase *Mundus Novus* (New World) was coined by a Venetian printer in 1504. He lit on it as a title for a letter written by the Florentine explorer Amerigo Vespucci following the latter's return from newly discovered Brazil. The phrase caught on. The revelation of an entirely unknown and inhabited world, credited to Vespucci, was far more sensational than Columbus's report of a few islands and a new route to the Indies.

Moreover, Vespucci's description of the New World, laden as it was with vivid accounts of cannibalism and sexual promiscuity among the natives, assured his account instant popularity. Columbus himself never used the phrase *New World.* His own characterization of the lands he discovered was *Other World,* a term perhaps more appropriate.

That other world was, of course, not new, but to this day we tend to date the history of the Americas in terms of the five centuries since Columbus's landing there—the relatively brief span since European intervention. Shakespeare comes to the point in *The Tempest* when he has Miranda exclaim, "O brave new world,/That has such people in 't!" and Prospero replies, "'Tis new to thee."

Where did Columbus think he was when he made his landfall?

He had no real idea. He imagined that he had reached the Indies, and he promptly spoke of the natives he encountered as Indians. But nothing he saw in the Caribbean coincided with descriptions of the East. Instead of sophisticated Orientals dressed in sumptuous brocaded coats, he found naked inhabitants who seemed gentle and naive. Instead of the glittering city with golden-roofed temples that Marco Polo had recounted, there were simple huts. It was all rather baffling. Columbus pressed on from island to island, and when he reached Cuba, which he named La Isla Juana, he followed its coast west. "I found it to be so long," he wrote, "that I thought it must be the mainland, the province of Catayo [in China]. And since there were neither towns nor cities on the coast, but only small villages, with the people of which I could not have speech because they all fled forthwith, I went forward on the same course, thinking that I should not fail to find great cities and towns."

Although no glittering citadels appeared on the horizon, the explorer and his sailors were quick to notice that the natives wore small gold pendants as nose ornaments, and Columbus took this as a sign that the Bahamian island on which he had first landed, which he called San Salvador, would perhaps turn out to be a steppingstone to Cathay.

His subsequent discovery of gold on the large island he named Hispaniola convinced him and his men that they had indeed landed in the outer reaches of the Indies, and this was what he believed when he commenced his return voyage to Spain on January 4, 1493.

How did he come up with the idea in the first place?

Nobody knows. But one thing is certain: It was not an original idea. A westward route had been suggested as far back as Aristotle. Columbus's interest in finding such a route may have arisen around 1476, when he was shipwrecked off the coast of Portugal and took up residence in Lisbon. At that time Portugal stood proudly at the head of European navigation. Columbus was then twenty-five years old. Intensely religious, he found his geographic convictions strengthened by passages from the Bible and from such predictions as one in Seneca's *Medea:* "An age will come after many years when the Ocean will loose the chains of things, and a great part of the earth will be opened up and a new sailor such as the one who was Jason's guide . . . will reveal a new world." Columbus longed to be that sailor.

Did it take Columbus long to get backing?

Years. He first presented the petition for his "Enterprise of the Indies," as he called it, to King John II of Portugal in 1484 or a bit earlier. It was turned over to a commission of experts just as it would be today. They rejected it.

When Columbus turned to King Ferdinand and Queen Isabella of Spain for support in 1486, his proposal was submitted to an assemblage of Spanish scholars and ecclesiastics known as the Talavera Commission. Again a rejection. The commission ruled that the distance was far greater than Columbus claimed, and the enterprise therefore not feasible. They were right on the first count, wrong on the second. Over the years Columbus persisted. Finally, through the intervention of Luis de Santangel, the keeper of the privy purse, who had befriended him at the Spanish court, he obtained Queen Isabella's permission in the spring of 1492. "By these presents," announced the royal decree, "we dispatch the noble man Christoforus Colon with three equipped caravels over the Ocean Seas toward the regions of India for certain reasons and purposes."

How can so many nations claim Columbus as one of their own?

Rival claims follow in the wake of any heroic accomplishment. Columbus was born in Genoa of Italian parents in 1451, and it has been insisted that he was a full-blooded Spaniard, a Catalan, or a Jew of Portuguese or Catalan descent, but the evidence suggests that he was a Catholic of Genoese origin. Whatever his background, he basked in that wondrous confluence of Arab, Jewish, and Christian genius that marked the intellectual world of Portugal and Spain during the early Renaissance. The undisputed facts are that his father was Domenico Colombo, and his mother was Susanna Fontanarossa, both of Genoa. They had two younger sons, Bartolomeo and Giacomo (later known as Diego), and a daughter, Bianchinetta. The family business was weaving. Domenico managed a decent living as a member of the clothiers' guild, but his prospects for improvement were never very bright.

Columbus left Genoa as a young and illiterate sailor. After living in Portugal and then Spain and acquiring their languages, he taught himself to read and write. He also taught himself Latin, the medium of communication of educated men; many of the books on which he relied for his navigational theories were in Latin.

In his writings Columbus more than once described himself as *un estranjero*. Indeed, the Spanish officers and sailors who were eventually to serve under him often resented the fact that he was a "foreigner." Although the population of fifteenth-century Spain was of a distinctly cosmopolitan mix, a fierce wave of nationalism was on the rise by the time Columbus settled there. The same year he sailed, Spain conquered the last of the Moors and ordered the expulsion of all unconverted Jews.

How did Columbus find his way?

A compass, dead reckoning, and luck. Latitude and longitude existed as concepts, but both were shrouded in guesswork. Latitude was reckoned by Ptolemaic *climata*—parallel zones arbitrarily laid down on a chart in terms of climate and, where practical, by the length of the longest day of the year, found to be directly proportional to the angular height of the sun. Longitude was arrived at through a complicated procedure by timing an eclipse. Like most mariners, Columbus couldn't manage it.

His indispensable instrument was a mariner's compass. A combination of the ancient "rose of the winds" and a magnetized needle, the compass had been in use long before Columbus sailed. Known by the Chinese, Arabs, and Phoenicians, it had been rediscovered by the Europeans in the fourteenth century. In Columbus's day the rose was a circular card on which a pattern of diamonds, lozenges, and lines marked the thirty-two compass points. No letters were used because most seamen could not read. Twelve winds were known to the ancients, but by Columbus's time the number had been reduced to eight; we indicate them today as N, NE, E, SE, S, SW, W, NW.

Perhaps most important, Columbus was a master at dead reckoning, a half-instinctual process that involved laying down compass courses, noting speed through the water, charting direction and strength of winds, being aware of currents, and constantly picking up where you had left off.

His double crossing over the "sea of darkness" is a near miracle of dead reckoning.

What qualifications did he bring to the job?

He had sailed in the Mediterranean and had been to Africa, England, Ireland, and allegedly as far north as Iceland. Having grown up in the maritime community of Genoa, he had begun seafaring when he was fourteen years old. At least that's what he says in his chronicles, though neither the records nor his claims are completely reliable. He also tells us in his log for December 21, 1492, that by then he had been at sea for twenty-three years "without leaving it for any time worth telling."

We have very little data on what kinds of ships he sailed on, in what capacities, or under whose banners. In any event, Genoese mariners were among the most renowned of the Middle Ages. It was the Genoese marine that the pope called upon during the First Crusade, in the eleventh century, to conduct a massive fleet from the southern ports of France to the eastern shores of the Mediterranean. During the following centuries, as the Mediterranean bustled with commerce and political intrigue, the republic of Genoa rose in power along with the republic of Venice. By the end of the thirteenth century the Genoese were attempting to find a water route to the Indies by way of Africa and in the process sailed far out into the Ocean Sea—or, as it was also known, the "green sea of gloom."

Did he have any real idea of the risks he was running?

He certainly did. But he was deeply devout, charged with a messianic zeal, and determined to take risks. Shipwrecks, drownings, mutinies, scurvy, gales, starvation—all were part of every sailor's job at the time. The Renaissance poet Luis de Camoëns detailed the seamen's working environment:

To tell thee all the dangers of the Deep
(Which humane Judgment cannot comprehend)
Suddain and fearfull storms, the Ayre that sweep;
Lightnings, that with the Ayre the Fire doe blend;
Black Hurracans; thick Nights; Thunders, that keep
The World alarm'd, and threaten the Last end:
Would be too tedious, indeed vain and mad,
Though a brasse Tongue, and Iron lungs I had.

Nevertheless, Columbus believed that the mariner must, as he put it, probe "the secrets of this world."

Seneca had prophesied, "The time will come when every land shall yield its hidden treasure; when men no more shall unknown course measure, for round the world no 'farthest land' shall be." Columbus knew such words well. They fired his imagination and allayed his fears.

How did Columbus recruit his crew?

Columbus was a stranger at Palos de la Frontera, the small coastal town where the Spanish monarchs had made provision for two of his ships. He had virtually no connections with either common sailors or officers and was therefore obliged to rely on the help of two prominent seafaring families. The more powerful was that of Martín Pinzón of Palos; the other was the family of Juan Niño, of the nearby Andalusian town of Moguer. Together with Columbus, the Pinzóns and Niños managed to recruit about ninety men and boys for the three vessels. Martín Pinzón himself assumed command of the *Pinta*, while Juan Niño (with whom Columbus developed a close friendship) sailed as master of the *Niña*.

We know the names of all but three of those who signed on for the epochal trip. They came primarily from towns and villages in Andalusia; all but four were Spaniards. Columbus was, of course, one of the foreigners. Each ship had a master, a captain, a pilot, a marshal, and a surgeon, supported by the usual complement of able seamen and cabin boys.

Did they sign on eagerly? Not everyone. Experienced sailors questioned the feasibility of such a trip westward, but all were paid the going wage by the crown, and despite legends to the contrary, no prisoners were used to pad the crews.

One officer on board the flagship *Santa María* was the scholar Luis de Torres, a converted Jew who could speak Arabic. He was meant to be the interpreter between Columbus and the grand khan of China. Columbus, of course, never encountered the grand khan, and a leader of China wouldn't have been likely to speak Arabic anyway, but Europeans believed that all languages stemmed from that tongue, and therefore it was best to be prepared.

Why isn't the New World named for him?

If the New World was destined to be named by Europeans, it should have been named after Columbus. A more appropriate European name would have been North and South Columbia. But the two continents were named instead after Amerigo Vespucci, who voyaged to the New World after Columbus. The name America was assigned by an Alsatian geographer named Martin Waldseemüller when he attempted to chart the New World discoveries in 1507. Because Vespucci was more aggressive in promoting himself, Waldseemüller believed the glory to be his. That Vespucci was indisputably the more popular explorer at this time we learn from Thomas More's *Utopia*, a book based on the Florentine's accounts: "Everyone's reading about the four voyages of Vespucci."

Renaissance geographers were skilled and conscientious scientists, but as they worked to locate obscure New World islands on their charts, they found the data vague and often misleading. The mapmakers could only put faith in intelligent guesses, a course taken by Wald-seemüller when he charted the discoveries of Columbus, Vespucci, and other early explorers as one continuous, continental land strip. By this bold and imaginative step, he in effect introduced a new hemisphere. The name America had been suggested for this new land mass by a fellow geographer and poet named Matthias Ringman. "I don't see why anyone should justly forbid naming it Amerige," he wrote, "land of Americus as it were, after its discoverer Americus, a man of true genius, or America, inasmuch as both Europe and Asia have received their names from women." The name caught on.

Is it true that Columbus's fleet brought syphilis back from the New World?

The disease indeed made its first epidemic appearance in Europe following Columbus's first voyage, when camp followers spread it among the soldiers of King Charles VIII during the French monarch's 1494 campaign to seize the kingdom of Naples. Several tracts of the period discuss the outbreak and indicate that until then the *morbus gallicus* (French disease) had been unknown in Europe. Many scholars hold that it was spread among women infected by Spanish soldiers who had sailed with Columbus to the New World and contracted it there. Whether or not the affliction had existed in Europe before, its first virulent manifestations did date from the Neapolitan campaign.

Columbus is silent on the subject in his writings. In any case, it was not a fit topic to raise with Queen Isabella, for whom, together with King Ferdinand, his reports were intended. But the Spanish chronicler Gonzalo Fernández de Oviedo y Valdés wrote of the New World origin of the disease as an unimpeachable fact. In his *General History of the Indies,* published in 1535, he discourses on it at some length, claiming that "up to the time King Charles passed through there [Italy], no such plague had been seen in those lands. But the truth is that from this island of Haiti or Hispaniola this disease spread to Europe, as has been said; and it is a very common thing here among the Indians, and they know how to cure it, and have very excellent herbs, trees and plants appropriate to this and other infirmities. . . . "

The disease became known in Europe by a string of names, most of them imputing blame for its spread: the French Pox, the German Sickness, the Polish Disease. Around 1512 Girolamo Fracastoro, an Italian physician and poet, wrote a Latin poem dramatizing the disorder's importation from the New World. He called the work "Syphilis or Morbus Gallicus," after a young shepherd named Syphilus who had invoked the wrath of the gods, and thus he coined the name by which the disease is known to this day.

Did Columbus make any attempt at colonizing on his first voyage?

Yes, but it was catastrophic. The tiny settlement was called La Navidad because the plan to set it up was made on Christmas Day of 1492. Located in a shallow bay off the northeast coast of the large island that Columbus called Hispaniola, the site was not the most advantageous, but then Columbus had not exactly chosen it. Nor had it been his intention to establish a colony. The heady step of planting Europeans in the New World came about as the result of the shipwreck of the *Santa María.* While Columbus slept on Christmas Eve, his helmsman ran the flagship aground on the reefs of a Haitian bay.

Ever optimistic, the explorer decided to interpret the woeful disaster as a sign "that our Lord had caused me to run aground at this place so that I might establish a settlement here." He had a tower and a fortress constructed out of the ship's timbers, and volunteers to man the settlement presented themselves eagerly, since word had got around that gold mines lay not far off in the territory of Cibao, a location that Columbus took to be the local name for Cipangu (Japan). Thirty-nine men, including three officers, were chosen to be the first Spanish settlers in the New World. Columbus left them with artillery, a year's supply of bread and wine, seeds, merchandise for trading, and the *Santa María's* small boat. He was confident that when he returned to the New World, the colony would be nothing less than a storehouse of gold. But only desolation greeted him on his second trip, in November of 1493. In their greed for treasure and in their lust for local women, the colonists had quarreled with one another and antagonized the natives. None survived.

To whom did Columbus report his first triumph?

To the king who had turned him down. Columbus's ship was so battered on the return that he was forced to drop anchor in a Portuguese seaport before moving on to Spain. After receiving the crown's permission to enter the outer harbor of Lisbon, he presented himself to King John II of Portugal on March 9, 1493, accompanied by some of the Indians whom he had brought back from the New World. Confronted with this evidence of the navigator's extraordinary discovery, the envious king attempted to make counterclaims of his own in the name of Portugal. After detaining Columbus for some tense days of interrogation, John II permitted the forty-two-year-old mariner to sail on.

Meanwhile, Columbus sent word of his discovery to the Spanish monarchs in Barcelona by a soon-to-be-famous letter that was forthwith printed and issued in many editions. A key passage reflects Columbus's pride in what he had done: "For although men have talked or written of these lands, all was conjecture, without getting a look at it, but amounted only to this, that those who heard for the most part listened and judged it more a fable than that there was anything in it, however small."

Columbus presented himself, at last, to King Ferdinand and Queen Isabella in Barcelona in late April 1493. By then he had already received the reward for which he had yearned: a communication from the Spanish monarchs welcoming him back, addressed to "Don Cristóbal Colón [Columbus], their Admiral of the Ocean Sea, Viceroy and Governor of the Islands that he hath discovered in the Indies." The illiterate sailor from Genoa had become a gentleman, an admiral, and a political power.

What happened to the six Indians that Columbus brought back to Spain?

They were received ceremoniously. Columbus organized a grand procession to the Spanish court, and as the Indians paraded through Barcelona in their exotic dress, crowds thronged to see them. What the Indians thought of it all, we shall never know.

In years ahead Columbus would exhibit a fierce authority over the inhabitants of the New World, but his first recorded impression of them is glowing: "Of anything they have, if you ask them for it, they never say no; rather they invite the person to share it, and show as much love as if they were giving their hearts; and whether the things be of value or of small price, at once they are content with whatever little thing of whatever kind may be given to them. . . . I gave them a thousand good, pleasing things which I had bought, in order that they might be fond of us, and furthermore might be made Christians and be inclined to the love and service of their Highnesses and of the whole Castilian nation, and try to help us and to give us of the things which they have in abundance and which are necessary to us."

Making them Christians was the highest priority. The six he brought back to Spain were promptly baptized and given Christian names, with King Ferdinand, Queen Isabella, and the infante Don Juan, their godparents. When Columbus embarked on his second voyage to the New World, in September of 1493, five of them returned with him. The sixth, named Don Juan, remained attached to the royal Spanish household. He died within two years.

How many voyages to the New World did Columbus make?

Four—in 1492, 1493, 1498, and 1502.

Columbus's second voyage was crowded with events, few of which redounded to the glory of either the explorer or Spain. Yet it began in the grandest manner. With a fleet of no fewer than seventeen ships and his imposing new title of admiral, Columbus set sail on September 25, 1493, from the ancient port city of Cádiz in Spain. The trip was to last more than two and a half years. Officially the goal was the expansion of Christendom through the acquisition of territories and the conversion of the New World natives, but the quest for gold always took priority. The admiral was instructed to ensure that the natives were "treated very well and lovingly" by all the Spanish expeditionaries. These numbered around thirteen hundred: gentlemen-adventurers, cavalry and infantry, farm laborers, a wide range of craftsmen, and five ecclesiastics to perform conversions. Horses were brought for the first time to the New World, along with cattle, other livestock, grains, and seeds. There were no women.

By November 3, all seventeen ships had successfully crossed the Ocean Sea. It was an amazing maritime feat; so large a Renaissance fleet had never gone so far in company. The fleet dropped anchor off a small Caribbean island, which Columbus named Marie Galante, after the nickname of his flagship.

There was much to be done. But first Columbus made his crew swear he was on the threshold of fabled Cathay. Having proved to the Renaissance world that the Ocean Sea was navigable, the admiral was now equally determined to prove that the Indies lay close to its western shores. As soon as he reached the New World on his second voyage, he began a systematic search for the Asian mainland. During nearly two months of the most skillful navigation, he made his way around hundreds of islands, giving many of them the names they hold today and describing the incomparable beauty of the region in terms evocative of a golden age. Groves of majestic palms on the shores of Cuba "seemed to reach the sky" above springs of water "of such goodness and so sweet, that no better could be found in the world." His men rested on the grass "by those springs amid the scent of the flowers which was marvellous, and the sweetness of little birds, so many and so delightful, and under the shade of those palms so tall and fair that it was a wonder to see it all."

The admiral insisted that Cuba was a "peninsular" island depending from the mainland of China, and with stores running low he sent his public notary to gather testimony supporting this shaky claim that he was on the threshold of Cathay. Depositions were taken from the men in Columbus's entourage to the effect that Cuba was part of a mainland. All eighty were willing so to swear. Anyone who suggested the contrary could be fined ten thousand maravedis and the loss of his tongue.

The expedition left behind three colonies. Two soon disappeared, but the third, planned by Columbus and built by his brother Bartolomeo after the admiral's return to Spain in early 1496, enjoyed a fine harbor and flourished. The brothers named it Santo Domingo after their father, and by early in the next century the town could boast a cathedral and a university. Today, as capital of the Dominican Republic, the busy port has a population of nearly 1.5 million and is the oldest continuously inhabited European city in the Western Hemisphere.

But this second foray into the New World also left a less happy legacy. Spaniards forced the Indians to hunt for gold and to share their provisions and, when they failed to submit, exterminated them. In 1494 Columbus sent to Spain about five hundred captured members of the Taino tribe—the same people of whom he had written "they show as much love as if they were giving their hearts." The three hundred who survived the passage were sold on the block in Seville. Here was the sorry inauguration of the slave trade between the Old World and the New.

Did anybody speak out against the murder and enslavement of the Indians?

Bartolomé de Las Casas, an eminent Spanish bishop, used the accounts of his father and uncle, who had sailed with Columbus, to frame his luminous *Apologia*. He devoted himself to the denunciation of the plundering and devastation of the new territories with the "loss of so many thousands of souls." Appalled by Spanish cruelties, Las Casas passionately insisted that the peoples of the New World "are our brothers, redeemed by Christ's most precious blood, no less than the wisest and most learned men in the whole world." Through books, sermons, and direct representation to the crown, he pleaded the cause of the oppressed Indians for more than half a century.

Why did Columbus go a third time?

No sooner had he returned from his second expedition than he petitioned the Spanish monarchs to finance yet a third. He insisted that he was certain to discover the mainland of Asia if allowed to press westward beyond the islands he had already discovered—and he was sure that territories to the south of where he had been would prove abundant in gold. After all, lands in the Indies located in the same latitude as those where the Portuguese had struck it rich in Africa (eight to ten degrees above the equator, in Sierra Leone) must be topographically equivalent in tropical heat, in gold, and in spices. This equivalency theory had been conceived by Aristotle in the fourth century B.C., and the Admiral of the Ocean Sea swallowed it whole.

King Ferdinand and Queen Isabella assented to a third voyage, yet it was some two years before written permission, money, and the requested fleet of eight ships became a reality. Wars with France and the kingdom of Naples were denuding Spanish coffers, and there were marriage alliances to negotiate that required staggering outlays. For example, no fewer than 130 vessels were assembled in an elaborately equipped flotilla to escort the king's daughter Joanna to Flanders for her marriage to the son of the Habsburg emperor. Columbus must have envied that fleet. But the Enterprise of the Indies no longer occupied center stage in the Iberian world. Vasco da Gama had just made it around the Cape of Good Hope to the *real* India in a stunning feat of navigation during the winter of 1497–98, and the Italian Giovanni Caboto was claiming islands off Nova Scotia for the English crown. Columbus's glory as an explorer was being eclipsed, and he knew it.

Any luck on the third time out?

Almost none. Columbus touched on the mainland of South America, in what today is Venezuela, on August 4, 1498. He thus became the first European on record ever to set foot on a continent of the Western Hemisphere. He had mistaken the horizontal stretch of the peninsula for an island and turned north without trying to sail around it.

For Columbus this so-called island nonetheless represented an astounding discovery; he believed it to be the doorway to the Earthly Paradise often cited in the Bible, in tales of antiquity, and in the medieval literature he knew so well.

His initial landing on the beautiful island of Trinidad was also one of the important discoveries of his third voyage. It had prompted the sensation that he was in this divine territory; the land and sea in this region appeared to swell in height somewhat "like a woman's breast," he observed. Pierre d'Ailly's *Imago Mundi* and Sir John Mandeville's *Travels,* two books that had stirred Columbus's imagination, claimed that the lands of the Earthly Paradise would swell almost to the height of the moon. Surely, then, Columbus was skirting the shores of Eden. If this was not Paradise, how could he account for the mysterious torrent of fresh waters—actually issuing from the delta of the Orinoco River—that mingled with the salt of the Ocean Sea?

The Earthly Paradise was believed the locus of a great spring that flowed underground and re-surfaced to become the four great rivers of the inhabited world: the Tigris, the Euphrates, the Ganges, and the Nile. The admiral would have little success in promoting this idea. Renaissance scholars were abandoning the fable-laden geography of the medieval cosmos.

The admiral's fortunes reached a nadir when he was arrested on Hispaniola for misman-agement of colonial affairs, by an official sent over to the New World by King Ferdinand and Queen Isabella. He was without question a poor administrator—by turns weak, stubborn, and horrifyingly ruthless. Yet few could have satisfactorily handled the crises that were contin-ually arising as part of Spain's conquest of the New World. There were rebellions and near re-bellions among the hundreds of Spaniards cut off from their families and the comforts of their homeland, and the greed for gold drove them to break up into factions and to savagely abuse the natives. Columbus was returned to Spain in October 1500 in chains, along with his brothers, Bartolomeo and Diego, who had been given a large measure of authority in colonial affairs.

Thus the explorer's third search for the splendors of Cathay in the name of the Spanish monarchs met its ignominious end.

It was a voyage that, indeed, appeared to have been ill fated from the start. It had begun with none of the excitement of the first and certainly little of the grandeur of the second. Co-lumbus's insistence on the magical reality of the Earthly Paradise struck his contemporaries as little more than the imaginings of a man obsessed with the idea that he was an agent of divine providence.

How did Columbus persuade anyone to let him make a fourth voyage?

"In Spain they judge me," he complained, "as if I had been governor of Sicily or of a prov-ince or city under an established government, and where the laws can be observed without fear of chaos. This is most unjust. I should be judged as a captain sent from Spain to the In-dies to conquer a numerous and warlike people."

Eventually the admiral was vindicated by the Spanish court, but the psychological dam-age to the infirm and aging man was profound. Now, more than ever, he wanted to seize those elusive riches, and this time he insisted that the wealth lay beyond a strait that led directly to the Indian Ocean. He proposed to find the strait.

Permission was long in coming, and humiliating when it arrived. The admiral would be accompanied by an official comptroller who was to keep a strict inventory of the gold, silver, pearls, and spicery that Columbus had long dangled before the imagination of the Spanish court, and the explorer would be under the jurisdiction of a Spanish governor whom the king and queen had appointed to replace him in the New World.

Thus began a gloomy voyage in a modest fleet of four caravels. He sailed past islands al-ready discovered but found no strait. He believed—correctly—that he was on an isthmus be-tween the waters but had neither the men nor the supplies to push through the jungles that separated him from becoming the discoverer of the Pacific.

His ships began to disintegrate. Two had to be abandoned. The admiral was frequently delirious, his men explosively dissatisfied. "What with the heat and dampness," wrote Colum-bus's fourteen-year-old son, Ferdinand, "our ship biscuit had become so wormy that, God help me, I saw many who waited for darkness to eat the porridge made of it, that they might not see the maggots."

In the holds of his rotting vessels, captive natives committed suicide by hanging them-selves from the low beams overhead, bending their knees in the cramped space to assure their death.

So ended the final voyage of Christopher Columbus.

What sort of man was he?

It would be foolish to conjure up Columbus as a dashing, brilliant seaman or even as a bold and enlightened explorer. He certainly was a great sailor, and his successful crossing of the Ocean Sea was an unparalleled feat of navigation. Yet very little comes through from the scant information we have on Columbus the man, or from his own writings, to suggest that he was the swashbuckling, decisive, and gallant Renaissance figure often portrayed in schoolbooks.

He was, rather, contained, inflexible, and high-minded. He was also capable of ruthlessness and extreme cruelty. That he was imaginative and intrepid there can be no doubt. And although he proved a weak and fumbling administrator, we do gain the sense of a magnetic personality: he was able to wed a woman who was by far his social superior, and he won the compassionate support of Queen Isabella for an enterprise that was decidedly risky. Like all those held up to heroic stature, he had that admirable mix of courage, single-mindedness, and zeal that saw him through overwhelming obstacles.

But if there was a single key to his character, it was his intense religiosity. Columbus had a fundamental belief in the Bible and a sense of destiny that was clearly messianic.

When he invoked mystical cosmology, the Bible, ancient legends, and empirical fact to authenticate his ideas, he gave no more weight to science than to prophecy. "God made me the messenger of the new heaven and the new earth of which he spoke in the Apocalypse of St. John . . . and he showed me the spot where to find it," he wrote, after having taken his little fleet across a forbidding sea on that first epochal voyage. Such a statement helps us understand the Genoese explorer as a figure in transition from the medieval world, with its roots in the real and the unreal, to that of the boldly questioning Renaissance.

What did his world make of what he found?

The voyages of discovery by Columbus and his followers provoked predictable excitement, yet for decades there was little understanding of the magnitude of what had transpired. Renaissance Europe had been guided by maps on which North America and South America were nonexistent; they did not suddenly jump into place. Scholars, merchants, and ecclesiastics found it inconceivable that the small islands first sighted by Columbus were not disconnected, negligible interruptions on the way to the Orient but part of a new land mass. Geographers worried that the astonishing disclosure of an undetected hemisphere would discredit traditional cosmography, built as it was on the precepts of classical antiquity and closely tied to biblical beliefs. That general bafflement prevailed is evident in the prelude to Sir Thomas More's *Utopia*, in which the author remarks with a palpable sigh: "Nowadays countries are always being discovered which were never mentioned in the old geography books." The process by which the Old World adjusted was slow, erratic, and frequently brutal. Acquisitiveness was stirred by the apparent sudden availability of silver and gold and the possibilities for territorial expansion; further, the New World's populations were viewed as the opportunity for mass conversions to Christianity. There was as much caution as curiosity, but the desire to know and the desire to convert were passionate forces in the Renaissance, and they ensured that the ultimate response of Christendom to what was once the dark side of the earth would be vigorous and decisive. Indeed, Europe could accept the New World only by imposing its dominion over it.

October 1991

III

THE JAMESTOWN FIASCO

Edmund S. Morgan

The first years of settlement at Jamestown were a disaster. Yet, many Europeans had settled in the new world successful before the English arrived along the Chesapeake in 1607. Why were the initial years so difficult? In the following passage, Edmund S. Morgan analyzes those tortuous years and the factors that created such turmoil and death, and why hope emerged by 1616.

The first wave of Englishmen reached Virginia at Cape Henry, the southern headland at the opening of Chesapeake Bay, on April 26, 1607. The same day their troubles began. The Indians of the Cape Henry region (the Chesapeakes), when they found a party of twenty or thirty strangers walking about or their territory, drove them back to the ships they came on. It was not the last Indian victory, but it was no more effective than later ones. In spite of troubles, the English were there to stay. They spent until May 14 exploring Virginia's broad waters and then chose a site that fitted the formula Hakluyt had prescribed. The place which they named Jamestown, on the James (formerly Powhatan) River, was inland from the capes about sixty miles, ample distance for warning of a Spanish invasion by sea. It was situated on a peninsula, making it easily defensible by land; and the river was navigable by oceangoing ships for another seventy-five miles into the interior, thus giving access to other tribes in case the local Indians should prove as unfriendly as the Chesapeakes.

Captain Christopher Newport had landed the settlers in time to plant something for a harvest that year if they put their minds to it. After a week, in which they built a fort for protection, Newport and twenty-one others took a small boat and headed up the river on a diplomatic and reconnoitering mission, while the settlers behind set about the crucial business of planting corn. Newport paused at various Indian villages along the way and assured the people, as best he could, of the friendship of the English and of his readiness to assist them against their enemies. Newport gathered correctly from his attempted conversations that one man, Powhatan, ruled the whole area above Jamestown, as far as the falls at the present site of Richmond. His enemies, the Monacans, lived above the falls (where they might be difficult to reach if Powhatan proved unfriendly). Newport also surmised, incorrectly, that the Chesapeake Indians who had attacked him at Cape Henry were not under Powhatan's dominion. He accordingly tried to make an alliance against the Chesapeakes and Monacans with a local chief whom he mistook for Powhatan. At the same time, he planted a cross with the name of King James on it (to establish English dominion) and tried to explain to the somewhat bewildered and justifiably suspicious owners of the country that one arm of the cross was Powhatan, the other himself, and that the fastening of them together signified the league between them.

If the Indians understood, they were apparently unimpressed, for three days later, returning to Jamestown, Newport found that two hundred of Powhatan's warriors had attacked the fort the day before and had only been prevented from destroying it by fire from the ships. The settlers had been engaged in planting and had not yet unpacked their guns from the cases in which they were shipped. That was a mistake they were not likely to repeat. But for the next ten years they seem to have made nearly every possible mistake and some that seem almost impossible. It would take a book longer than this to recount them all, and the story has already been told many times. But if we are to understand the heritage of these ten disastrous years for later Virginia history, we should look at a few of the more puzzling episodes and then try to fathom the forces behind them.

Skip over the first couple of years, when it was easy for Englishmen to make mistakes in the strange new world to which they had come, and look at Jamestown in the winter of 1609-10. It is three planting seasons since the colony began. The settlers have fallen into an uneasy truce with the Indians, punctuated by guerrilla raids on both sides, but they have had plenty of time in which they could have grown crops. They have obtained corn from the Indians and supplies from England. They have firearms. Game abounds in the woods; and Virginia's rivers are filled with sturgeon in the summer and covered with geese and ducks in the winter. There are five hundred people in the colony now. And they are starving. They scour the woods listlessly for nuts, roots, and berries. And they offer the only authentic examples of cannibalism witnessed in Virginia. One provident man chops up his wife and salts down the pieces. Others dig up graves to eat the corpses. By spring only sixty are left alive.

Another scene, a year later, in the spring of 1611. The settlers have been reinforced with more men and supplies from England. The preceding winter has not been as gruesome as the one before, thanks in part to corn obtained from the Indians. But the colony still is not growing its own corn. The governor, Lord De la Warr, weakened by the winter, has resumed to England for his health. His replacement, Sir Thomas Dale, reaches Jamestown in May, a time when all hands could have been used in planting. Dale finds nothing planted except "some few seeds put into a private garden or two." And the people he finds at "their daily and usuall workes, bowling in the streetes."

It is evident that the settlers, failing to plant for themselves, depend heavily on the Indians for food. The Indians can finish them off at any time simply by leaving the area. And the Indians know it. One of them tells the English flatly that "we can plant any where . . . and we know that you cannot live if you want [i.e., lack] our harvest, and that reliefe we bring you." If the English drive out the Indians, they will starve.

With that in mind, we look back a year on a scene in the summer following the starving, cannibal winter. It is August, when corn is ripening. The governor has been negotiating with Powhatan about some runaway Englishmen he is thought to be harboring. Powhatan returns "noe other than prowde and disdaynefull Answers," and so the governor sends George Percy "to take Revendge upon the Paspeheans and Chiconamians [Chickahominiesl]," the tribes closest to Jamestown. Percy, the brother of the Earl of Northumberland and the perennial second in command at Jamestown, takes a group of soldiers up the James a few miles by boat and then marches inland three miles to the principal town of the Paspaheghs. They fall upon the town, kill fifteen or sixteen Indians, and capture the queen of the tribe and her children.

Percy then has his men burn the houses and "cutt downe their Corne groweinge about the Towne." He takes the queen and her children back to his boats and embarks for Jamestown, but his men "begin to murmur because the queen and her Children weare spared." Percy therefore obliges them by throwing the children overboard "and shoteinge owtt their Braynes in the water." Meanwhile he sends another party under Captain James Davis to attack another Indian town (presumably a Chickahominy town), where again they cut down the corn and burn the houses. Upon resuming to Jamestown, Percy hears that the governor is displeased that the queen of the Paspaheghs has been spared. Davis wants to burn her, but Percy, "haveinge scene so mutche Bloodshedd that day," insists that she merely be put to the sword. So she is led away and stabbed.

Thus the English, unable or unwilling to feed themselves, continually demanding corn from the Indians, take pains to destroy both the Indians and their corn.

One final scene. It is the spring of 1612, and Governor Dale is supervising the building of a fort at Henrico, near the present site of Richmond. He pauses to deal with some of his men, Englishmen, who have committed a serious crime.

It is not easy to make sense out of the behavior displayed in these episodes. How to explain the suicidal impulse that led the hungry English to destroy the corn that might have fed them and to commit atrocities upon the people who grew up? And how to account for the seeming unwillingness or incapacity of the English to feed themselves? Although they had invaded Indian territory and quarreled with the owners, the difficulty of obtaining land was not great. The Indians were no match for English weapons. Moreover, since the Indians could afford to give up the land around Jamestown as well as Henrico without seriously endangering their own economy, they made no concerted effort to drive the English out. Although Indian attacks may have prevented the English from getting a crop into the ground in time for a harvest in the fall of 1607, the occasional Indian raids thereafter cannot explain the English failure to grow food in succeeding years. How, then, can we account for it?

The answer that comes first to mind is the poor organization and direction of the colony. The government prescribed by the charter placed full powers in a council appointed by the king, with a president elected by the other members. The president had virtually no authority of his own; and while the council lasted, the members spent most of their time bickering and intriguing against one another and especially against the one man who had the experience and the assurance to take command. The names of the councillors had been kept secret (even from themselves) in a locked box, until the ships carrying the first settlers arrived in Virginia. By that time a bumptious young man named John Smith had made himself unpopular with Captain Christopher Newport (in command until their arrival) and with most of the other gentlemen of consequence aboard. When they opened the box, they were appalled to find Smith's name on the list of councillors. But during the next two years Smith's confidence in himself and his willingness to act while others talked overcame most of the handicaps imposed by the feeble frame of government. It was Smith who kept the colony going during those years. But in doing so he dealt more decisively with the Indians than with his own quarreling countrymen, and he gave an initial turn to the colony's Indian relations that was not quite what the company had intended.

Smith, the son of a yeoman, was a rare combination of actor and man of action. He had already won his spurs fighting against the Turks in Hungary, where, as he tells it, he won all the battles except the last, in which he was captured, enslaved, and then rescued by a fair princess. With her assistance he made his escape, then trekked across Europe and was back in England to join the Jamestown expedition at the age of twenty-seven. In spite of his youth, he may have had more experience than anyone else at Jamestown in making war, in living off the land, and in communicating with people whose language he did not know. Certainly he showed more aptitude than anyone else in all these matters. And it was probably his ability to deal with the Indians that prevented them from destroying or starving the settlement.

When the supplies ran out in the first autumn, Smith succeeded in trading with the Indians for corn. Then, on an exploring expedition up the Chickahominy River, he was made a prisoner and brought before Powhatan. This was the point at which another fair princess, Pocahontas, stepped in to save his life—or so Smith later told it; and in spite of the skepticism engendered by the larger-than-life view of himself that Smith always affected, there seems to be no good reason to doubt him. In any case, he resumed unharmed; and while he remained in Virginia (until the fall of 1609), he conducted most of the colony's relations (both with Powhatan and with the tribes under Powhatan's dominion).

Smith took a keener interest in the Indians than anyone else in Virginia for a century to come. The astonishingly accurate map he made of the country shows the locations of the different tribes, and his writings give us most of the information we will ever have about them. But his interest in them was neither philanthropic nor philosophic. As he came to know them, he was convinced that they could be incorporated into the English settlement, but he scorned the notion that gentleness was the way to do it. Although Smith looks a little like a latterday Drake or Hawkins, he did not see the Indians as Drake saw the Cimarrons. His own model seems to have been Hernando Cortez, and he would gladly have made Powhatan his **Montezuma**.[1] He was disgusted when orders came from the company requiring that the settlers give the old chief a formal coronation, designed to make him a proper king, ally, and in some sense a vassal of King James. Smith witnessed the ceremony with undisguised contempt. Powhatan himself submitted with ill grace to the dignity thus thrust upon him and made it plain that he did not consider himself anybody's vassal and that he needed none of the proffered English assistance against his enemies.

Smith was sure that kindness was wasted on savages, and within weeks he was successfully bullying and browbeating Powhatan out of hundreds of bushels of corn. Years later, as he reflected in England on the frustrations that continued to beset Virginia, he was sure he had been right, that the Spanish had shown the way to deal with Indians. The English should have learned the lesson of how the Spanish "forced the treacherous and rebellious **Infidels**[2] to doe all manner of drudgery worke and every for them, themselves living like Souldiers upon the fruits of their labours." John Smith's idea of the proper role of the Virginia Indians in English Virginia was something close to slavery. Given the superiority of English arms, he had no doubt of his ability to conquer the lot of them with a handful of men, just as Cortez had conquered the much more populous and formidable **Aztecs**.[3] Once conquered, they could forthwith be put to work for their conquerors.

Smith was not afraid of work himself; and in the absence of Indian slaves he bent his efforts as much toward getting work out of Englishmen as he did toward supplying their deficiencies from Indian larders. In these first years many Englishmen perceived that the Indians had a satisfactory way of living without much work, and they slipped away "to live Idle among the Savages." Those who remained were so averse to any kind of labor, Smith reported, "that had they not beene forced nolens volens perforce to gather and prepare their victual! they would all have starved, and have eaten one another." While the governing council ruled, under the presidency of men of greater social prestige than Smith, he could make little headway against the jealousies and intrigues that greeted all his efforts to organize the people either for

---

1. **Montezuma:** Last Aztec emperor in Mexico (1502–1520).

2. **Infidels:** One who has no religious beliefs.

3. **Aztecs:** A member of the Indian people of Central Mexico noted for their civilization before Cortes invaded Mexico in 1519.

planting or for gathering food. But month by month other members of the council died or returned to England; and by the end of 1608 Smith was left in complete control. He divided the remaining settlers into work gangs and made them a little speech, in which he told them they could either work or starve: "How so ever you have bin here to fore tolerated by the authoritie of the Councell from that I have often commanded you, yet seeing nowe the authoritie resteth wholly in my selfe; you must obey this for a law, that he that will not worke, shall not eate (except by sicknesse he be disabled)." He did not except himself from the rule and assured them that "every one that gathereth not every day as much as I doe, the next dale shall be set beyond the river, and for ever bee banished from the fort, and live there or starve." And lest this only produce a general exodus to the Indians, Smith used his influence with the neighboring tribes to apply the same discipline to any settler who dared choose that course. As a result, in the winter of 1608-9 he lost only seven or eight men.

Had Smith been left in charge, it is not impossible that he would have achieved a society which, in one way or another, would have included the Indians. They might have had a role not much better than the Spanish assigned them, and they might have died as rapidly as the Arawaks from disease and overwork. But it is unlikely that the grisly scenes already described would have taken place (they all occurred after his departure). In spite of his eagerness to subdue the Indians, Smith was in continual contact and communication with them. He bullied and threatened and browbeat them, but we do not read of any atrocities committed upon them under his direction, nor did he feel obliged to hang, break, or burn any Englishman who went off to live with them.

But the Virginia Company in 1609 was not yet ready to abandon its goal of making its own way in Virginia and sharing the country with the Indians on more favorable terms than Smith would have allowed them. The members of the council who returned to England complained of Smith's overbearing ways, with Englishmen as well Indians. So the company decided not to leave the colony in the hands of so pushy a young man. At the same time, however, they recognized that the conciliar form of government was ineffective, and that a firmer authority was necessary to put their lazy colonists to work. They accordingly asked, and were given, a new charter, in which the king relinquished his government of the colony. Henceforth the company would have full control and would rule through a governor who would exercise absolute powers in the colony. He would be assisted by a council, but their advice would not be binding on him. In fact, he would be as much a military commander as a governor, and the whole enterprise would take on a more military character.

For the next eight or nine years whatever evils befell the colony were not the result of any diffusion of authority except when the appointed governor was absent—as happened when the first governor, Lord De la Warr, delayed his departure from England and his deputy, Sir Thomas Gates, was shipwrecked en route at Bermuda. The starving winter of 1609-10 occurred during this interval; but Gates arrived in May, 1610, followed by De la Warr himself in June. Thereafter Virginia was firmly governed under a clear set of laws, drafted by Gates and by De la Warr's subsequent deputy, Sir Thomas Dale. The so-called Lawes Divine, Morall and Martiall were mostly martial, and they set the colonists to work with military discipline and no pretense of gentle government. They prescribed that the settlers be divided into work gangs, much as Smith had divided them, each of which would proceed to its assigned tasks at regular hours. At the beating of a drum, the master of each gang would set them to work and "not suffer any of his company to be negligent, and idle, or depart from his works" until another beat of the drums allowed it.

The *Laws* prescribed death for a variety of crimes, including rape, adultery, theft, lying, sacrilege, blasphemy, or doing or saying anything that might "tend to the derision" of the Bible.

On a more practical level, in order to increase the livestock which had by this time been brought over, the *Laws* made it death to kill any domestic animal, even a chicken. It was also death, in weeding a garden, to take an ear of corn or a bunch of grapes from it, death too to trade privately with anyone on the ships that came to the colony. And the punishments were inflicted with an arbitrary rigor that became a scandal. For stealing two or three pints of oatmeal a man had a needle thrust through his tongue and was then chained to a tree until he starved.

The *Laws* did not even contemplate that the Indians would become a part of the English settlement. Though the company had frowned on Smith's **swashbuckling**[4] with Indians, it was disenchante with Powhatan and convinced that he and those under his dominion did need to be dealt with more sternly. Sir Thomas Gates was instructed to get some Indian children to bring up in the English manner, free of their parents' evil influence. And he was also told to subjugate the neighboring tribes, to make them pay tribute, and to seize the chiefs of any that refused. If he wanted to make friends with any Indians, they must be "those that are farthest from you and enemies unto those amonge whom you dwell." The company's new attitude was incorporated in several provisions of the *Laws*. When Indians came to Jamestown to trade or visit, they were to be placed under guard to prevent them from stealing anything; no inhabitant was to speak to them without the governor's permission; and the settlers were forbidden on pain of death to "runne away from the Colonie, to Powhatan, or any savage Werowance else whatsoever." The company's desire to bring the Indians into the community had given way to an effort to keep settlers and Indians apart.

In their relations to the Indians, as in their rule of the settlers, the new governing officers of the colony were ruthless. The guerrilla raids that the two races conducted against each other became increasingly hideous, especially on the part of the English. Indians coming to Jamestown with food were treated as spies. Gates had them seized and killed "for a Terrour to the Reste to cawse them to desists from their subtell practyses." Gates showed his own subtle practices by enticing the Indians at Kecoughtan (Point Comfort) to watch a display of dancing and drumming by one of his men and then "espyeinge a fltteinge oportunety fell in upon them putt fyve to the sworde wownded many others some of them beinge after fownde in the woods with Sutche extraordinary Lardge and mortall wownds that itt seemed strange they Cold flye so far." It is possible that the rank and file of settlers aggravated the bad relations with the Indians by unauthorized attacks, but unauthorized fraternization seems to have bothered the governors more. The atrocities committed against the queen of the Paspaheghs; though apparently demanded by the men, were the work of the governing officers, as were the atrocities committed against the Englishmen who fled to live with the Indians.

John Smith had not had his way in wishing to reduce the Indians to slavery, or something like it, on the Spanish model. But the policy of his successors, though perhaps not with company approval, made Virginia look far more like the Hispaniola of Las Casas than it did when Smith was in charge. And the company and the colony had few benefits to show for all the rigor. At the end of ten years, in spite of the military discipline of work gangs, the colonists were still not growing enough to feed themselves and were still begging, bullying, and buying corn from the Indians whose lands they scorched so deliberately. We cannot, it seems, blame the colony's failures on lax discipline and diffusion of authority. Failures continued and atrocities multiplied after authority was made absolute and concentrated in one man.

Another explanation, often advanced, for Virginia's early troubles, and especially for its failure to feed itself, is the collective organization of labor in the colony. All the settlers were

---

4. **swashbuckling:** A flamboyant swordsman or adventurer.

expected to work together in a single community effort, to produce both their food and the exports that would make the company rich. Those who held shares would ultimately get part of the profits, but meanwhile the incentives of private enterprise were lacking. The work a man did bore no direct relation to his reward. The laggard would receive as large a share in the end as the man who worked hard.

The communal production of food seems to have been somewhat modified after the reorganization of 1609 by the assignment of small amounts of land to individuals for private gardens. It is not clear who received such allotments, perhaps only those who came at their own expense. Men who came at company expense may have been expected to continue working exclusively for the common stock until their seven-year terms expired. At any rate, in 1614, the year when the first shipment of company men concluded their service, Governor Dale apparently assigned private allotments to them and to other independent "farmers." Each man got three acres, or twelve acres if he had a family. He was responsible for growing his own food plus two and a half barrels of corn annually for the company as a supply for newcomers to tide them over the first year. And henceforth each "farmer" would work for the company only one month a year.

By this time Gates and Dale had succeeded in planting settlements at several points along the James as high up as Henrico, just below the falls. The many close spaced tributary rivers and creeks made it possible to throw up a **palisade**[5] between two of them to make a small fortified peninsula. Within the space thus enclosed by water on three sides and palisaded on the fourth, the settlers could build their houses, dig their gardens, and pasture their cattle. It was within these enclaves that Dale parceled out private allotments. They were affirmations of an expectation that would linger for a century, that Virginia was about to become the site of thriving cities and towns. In point of fact, the new "cities" scarcely matched in size the tiny villages from which Powhatan's people threatened them. And the "farmers" who huddled together on the allotments assigned to them proved incapable of supporting themselves or the colony with adequate supplies of food.

According to John Rolfe, a settler who had married John Smith's fair Pocahontas, the switch to private enterprise transformed the colony's food deficit instantly to a surplus: instead of the settlers seeking corn from the Indians, the Indians sought it from them. If so, the situation did not last long. Governor Samuel Argall, who took charge at the end of May, 1617, bought 600 bushels from the Indians that fall, "which did greatly relieve the whole Colonie." And when Governor George Yeardley relieved Argall in April, 1619, he found the colony "in a great scarcity for want of corn" and made immediate preparations to seek it from the Indians. If, then, the colony's failure to grow food arose from its communal organization of production, the failure was not overcome by the switch to private enterprise.

Still another explanation for the improvidence of Virginia's pioneers is one that John Smith often emphasized, namely, the character of the immigrants. They were certainly an odd assortment, for the most conspicuous group among them was an extraordinary number of gentlemen. Virginia, as a patriotic enterprise, had excited the imagination of England's nobility and gentry. The shareholders included 32 present or future earls, 4 countesses, and 3 viscounts (all members of the nobility) as well as hundreds of lesser gentlemen, some of them perhaps retainers of the larger men. Not all were content to risk only their money. Of the 105 settlers who started the colony, 36 could be classified as gentlemen. In the first of 120 additional settlers, 28

---

5. **palisade:** A line of lofty, steep cliffs, usually along a river.

were gentlemen, and in the second supply of 70, again 28 were gentlemen. These numbers gave Virginia's population about six times as large a proportion of gentlemen as England had.

Gentlemen, by definition, had no manual skill, nor could they be expected to work at ordinary labor. They were supposed to be useful for "the force of knowledge, the exercise of counsell"; but to have ninety-odd wise men offering advice while a couple of hundred did the work was inauspicious, especially when the wise men included "many unruly gallants packed thether by their friends to escape il destinies" at home.

What was worse, the gentlemen were apparently accompanied by the personal attendants that gentlemen thought necessary to make life bearable even in England. The colony's laborers "were for most part footmen, and such as they that were Adventurers brought to attend them, or such as they could perswade to goe with them, that never did know what a dayes worke was." Smith complained that he could never get any real work from more than thirty out of two hundred, and he later argued that of all the people sent to Virginia, a hundred good laborers "would have done more than a thousand of those that went."

The company may actually have had little choice in allowing gentlemen and their servants to make so large a number of their settlers. The gentlemen were paying their own way, and the company perhaps could not afford to deny them. But even if unencumbered by these volunteers, the colony might have foundered on the kind of settlers that the company itself did want to send. What the company wanted for Virginia was a variety of craftsmen. Richard Hakluyt had made up a list for Walter Raleigh that suggests the degree of specialization contemplated in an infant settlement: Hakluyt wanted both carpenters and joiners, tallow chandlers and wax chandlers, bowstave preparers and bowyers, fietchers and arrowhead makers, men to rough-hew pikestaffs and other men to finish them. In 1610 and again in 1611 the Virginia Company published lists of the kind of workers it wanted. Some were for building, making tools, and other jobs needed to keep the settlers alive, but the purpose of staying alive would be to see just what Virginia was good for and then start sending the goods back to England. Everybody hoped for gold and silver and jewels, so the colony needed refiners and mineral men. But they might have to settle for iron, so send men with all the skills needed to smelt it. The silk grass that Harlot described might produce something like silk, and there were native mulberry trees for growing worms, so send silk dressers. Sturgeon swam in the rivers, so send men who knew how to make caviar. And so on. Since not all the needed skills for Virginia's potential products were to be found in England, the company sought them abroad: glassmakers from Italy, **millwrights**[6] from Holland, pitch boilers from Poland, vine dressers and saltmakers from France. The settlers of Virginia were expected to create a more complex, more varied economy than England itself possessed. As an extension of England, the colony would impart its variety and health to the mother country.

If the company had succeeded in filling the early ships for Virginia with as great a variety of specialized craftsmen as it wanted, the results might conceivably have been worse than they were. We have already noticed the effect of specialization in England itself, where the division of labor had become a source not of efficiency but of idleness. In Virginia the effect was magnified. Among the skilled men who started the settlement in 1607 were four carpenters, two bricklayers, one mason (apparently a higher skill than bricklaying), a blacksmith, a tailor, and a barber. The first "supply" in 1608 had six tailors, two goldsmiths, two refiners, two apothecaries, a blacksmith, a gunner (*i.e.*, gunsmith?), a cooper, a tobacco pipe maker, a jeweler, and a perfumer. There were doubtless others, and being skilled they expected to be paid and fed

---

6. **millwright:** A person who designs, builds, or repairs mills or mill machinery.

for doing the kind of work for which they had been hired. Some were obviously useful. But others may have found themselves without means to use their special talents. If they were conscientious, the jeweler may have spent some time looking for jewels, the goldsmiths for gold, the perfumer for something to make perfume with. But when the search proved futile, it did not follow that they should or would exercise their skilled hands at any other tasks. It was not suitable for a perfumer or a jeweler or a goldsmith to put his hand to the hoe. Rather, they could join the gentlemen in genteel loafing while a handful of ordinary laborers worked at the ordinary labor of growing and gathering food.

The laborers could be required to work at whatever they were told to; but they were, by all accounts, too few and too feeble. The company may have rounded them up as it did in 1609 when it appealed to the mayor of London to rid the city of its "swarme of unnecessary inmates" by sending to Virginia any who were destitute and lying in the streets.

The company, then, partly by choice, partly by necessity, sent to the colony an over-supply of men who were not prepared to tackle the work essential to settling in a wilderness. In choosing prospective Virginians, the company did not look for men who would be particularly qualified to keep themselves alive in a new land. The company never considered the problem of staying alive in Virginia to be a serious one. And why should they have? England's swarming population had had ample experience in moving to new areas and staying alive. The people who drifted north and west into the pasture-farming areas got along, and the lands there were marginal, far poorer than those that awaited the settlers of tidewater Virginia. Though there may have been some farmers among the early settlers, no one for whom an occupation is given was listed as a husbandman or yeoman. And though thirty husbandmen were included in the 1611 list of men wanted, few came. As late as 1620 the colony reported "a great scarcity, or none at all" of "husbandmen truely bred," by which was meant farmers from the arable regions. In spite of the experience at Roanoke and in spite of the repeated starving times at Jamestown, the company simply did not envisage the provision of food as a serious problem. They sent some food supplies with every ship but never enough to last more than a few months. After that people should be able to do for themselves.

The colonists were apparently expected to live from the land like England's woodland and pasture people, who gave only small amounts of time to their small garden plots, cattle, and sheep and spent the rest in spinning, weaving, mining, handicrafts, and loafing. Virginians would spend their time on the more varied commodities of the New World. To enable them to live in this manner, the company sent cattle, swine, and sheep: and when Dale assigned them private plots of land, the plots were small, in keeping with the expectation that they would not spend much time at farming. The company never intended the colony to supply England with grain and did not even expect that agricultural products might be its principal exports. They did want to give sugar, silk, and wine a try, but most of the skills they sought showed an expectation of setting up extractive industries such as iron mining, smelting, salt-making, pitch making, and glassmaking. The major part of the colonists' work time was supposed to be devoted to processing the promised riches of the land for export; and with the establishment of martial law the company had the means of seeing that they put their shoulders to the task.

Unfortunately, the persons charged with directing the motley work force had a problem, quite apart from the overload of gentlemen and specialized craftsmen they had to contend with. During the early years of the colony they could find no riches to extract. They sent back some cedar wood, but lumber was too bulky a product to bear the cost of such long transportation to market. Sassafras was, available in such quantities that the market for it quickly collapsed. The refiners found no gold or silver or even enough iron to be worth mining. Silk grass and silk proved to be **will-o'-the-wisp**.[7]

The result was a situation that taxed the patience both of the leaders and of the men they supervised. They had all come to Virginia with high expectations. Those who came as servants of the company had seven years in which to make their employers rich. After that they would be free to make themselves rich. But with no prospect of riches in sight for anybody, it was difficult to keep them even at the simple tasks required for staying alive or to find anything else for them to do.

The predicament of those in charge is reflected in the hours of work they prescribed for the colonists, which contrast sharply with them specified in the English Statute of Artificers. There was no point in demanding dawn-to-dusk toil unless there was work worth doing. When John Smith demanded that men work or starve, how much work did he demand? By his own account, "4 hours each day was spent in worke, the rest in pastimes and merry exercise." The governors who took charge after the reorganization of 1609 were equally modest in their demands.

To have grown enough corn to feed the colony would have required only a fraction of the brief working time specified, yet it was not grown. Even in their free time men shunned the simple planting tasks that sufficed for the Indians. And the very fact the the Indians did grow corn may be one more reason why the colonists did not. For the Indians presented a challenge that Englishmen were not prepared to meet, a challenge to their image of themselves, to their self-esteem, to their conviction of their own superiority over foreigners, and especially over barbarous foreigners like the Irish and the Indians.

If you were a colonist, you knew that your technology was superior to the Indians'. You knew that you were civilized, and they were savages. It was evident in your firearms, your clothing, your housing, your government, your religion. The Indians were supposed to be overcome with admiration and to join you in extracting riches from the country. But your superior technology had proved insufficient to extract anything. The Indians, keeping to themselves, laughed at your superior methods and lived from the land more abundantly and with less labor than you did. They even furnished you with the food that you somehow did not get around to growing enough of yourselves. To be thus condescended to by heathen savages was intolerable. And when your own people started deserting in order to live with them, it was too much. If it came to that, the whole enterprise of Virginia would be over. So you killed the Indians, tortured them, burned their villages, burned their cornfields. It proved your superiority in spite of your failures. And you gave similar treatment to any of your own people who succumbed to the savage way of life. But you still did not grow much corn. That was not what you had come to Virginia for.

By the time the colony was ten years old and an almost total loss to the men who had invested their lives and fortunes in it, only one ray of hope had appeared. It had been known, from the Roanoke experience, that the Indians grew and smoked a kind of tobacco; and tobacco grown in the Spanish West Indies was already being imported into England, where it sold at eighteen shillings a pound. Virginia tobacco had proved, like everything else, a disappointment; but one of the settlers, John Rolfe, tried some seeds of the West Indian variety, and the result was much better. The colonists stopped bowling in the streets and planted tobacco in them— and everywhere else that they could find open land. In 1617, ten years after

---

7. **will-o'-the-wisp:** A delusive or misleading goal.

the first landing at Jamestown, they shipped their first cargo to England. It was not up to Spanish tobacco, but it sold at three shillings a pound.

To the members of the company it was proof that they had been right in their estimate of the colony's potential. But the proof was bitter. Tobacco had at first been accepted as a medicine, good for a great variety of ailments. But what gave it its high price was the fact that people had started smoking it for fun. Used this way it was considered harmful and faintly immoral. People smoked it in taverns and brothels. Was Virginia to supplement England's economy and redeem her rogues by pandering to a new vice? The answer, of course, was yes. But the men who ran the Virginia Company, still aiming at ends of a higher nature, were not yet ready to take yes for an answer.

Indians in the Land

A Conversation between William Cronon and Richard White

The noble denizen of the deep, the terrible savage, or the primitive innocent, are all pic-tures of the American Indian. In recent years historians have tried to put those first Amer-icans into a more realistic perspective using new tools of analysis and new use of sources. The following conversation between William Cronon and Richard White place the Indi-ans in the natural environment and their relationship with it. In discussing the natives use of the environment, valuable new insights into their lives are gleaned.

When the historian Richard White wrote his first scholarly article about Native American en-vironmental history in the mid-1970s, he knew he was taking a new approach to an old field, but he did not realize just how new it was. "I sent it to a historical journal," he reports, "and I never realized the U.S. mail could move so fast. It was back in three days. The editor told me it wasn't history."

Times have changed. The history of how Native Americans have lived in, used, and al-tered the environment of North America has emerged as one of the most exciting new fields in historical scholarship. It has changed our understanding not only of Native Americans but of the American landscape itself. To learn more about what historians in the field have been discovering, American Heritage asked two of its leading practitioners, Richard White and William Cronon, to meet and talk about their subject.

White, who is thirty-nine, teaches at the University of Utah. While earning his B.A. from the University of California at Santa Cruz in the late 1960s, he became involved in Native American politics. He wrote his doctoral dissertation at the University of Washing-ton on the environmental history of Island County, Washington. That work, which became his first book—*Land Use, Environment, and Social Change*—earned him the Forest History Society's prize for the best book published in 1979–1980. This was followed by *The Roots of Dependency*, an environmental history of three Native American tribes: the Choctaws of the Southeast, the Pawnees of the Great Plains, and the Navajos of the Southwest. In it he showed how each had gradually been forced into economic dependency on the now-domi-nant white society.

William Cronon, thirty-two, teaches history at Yale University. His first book, *Changes in the Land: Indians, Colonists, and the Ecology of New England*, examined the different ways Na-tive Americans and colonists had used the New England landscape. It won the Francis Park-man Prize in 1984. Cronon recently became a MacArthur Fellow, and is working on several projects in environmental history and the history of the American West.

This conversation, which was arranged and edited by William Cronon, took place late in 1985 at Richard White's home in Salt Lake City.

William Cronon If historians thought about the environment at all up until a few years ago, they thought of it in terms of an older school of American historians who are often called "environmental determinists." People like Frederick Jackson Turner argued that Europeans came to North America, settled on the frontier, and began to be changed by the environment.

Richard White In a delayed reaction to Turner, historians in the late 1960s and early 1970s reversed this. They began to emphasize a series of horror stories when they wrote about the environment. The standard metaphor of the time was "the rape of the earth," but what they were really describing was the way Americans moving west cut down the forests, ploughed the land, destroyed the grasslands, harnessed the rivers—how they in effect transformed the whole appearance of the North American landscape.

WC Since then, I think, we've realized that both positions are true, but incomplete. The real problem is that human beings reshape the earth as they live upon it, but as they reshape it, the new form of the earth has an influence on the way those people can live. The two reshape each other. This is as true of Indians as it is of European settlers.

RW My first connections with Indians in the environment was very immediate. I became interested because of fishing-rights controversies in the Northwest, in which the Indians' leading opponents included several major environmental organizations. They argued that Indians were destroying the fisheries. What made this odd was that these same groups also held up Indians as sort of primal ecologists. I remember reading a Sierra Club book which claimed that Indians had moved over the face of the land and when they left you couldn't tell they'd ever been there. Actually, this idea demeans Indians. It makes them seem simply like an animal species, and thus deprives them of culture. It also demeans the environment by so simplifying it that all changes come to seem negative—as if somehow the ideal is never to have been here at all. It's a crude view of the environment, and it's a crude view of Indians.

WC Fundamentally, it's an ahistorical view. It says not only that the land never changed—"wilderness" was always in this condition—but that the people who lived upon it had no history, and existed outside of time. They were "natural."

RW That word *natural* is the key. Many of these concepts of Indians are quite old, and they all picture Indians as people without culture. Depending on your view of human nature, there are two versions. If human beings are inherently evil in a Calvinistic sense, then you see Indians as inherently violent and cruel. They're identified with nature, but it's the nature of the howling wilderness, which is full of Indians. But if you believe in a beneficent nature, and a basically good human nature, then you see Indians as noble savages, people at one with their environment.

WC To understand how Indians really did view and use their environment, we have to move beyond these notions of "noble savages" and "Indians as the original ecologists." We have to look instead at how they actually lived.

RW Well, take the case of fire. Fire transformed environments all over the continent. It was a basic tool used by Indians to reshape landscape, enabling them to clear forests to create grasslands for hunting and fields for planting. Hoe agriculture—as opposed to the plow agriculture of the Europeans—is another.

WC There's also the Indians' use of "wild" animals—animals that were not domesticated, not owned in ways Europeans recognized. Virtually all North American Indians were intimately linked to the animals around them, but they had no cattle or pigs or horses.

RW What's hardest for us to understand, I think, is the Indians' different way of making sense of species and the natural world in general. I'm currently writing about the Indians of the Great Lakes region. Most of them thought of animals as a species of *persons*. Until you grasp that fact, you can't really understand the way they treated animals. This is easy to romanticize—it's easy to turn it into a "my brother the buffalo" sort of thing. But it wasn't. The Indians *killed* animals. They often overhunted animals. But when they overhunted, they did so within the context of a moral universe that both they and the animals inhabited. They conceived of animals as having, not rights—that's the wrong word—but *powers*. To kill an animal was to be involved in a social relationship with the animal. One thing that has impressed me about Indians I've known is their realization that this is a harsh planet, that they survive by the deaths of other creatures. There's no attempt to gloss over that or romanticize it.

WC There's a kind of debt implied by killing animals.

RW Yes. You incur an obligation. And even more than the obligation is your sense that those animals have somehow surrendered themselves to you.

WC There's a gift relationship implied . . .

RW . . . which is also a *social* relationship. This is where it becomes almost impossible to compare Indian environmentalism and modern white environmentalism. You cannot take an American forester or an American wildlife manager and expect him to think that he has a special social relationship with the species he's working on.

WC Or that he owes the forest some kind of gift in return for the gift of wood he's taking from it.

RW Exactly. And it seems to me hopeless to try to impose that attitude onto Western culture. We distort Indian reality when we say Indians were conservationists—that's not what conservation means. We don't give them full credit for their view, and so we falsify history.

Another thing that made Indians different from modern Euro-Americans was their commitment to producing for *security* rather than for maximum yield. Indians didn't try to maximize the production of any single commodity. Most tried to attain security by diversifying their diet, by following the seasonal cycles: they ate what was most abundant. What always confused Europeans was why Indians didn't simply concentrate on the most productive part of the cycle: agriculture, say. They could have grown more crops and neglected something else. But once you've done that, you lose a certain amount of security.

WC I like to think of Indian communities having a whole series of ecological nets under them. When one net failed, there was always another underneath it. If the corn died, they could always hunt deer or gather wild roots. In hard times—during an extended drought, for instance—those nets became crucial.

All of this was linked to seasonal cycles. For me, one of the best ways of understanding the great diversity of environmental practices among Indian peoples is to think about the different ways they moved across the seasons of the year. Because the seasons of North America differ markedly between, say, the Eastern forests and the Great Plains and the Southwestern deserts, Indian groups devised quite different ways of life to match different natural cycles.

New England is the region I know best. For Indians there, spring started with hunting groups drawing together to plant their crops after having been relatively dispersed for the winter. While women planted beans, squash, and corn, men hunted the migrating fish and birds. They dispersed for summer hunting and gathering while the crops matured, and then reassembled in the fall. The corn was harvested and great celebrations took place. Then, once the harvest was done and the corn stored in the ground, people broke up their villages and fanned out in small bands for the fall hunt, when deer and other animals were at their fattest. The hunt went on until winter faded and the season of agriculture began again. What they had was agriculture during one part of the year, gathering going on continuously, and hunting concentrated in special seasons. That was typical not just of the Indians of New England but of eastern Indians in general.

RW For me the most dramatic example of seasonal changes among Indian peoples would be the horticulturists of the eastern Great Plains. The Pawnees are the example I know best. Depending on when you saw the Pawnees, you might not recognize them as the same people. If you came upon them in the spring or early fall, when they were planting or harvesting crops, you would have found a people living in large, semi-subterranean earth lodges and surrounded by scattered fields of corn and beans and squash. They looked like horticultural people. If you encountered the Pawnees in early summer or late fall, you would have thought you were seeing Plains nomads—because then they followed the buffalo, and their whole economy revolved around the buffalo. They lived in tepees and were very similar, at least in outward appearance, to the Plains nomads who surrounded them.

For the Pawnees, these cycles of hunting and farming were intimately connected. One of my favorite examples is a conversation in the 1870s between the Pawnee Petalesharo and a Quaker Indian agent who was trying to explain to him why he should no longer hunt buffalo. Suddenly a cultural chasm opens between them, because Petalesharo is trying to explain that the corn will not grow without the buffalo hunt. Without buffalo to sacrifice at the ceremonies, corn will not come up and the Pawnee world will cease. You see them talking, but there's no communication.

WC It's difficult for a modern American hearing this to see Petalesharo's point of view as anything other than alien and wrong. This notion of sacrificing buffalo so corn will grow is fundamental to his view of nature, even though it's utterly different from what *we* mean when we call him a conservationist.

RW And yet, if you want to understand people's actions historically, you have to take Petalesharo seriously.

WC Environmental historians have not only been reconstructing the ways Indians used and thought about the land, they've also been analyzing how those things changed when the Europeans invaded. A key discovery of the last couple of decades had been our radically changed sense of how important European disease was in changing Indian lives.

RW It was appalling. Two worlds that had been largely isolated suddenly came into contact. The Europeans brought with them diseases the Indians had never experienced. The resulting death rates are almost impossible to imagine: 90 to 95 percent in some places.

WC The ancestors of the Indians came to North America from ten to forty thousand years ago. They traveled through an Arctic environment in which many of the diseases common to temperate and tropical climates simply couldn't survive. They came in groups that were biologically too small to sustain those diseases. And they came without the domesticated animals with which we share several of our important illnesses. Those three circumstances meant that Indians shed many of the most common diseases of Europe and Asia. Measles, chicken pox, smallpox, and many of the venereal diseases vanished during migration., For over twenty thousand years, Indians lived without encountering these illnesses, and so lost the antibodies that would ordinarily have protected them.

RW Most historians would now agree that when the Europeans arrived, the Indian population of North America was between ten and twelve million (the old estimate was about one million). By the early twentieth century it had fallen to less than five hundred thousand. At the same time, Indian populations were also under stress from warfare. Their seasonal cycles were being broken up, and they were inadequately nourished as a result. All these things contributed to the tremendous mortality they suffered.

WC Part of the problem was biological; part of it was cultural. If a disease arrived in mid-summer, it had quite different effects from one that arrived in the middle of the winter, when people's nutrition levels were low and they were more susceptible to disease. A disease that arrived in spring, when crops had to be planted, could disrupt the food supply for the entire year. Nutrition levels would be down for the whole subsequent year, and new diseases would find readier victims as a result.

RW The effects extended well beyond the original epidemic—a whole series of changes occurred. If Indian peoples in fact shaped the North American landscape, this enormous drop in their population changed the way the land looked. For example, as the Indians of the Southeast died in what had once been a densely populated region with a lot of farmland, cleared areas reverted to grassy woodland. Deer and other animal populations increased in response. When whites arrived, they saw the abundance of animals as somehow natural, but it was nothing of the sort.

Disease also dramatically altered relationships among Indian peoples. In the 1780s and 1790s the most powerful and prosperous peoples on the Great Plains margins were the Mandans, the Arikaras, the Hidatsas, the Pawnees, all of whom raised corn as part of their subsistence cycles. Nomadic, nonagricultural groups like the Sioux were small and poor. Smallpox changed all that. Those peoples living in large, populous farming villages were precisely those who suffered the greatest death rates. So the group that had once controlled the region went into decline, while another fairly marginal group rose to historical prominence.

WC That's a perfect example of biological and cultural interaction, of how complex it is. A dense population is more susceptible to disease than a less dense one: that's a biological observation true of any animal species. But which Indian communities are dense and which are not, which ones are living in clustered settlements and which ones are scattered thinly on the ground—these aren't biological phenomena but *cultural* ones.

RW Perhaps the best example of this is the way different Plains Indians responded to the horse, which, along with disease, actually preceded the arrival of significant numbers of Europeans in the region. The older conception of what happened is that when the horse arrived, it transformed the world. That may have been true for the Sioux, but not for the Pawnees. The Sioux became horse nomads; the Pawnees didn't. They were not willing to give up the security of raising crops. For them, the horse provided an ability to hunt buffalo more efficiently, but they were not about to rely solely on buffalo. If the buffalo hunt failed, and they had neglected their crops, they would be in great trouble. As far as I know, there is no agricultural group, with the exception of the Crows and perhaps the Cheyennes, that *willingly* gave up agriculture to rely solely on the buffalo. The people like the Sioux who became Plains nomads had always been hunters and gatherers, and for them horses represented a *more* secure subsistence, not a less secure one.

WC It's the ecological safety net again. People who practiced agriculture were reluctant to abandon it, because it was one of their strongest nets.

RW And they didn't. When given a choice, even under harsh circumstances, people tried to integrate the horse into their existing economy, not transform themselves.

The horse came to the Sioux at a time when they were in trouble. Their subsistence base had grown precarious: the buffalo and beavers they'd hunted farther east were declining, and the decline of the farming villages from disease meant the Sioux could no longer raid or trade with them for food. The horse was a godsend: buffalo hunting became more efficient, and the buffalo began to replace other food sources. Having adopted the horse, the Sioux moved farther out onto the Plains. By the time they had their famous conflicts with the United States in the 1860s and 1870s, they were the dominant people of the Great Plains. Their way of life was unimaginable without the horse and buffalo.

WC The result was that the Sioux reduced the number of ecological nets that sustained their economy and way of life. And although the bison were present in enormous numbers when the Sioux began to adopt the horse, by the 1860s the bison were disappearing from the Plains; by the early eighties they were virtually gone. That meant the Sioux's main ecological net was gone, and there wasn't much left to replace it.

RW To destroy the buffalo was to destroy the Sioux. Of course, given time, they might have been able to replace the buffalo with cattle and become a pastoral people. That seems well within the realm of historical possibility. But they were never allowed that option.

WC Disease and the horse are obviously important factors in Indian history. But there's a deeper theme underlying these things. All North American Indian peoples eventually found themselves in a relationship of dependency with the dominant Euro-American culture. At some point, in various ways, they ceased to be entirely autonomous peoples, controlling their own resources and their own political and cultural life. Is environmental history fundamental to explaining how this happened?

RW I think it's absolutely crucial. Compare the history of European settlement in North America with what happened in Asia and Africa. Colonialism in Asia and Africa was very important, but it was a passing phase. It has left a strong legacy, but Africa is nonetheless a continent inhabited by Africans, Asia a continent inhabited by Asians. American Indian peoples, on the other hand, are a small minority in North America. Part of what happened was simply the decline in population, but as we've said, that decline was not simple at all. To understand it, we have to understand environmental history.

Many Indians were never militarily conquered. They nonetheless became dependent on whites, partly because their subsistence economy was systematically undercut. Virtually every American Indian community eventually had to face the fact that it could no longer feed or shelter itself without outside aid. A key aspect of this was the arrival of a market economy in which certain resources came to be overexploited. The fur trade is the clearest example of this.

WC No question. The traditional picture of the fur trade is that Europeans arrive, wave a few guns and kettles and blankets in the air, and Indians come rushing forward to trade. What do they have to trade? They have beaver pelts, deerskins, bison robes. As soon as the incentive is present, as soon as those European goods are there to be had, the Indians sweep across the continent, wipe out the fur-bearing animals, and destroy their own subsistence. That's the classic myth of the fur trade.

RW It simply didn't happen that way. European goods often penetrated Indian communities slowly; Indian technologies held on for a long time. Indians wanted European goods, but for reasons that could be very different from why we think they wanted them.

WC One of my favorite examples is the kettle trade. Indians wanted kettles partly because you can put them on a fire and boil water and they won't break. That's nice. But many of those kettles didn't stay kettles for long. They got cut up and turned into arrowheads that were then used in the hunt. Or they got turned into high-status jewelry. Indians valued kettles because they were such an extraordinarily flexible resource.

RW The numbers of kettles that have turned up in Indian graves proves that their value was not simply utilitarian.

WC The basic facts of the fur trade are uncontestable. Europeans sought to acquire Indian furs, food, and land; Indians sought to acquire European textiles, alcohol, guns, and other metal goods. Indians began to hunt greater numbers of fur-bearing animals, until finally several species, especially the beaver, were eliminated. Those are the two end points of the fur-trade story. But understanding how to get from one to the other is very complicated. Why did Indians engage in the fur trade in the first place? That's the question.

RW We tend to assume that exchange is straightforward, that it's simply giving one thing in return for another. That is not how it appeared to Indian peoples.

WC Think of the different ways goods are exchanged. One is how we usually perceive exchange today: we go into the local supermarket, lay down a dollar, and get a candy bar in return. Many Europeans in the fur trade thought that was what they were doing—giving a gun, or a blanket, or a kettle and receiving a number of furs in return. But for the Indians the exchange looked very different.

RW To see how Indians perceived this, consider two things we all know, but which we don't ordinarily label as "trade." One is gifts. There's no need to romanticize the giving of gifts. Contemporary Americans exchange gifts at Christmas or at weddings, and when those gifts are exchanged, as anybody who has received one knows, you incur an obligation. You often have relatives who never let you forget the gift they've given you, and what you owe in return. There's no *price* set on the exchange, it's a *gift*, but the obligation is very real. That's one way Indians saw exchange. To exchange goods that way, the two parties at least had to pretend to be friends.

At the other extreme, if friendship hadn't been established, goods could still change hands, but here the basis of exchange was often simple theft. If you had enemies, you could rob them. So if traders failed to establish some friendship, kinship, or alliance, Indians felt perfectly justified in attacking them and taking their goods. In the fur trade there was a fine line between people who sometimes traded with each other and sometimes stole from each other.

WC To make that more concrete, when the Indian handed a beaver skin to the trader, who gave a gun in return, it wasn't simply two goods that were moving back and forth. There were symbols passing between them as well. The trader might not have been aware of all those symbols, but for the Indian the exchange represented a statement about their friendship. The Indian might expect to rely on the trader for military support, and to support him in return. Even promises about marriage, about linking two communities together, might be expressed as goods passed from hand to hand. It was almost as if a language was being spoken when goods were exchanged. It took a long time for the two sides to realize they weren't speaking the same language.

RW Right. But for Indians the basic meanings of exchange were clear. You gave generously to friends; you stole from enemies. Indians also recognized that not everybody could be classified simply as a friend or an enemy, and this middle ground is where trade took place.

But even in that middle ground, trade always began with an exchange of gifts. And to fail to be generous in your gifts, to push too hard on the price—Indians read that as hostility. When Europeans tried to explain the concept of a "market" to Indians, it bewildered them. The notion that demand for furs in London could affect how many blankets they would receive for a beaver skin in Canada was quite alien to them. How on earth could events taking place an ocean away have anything to do with the relationship between two people standing right here who were supposed to act as friends and brothers toward each other?

WC So one thing Indian peoples had trouble comprehending at certain stages in this dialogue was the concept of *price*: the price of a good fluctuating because of its abundance in the market. Indian notions were much closer to the medieval "just price." This much gunpowder is always worth this many beaver skins. If somebody tells me they want twice as many skins for the same gunpowder I bought last year at half the price, suddenly they're being treacherous. They're beginning to act as an enemy.

RW Or in the words Algonquians often used, "This must mean my father doesn't love me any more." To Europeans that kind of language seems ludicrous. What in the world does love have to do with giving a beaver skin for gunpowder? But for Indians it's absolutely critical.

Of course, exchange became more commercial with time. Early in the fur trade, Indians had received European goods as gifts, because they were allies against other Indians or other Europeans. But increasingly they found that the only way to receive those goods was through direct economic exchange. Gift giving became less important, and trading goods for set prices became more important. As part of these commercial dealings, traders often advanced loans to Indians before they actually had furs to trade. By that mechanism, gifts were transformed into debts. Debts could in turn be used to coerce greater and greater hunting from Indians.

WC As exchange became more commercial, the Indians' relationship to animals became more commercial as well. Hunting increased with the rise in trade, and animal populations declined in response. First the beaver, then the deer, then the bison disappeared from large stretches of North America. As that happened, Indians found themselves in the peculiar position of relying more and more on European goods but no longer having the furs they needed to acquire them. Worse, they could no longer even *make* those same goods as they once had, in the form of skin garments, wild meat, and so on. That's the trap they fell into.

RW And that becomes dependency. That's what Thomas Jefferson correctly and cynically realized when he argued that the best way for the United States to acquire Indian lands was to encourage trade and have government storehouses assume Indian debts. Indians would have no choice but to cede their lands to pay their debts, and they couldn't even renounce those debts because they now needed the resources the United States offered them in order to survive. Not all tribes became involved in this, but most who relied on the fur trade eventually did.

Of course, the effects go both ways. As whites eliminated Indians and Indian control, they were also, without realizing it, eliminating the forces that had shaped the landscape itself. The things they took as natural—why there were trees, why there weren't trees, the species of plants that grew there—were really the results of Indian practices. As whites changed the practices, those things vanished. Trees began to reinvade the grassland, and forests that had once been open became closed.

WC Once the wild animals that had been part of the Indians' spiritual and ecological universe began to disappear, Europeans acquired the land and began to transform it to match their assumptions about what a "civilized" landscape should look like. With native animals disappearing, other animals could be brought in to use the same food supply that the deer, the moose, and the bison had previously used. And so the cow, the horse, the pig—the animals so central to European notions of what an animal universe looks like—began to move across the continent like a kind of animal frontier. In many instances the Indians turned to these domesticated European species to replace their own decreasing food supply and so adopted a more pastoral way of life. As they lost their lands, they were then stuck with the problem of feeding their animals as well as themselves.

RW The Navajos are a good example of this. We tend to forget that Indians don't simply vanish when we enter the twentieth century. The Navajos are perhaps the group who maintained control over their own lands for the longest time, but their control was increasingly subject to outside pressures. They very early adopted European sheep, which became more and more important to their economy, both because wild foods were eliminated and because the government strongly encouraged the Navajos to raise more sheep. They built up prosperous herds but were gradually forced to confine them to the reservation instead of the wider regions they had grazed before.

The result was a crisis on the Navajo reservation. The land began to erode. By the 1920s and 1930s the Navajos had far more sheep than could be sustained during dry years. And here's where one of the more interesting confrontations between Indians and conservationists took place. The government sought to reduce Navajo stock, but its own motives were mixed. There was a genuine fear for the Navajos, but the main concern had to do with Boulder Dam. Conservationists feared Lake Mead was going to silt up, and that the economic development of the Southwest would be badly inhibited.

What they didn't understand were the causes of erosion. They blamed it all on Navajo sheep, but it now appears that there was a natural gullying cycle going on in the Southwest. Anybody familiar with the Southwest knows that its terrain is shaped by more than sheep and horses, no matter how badly it is overgrazed. So the result of government conservation policy for the Navajos was deeply ironic. Having adjusted to the European presence, having prospered with their sheep, they found their herds being undercut by the government for the good of the larger economy. It's a classic case of Indians—as the poorest and least powerful people in a region—forced to bear the brunt of economic-development costs. So the Navajo economy was again transformed. As the Navajos became poorer and poorer, they grew more willing to lease out oil and allow strip mining on the reservation. They found.themselves in the familiar situation of being forced to agree to practices that were harmful, even in their view, to the land. They had to do it in order to survive, but they were then attacked by white conservationists for abandoning their own values.

WC A real no-win situation.

RW There are lessons in all this. We can't copy Indian ways of understanding nature, we're too different. But studying them throws our own assumptions into starker relief and suggests shortcomings in our relationships with nature that could cost us dearly in the long run.

WC I think environmental history may be capable of transforming our perspective, not just on Indian history, but on all human history. The great arrogance of Western civilization in the industrial and postindustrial eras has been to imagine human beings existing somehow apart from the earth. Often the history of the industrial era has been written as if technology has liberated human beings so that the earth has become increasingly irrelevant to modern civilization—when in fact all history is a long-standing dialogue between human beings and the earth. It's as if people are constantly speaking to the earth, and the earth is speaking to them. That's a way of putting it that Indians would be far more capable of understanding than most modern Americans. But this dialogue, this conversation between earth and the inhabitants of earth, is fundamental to environmental history. With it we can try to draw together all these pieces—human population changes, cultural changes, economic changes, environmental changes—into a complicated but unified history of humanity upon the earth. That, in rather ambitious terms, is what environmental historians are seeking to do.

August 1986

$\vee$

VERDICTS OF HISTORY:
THE BOSTON MASSACRE

Thomas J. Fleming

This relatively minor incident in the tension torn Boston of 1770 has long fascinated historians. Why did the shootings take place? Why did Bostonians rally to the death of 5 very common citizens? Why did prominent radicals John Adams and Josiah Quincy defend the soldiers? Thomas Fleming gives an in-depth look at this turbulent moment and proposes some interesting conclusions in the following analysis.

"The Jurors for the said Lord the King upon oath present that Thomas Preston, Esq.; William Wemms, laborer; James Hartegan, laborer; William McCauley, laborer; Hugh White, laborer; Matthew Killroy, laborer; William Warren, laborer; John Carroll, laborer and Hugh Montgomery, laborer, all now resident in Boston in the County of Suffolk, . . . not having the fear of God before their eyes, but being moved and seduced by the instigation of the devil and their own wicked hearts, did on the 5th day of this instant March, at Boston aforesaid within the county aforesaid with force and arms feloniously, willfully and of their malice aforethought assault one Crispus Attucks, then and there being in the peace of God and of the said Lord the King and that the said William Warren, with a certain handgun of the value of 20 shillings, which he the said William Warren then and there held in both his hands charged with gunpowder and two leaden bullets, then and there feloniously, willfully and of his malice aforethought, did shoot off and discharge at and against the said Crispus Attucks, and that the said William Warren, with the leaden bullets as aforesaid out of the said handgun then and there by force of the said gunpowder so shot off and discharged as aforesaid did then and there feloniously, willfully and of his malice aforethought, strike, penetrate and wound the said Crispus Attucks in and upon the right breast a little below the right pap of him the said Crispus and in and upon the left breast a little below the left pap . . . of which said mortal wounds the said Crispus Attucks then and there instantly died."

Thus did the citizens of Boston indict nine British soldiers for murder. (The designation of the soldiers as "laborers" in the indictment emphasized that they were being tried as ordinary citizens—and also that they often eked out their pay by working for hire in and around Boston.)

Never before in the history of Massachusetts had a trial aroused such intense, complex political and personal passion. Although his name stands alone in the indictment, Crispus Attucks was not the only victim. Four other Bostonians were also dead in what Samuel Adams, through his mouthpiece Benjamin Edes, publisher of the *Boston Gazette,* promptly called "a horrid massacre." For Adams and his friends in the Liberty party, the trial could have only one possible outcome. Paul Revere summed it up in the verse beneath his famous engraving of the scene.

> *But know, Fate summons to that awful Goal*
> *Where Justice strips the Murd'rer of his Soul:*
> *Should venal C[our]ts the scandal of the land*
> *Snatch the relentless Villain from her Hand*
> *Keen Execrations on this Plate inscrib'd*
> *Shall reach a Judge who never can be brib'd.*

The gist of what happened, whether baldly or passionately stated, was simple enough. Parliament's passage of the Townshend duties (import taxes on lead, paper, glass, tea) had inspired a series of riots and assaults on Royal officials which the magistrates and watchmen of Boston seemed helpless to prevent. On October 1, 1768, the Crown had landed two regiments of Royal troops to keep the peace. Relations between the townspeople and the soldiers had started poor and deteriorated steadily. After eighteen months, tempers on both sides were sputtering ominously.

Ironically, Parliament was about to repeal the Townshend duties, except for the tiny tax on tea, but the news had not reached Boston when the explosion occurred. At about eight o'clock on the moonlit night of March 5, 1770, a sentry on duty before the hated Custom House gave an impudent apprentice boy a knock on the ear with his gun. An unruly crowd gathered. Someone rang the bells in a nearby church. This signal, ordinarily a summons to fight fire, drew more people into the street. The frightened sentry called out the main guard. Seven men led by a corporal responded, and were shortly joined by Captain Thomas Preston. A few minutes later, a volley of shots left five "martyrs" dead or dying in the snow and six other men painfully wounded.

For a few hours Boston teetered on the brink of a blood bath. The well-armed Sons of Liberty outnumbered the British regiments ten to one, and the local militia was swiftly bolstered by hundreds of farmers who swarmed in from the countryside. Only a desperate speech by Lieutenant Governor Thomas Hutchinson, in which he promised to arrest the soldiers and charge them with murder, calmed the enraged city enough to restore an uneasy semblance of peace.

On the morning after the bloodshed, John Adams was in his office beside the Town House steps. Through the door came a tearful, wailing man, James Forest, known about Boston as a British toady and scornfully called "the Irish infant." The accused leader of the arrested British soldiers, Captain Preston, had begged him to find a lawyer posthaste. This had proved very difficult. Finally, young Josiah Quincy, Jr., from John Adams' home town of Braintree, had expressed a willingness on one condition—that John Adams join him in the defense. One other lawyer, Robert Auchmuty, a staunch conservative, had volunteered with the same proviso.

The challenge aroused all the latent conservatism in the thirty-four-year-old John Adams' pugnacious spirit. For a decade he had watched his distant cousin Samuel construct a "political engine" in Boston, discovering under his tutelage "the wheels . . . cogs or pins, some of them dirty ones, which composed the machine and made it go." Though he wrote convincing defenses of the Liberty party position in the *Boston Gazette,* John often signed himself

"Clarendon" (the British lord who had done his utmost to prevent Cromwell's excesses in the English civil war), and politely declined to harangue town meetings in the demagogic style of cousin Samuel and his friends Dr. Joseph Warren and James Otis. John took an even dimmer view of the violent tendencies of the Sons of Liberty—and obviously saw a direct connection between their terrorist tactics and the frightened state of the Boston bar.

Years later, John Adams recalled that he had "no hesitation" in accepting the case. He told Forest "that Council ought to be the very last thing that an accused person should want [*i.e.*, lack] in a free country. That the bar ought in my opinion to be independent and impartial at all times and in every circumstance."

This was a noble ideal, but John Adams knew that it was far from the reality of Boston in 1770. The city was ruthlessly divided into King's men and Liberty men. Doctors, lawyers, even clergymen, were chosen for their fiercely partisan political opinions. Adams himself had made his irrevocable choice in 1768, when he refused Thomas Hutchinson's offer to make him advocate general of the Court of Admiralty. Since that time the vast proportion of his law practice had come from Liberty clients.

Nevertheless Adams solemnly accepted a guinea from James Forest as a retainer to seal the agreement. He warned the overwrought Irishman that this would be "as important a cause as had ever been tried in any court or country of the world." Neither he nor Captain Preston could, of course, expect anything more than "fact, evidence and law would justify."

"Captain Preston," Forest answered, "requested and desired no more . . . as God Almighty is my judge I believe him an innocent man."

It was only a few days before the surprising news of Adams' decision had made a complete circuit of Boston and its environs. Rocks were flung through the windows of the Adams home. Boys jeered him on the streets. Josiah Quincy got a letter from his father in Braintree: "My Dear Son, I am under great affliction at hearing the bitterest reproaches uttered against you, for having become an advocate for those criminals who are charged with the murder of their fellow citizens. Good God! Is it possible? I will not believe it."

Young Quincy wrote his father a spirited defense of his decision. Tall and handsome, he was a fervent Liberty man, but above all an idealist. And he could afford to be reckless. He already knew he was suffering from tuberculosis, which was to cut short his brilliant career five years later. John Adams, with an established practice and a wife, and three children to support, had no such motive. Nor was his temperament in the least inclined to enthusiasm. A worrier by nature, he sometimes expressed awed amazement at Sam Adams, who let the citizens of Boston pay his debts and lived "like the grasshopper" from day to day. John had always self-consciously planned his career. "The art of living," he once told Cousin Samuel, had cost him "much musing and pondering and anxiety."

Adams' morale did not improve when Cousin Samuel convened a town meeting of three thousand roaring adherents to demand the immediate expulsion of the two regiments. Lieutenant Governor Thomas Hutchinson yielded one regiment, then (literally trembling with anguish) yielded both, and the soldiers trudged through a barrage of derision to boats that took them to Castle William, far out in Boston Harbor.

Sam Adams' next move was a vigorous prosecution of a trial by newspaper. Ninety-six depositions from eyewitnesses were recorded by John Hodgson, the only shorthand writer in Boston, and solemnly sworn to before justices of the peace. They were attached to a twenty-two-page report compiled by the Boston selectmen and published and distributed throughout the province, but not in Boston. The Liberty men piously declared they did not want to prejudice anyone against the defendants.

As propaganda the book was a masterful document. The ninety-six witnesses were all but unanimous in their pro-Liberty description of the murder scene. Only one man had anything even faintly favorable to say for the soldiers, and editorial comments declared him to be a liar. The rest agreed that they were all in the streets of Boston that night on utterly peaceful errands—visiting friends, attending church meetings—when they were attacked by soldiers armed with bayonets, swords, and cutlasses.

But Samuel Adams was not the only person interested in compiling a version of what happened on the night of March 5. In New York, General Thomas Gage, commander in chief of all British troops in North America, wrote to Lieutenant Colonel Dalrymple, the commander of the Boston garrison.

> It is absolutely necessary everything relating to the unhappy affair of the 5th of March should appear as full as it is possible upon Captain Preston's tryal. Not only what happened on the said night should be circumstantially made to appear, but also every insult and attack made upon the troops previous thereto with the pains taken by the military to prevent quarrels between the soldiers and inhabitants. If such things cannot be introduced at the tryal, affidavits should, however, be procured of these several circumstances and printed with the tryal which ought to be taken down for the purpose. . . .

Thus from the very start the trial became far more than a matter of determining the guilt or innocence of the arrested soldiers. The King's men were out to win a conviction against the mob-rule tactics of Samuel Adams. The Liberty men were as fiercely determined to pillory Parliament's use of armed force to suppress their political rights.

Between these two bitter determined groups of men stood the prisoners and their uneasy lawyers. Ironically, after the frantic search for defense attorneys, the Crown had almost as much trouble finding men willing to serve on the prosecution side. Jonathan Sewall, the colony's attorney general, handed up the indictment and disappeared from Boston, declaring that he would never appear in another court in that town. This may have been in part a maneuver to delay the trial. In the weeks succeeding the Massacre, Boston's inflamed state of mind made the possibility of an objective jury almost laughable.

But Samuel Adams was not to be easily put off. On the thirteenth of March, a town meeting resolved "That the selectmen be desired to employ one or more counsel to offer to the King's attorney as assistants to him in the trial of the murtherers now committed; and in case the King's attorney should refuse such assistance and the relatives of those persons who were murthered should apply for it, that then the town will bear the expense that may accrue thereby." The court soon appointed Samuel Quincy, Josiah Quincy's elder brother and a convinced Tory, to head the prosecution. Assisting him as the town's designee was attorney Robert Treat Paine, a staunch Liberty man.

On March 14, the day after the term opened, two of the judges declared themselves ill and announced a determination to adjourn to the second Tuesday in June. A committee of Liberty men swiftly appeared in court, with Samuel Adams and John Hancock as their spokesmen. In his quavering voice, gesturing with his palsied hands, Adams made what one observer called "a *very pathetic* [emotional] speech," calling on the court to proceed to the trial without delay. Governor Hutchinson described Adams as followed by "a vast concourse of people." The terrified judges, Hutchinson reported, "altered their determination and resolved to go on with the business. This, they assured me, was contrary to their inclination but they were under duress and afraid to offend the town."

Captain Thomas Preston, meanwhile, tried to launch a small propaganda campaign on his own behalf. An Anglo-Irishman, forty years old with fifteen years of army service on his record, he was, compared to the other British soldiers in the prison, well liked by the people of Boston. Various letters describe him as "amiable" and as being "a benevolent, humane man." Hoping no doubt to enlarge this image, he had the following "card" published in the *Boston Gazette*.

> Messieurs Edes and Gill, permit me thro' the channel of your Paper, to re-
> turn my Thanks in the most publick Manner to the Inhabitants in general of
> this Town—who throwing aside all *Party* and Prejudice, have with the ut-
> most Humanity and Freedom stept forth Advocates for Truth in Defence of
> my injured Innocence, in the late unhappy Affair that happened on Monday
> Night last: and to assure them, that I shall ever have the highest Sense of the
> *Justice* they have done me, which will be ever gratefully remembered, by
> Their most obliged and most obedient humble Servant, Thomas Preston.

In New York, this gesture struck General Gage as the height of folly. "I can't be a proper judge at this distance," he wrote to Colonel Dalrymple, "but I wish he may not have been too premature in that measure; and if a legal proceedings are hereafter made use of against him, they will justify themselves by his own words."

Through late March and April, Samuel Adams kept his town meeting in almost continu-ous session by endlessly delaying matters of business. This gave him a perfectly legal device to maintain a relentless pressure on Governor Hutchinson and the judges.

The beleaguered Hutchinson decided that he would have to offer his enemies a sacri-fice to allay their ferocity. Two weeks before the Massacre, a Custom House employee, Ebenezer Richardson, had gotten into a brawl with some boys who chased him home with a barrage of icy snowballs, stones, and brickbats. They continued the bombardment on his house, smashing most of the windows. The enraged Tory suddenly thrust a musket loaded with birdshot from an upstairs window. "By God," he shouted, "I'll make a lane through you." The gun boomed and most of the charge struck a twelve-year-old boy, who died that night. For Samuel Adams, Richardson was, of course, a very small fish. But his case did, in sequence of time, come first. Adams was therefore helpless to object when the judges moved to put Richardson in the dock.

Richardson had even more trouble procuring legal aid than Preston and his soldiers. Not a single attorney volunteered, and when the court appointed Samuel Fitch, he agreed to serve under violent protestations of duress, then became conveniently ill when the case went to trial. The court then appointed Josiah Quincy, Jr., an equally reluctant if more idealistic advocate. Only recently have we learned that the man who directed Richardson's defense was John Ad-ams. The notes and documents pertaining to the case were discovered in John's legal files by the editors of the Adams Papers. With Samuel Quincy and Robert Treat Paine handling the pros-ecution, Richardson's case became almost a rehearsal for the Massacre trial.

"A vast concourse of rabble," as one Tory described his fellow Bostonians, packed the courtroom. They growled their disapproval when the three judges unanimously agreed that from the testimony of witnesses on both sides, the charge against Richardson could amount to no more than manslaughter. Justice Peter Oliver went even further and declared to the jury that in his opinion the case was justifiable homicide. Whereupon an improper Bostonian shouted from the crowd: "Damn that judge. If I was nigh him I would give it to him." When Oliver finished speaking, someone in the crowd roared out: "Remember, Jury, you are on oath. Blood requires blood."

The jury found Richardson guilty of first-degree murder, and only vigorous exertion by the sheriff and town constables prevented the mob from taking him outside and hanging him on the spot.

The judges, aghast at the jury's complete disregard of their charge, refused to sentence Richardson. He was remanded to jail, where he was to languish for another two years. His case, however, made it look certain that trying Preston and the soldiers right away would result in their conviction. "Procrastination is our only course as things are now situated," wrote Colonel Dalrymple to General Gage.

Samuel Adams and his friends continued to agitate for instant justice. Once more they appeared in the courtroom and harangued the judges, threatening to withhold their salaries if they delayed any longer. But Hutchinson, who had the courage of his convictions, finally won the seesaw battle. Under his direction, the court constantly met and adjourned, met and adjourned. Then Hutchinson shifted the next meeting of the judiciary to Cambridge, proclaiming it a necessity to avoid the threats of the Boston mob. This inspired (on June 1, 1770) what Hutchinson ironically called "a jovial celebration . . . at Boston in opposition to me," which involved roasting an ox whole on the Common and a great dinner at Faneuil Hall. While toasts were being drunk to liberty, the judges quietly adjourned the court *sine die* (without setting a day to reconvene), automatically continuing to the next term the question of the soldiers' fate. Hutchinson wrote proudly to Gage, describing how he had "procured without any tumult a continuance of the trial to the next term."

Through the hot Boston summer Preston and his men sat in their cells. Preston's fortunes, which seemed for a while to be rising, took a sharp downward turn when a Tory version of the Massacre, first published in England, appeared in the *Boston Gazette*. The Captain was soon writing Gage that he feared the mob was planning an attack on the jail to murder him and his men in their cells. Though Hutchinson doubted that the Liberty people would make such an attack before the trial, he recommended to Sheriff Steven Greenleaf that he take the keys from the jailkeeper at night, just in case.

Meanwhile, Hutchinson was having his troubles with the judges. Twice during the summer, Chief Justice Benjamin Lynde, who was over seventy, came to him with his resignation. Justice Edmund Trowbridge was at least as terrified. Only Judge Peter Oliver stood firm, ignoring personal threats in the newspapers. Another worry was the lack of enthusiasm which the Tories anticipated in the soldiers' attorneys. Loyalist Auchmuty bluntly told Hutchinson he did not think Preston had a chance.

Nevertheless, early in September, with Hutchinson's approval, Preston began to press for a trial. Actually Hutchinson was still certain Preston would be found guilty, but he wanted the matter settled early in the fall, with sentencing delayed until the opening of the March term. This might give him time to get a ship to England and back with a King's pardon to save Preston's neck.

The justices, however, reserved their own opinion of when they should risk their lives by bringing Preston to trial: they went on circuit into the country. First, however, they did bring the Captain and his eight soldiers into the courtroom for arraignment. Each pleaded "Not guilty," and "for trial put himself upon God and the country."

At this point John Adams played a surprise card, one he had been holding very close to his vest. He made a motion to try Captain Preston and the soldiers separately. The court granted it. The soldiers immediately decided they were to be the sacrificial lambs, and forwarded a plaintive petition to the court: "May it please Your Honors, we poor distressed prisoners beg that ye would be so good as to lett us have our trial at the same time with our Captain, for we did our Captain's orders and if we don't obey his command we should have been confined and shott for not doing it. . . . " This only confirmed defense fears that Preston and his men would each accuse the other if tried jointly, and in the confusion the jury would decide to hang them all. But as we shall soon see, this was not the only reason for Adams' unexpected motion.

Not until October 24, 1770, did the judges return and the lawyers assemble to impanel a jury to decide Captain Preston's fate. Almost immediately it became evident that the court and all the lawyers were involved in a curious kind of collusion. Adams, the acknowledged leader of the defense, challenged every juror who came from within the city limits of Boston, quickly rejecting the eighteen men who had been selected by the Boston town meeting of August 24, 1770. When the legally summoned jurors were used up, it was the custom of the day to allow the sheriff to contribute "talesmen." By no coincidence, every talesman produced by the sheriff for Preston's trial came from outside Boston. Indeed, a study of the jury list reveals that five of the twelve selected were later Loyalist exiles.

These maneuvers must have been obvious to Samuel Adams. They were beyond all doubt known to John Adams and Josiah Quincy. Why did Samuel Adams by silence and inaction give tacit approval? A nod from him, and his well-disciplined bullyboys could have filled the courtroom as they did at Richardson's trial and terrified the judges and jurors into submission. But there is no evidence of any disorder during Preston's trial, nor at the trial of the soldiers. The change of tactics is startling, and there is nothing in the written evidence of the Massacre story that explains it.

The answer must lie in the political struggle that surrounded the trials. By this time, John Adams and Josiah Quincy had, thanks to a liberal supply of sovereigns from General Gage, obtained depositions from dozens of people who had been witnesses to various aspects of the bloody deed. These statements conflicted so totally with the evidence advanced by the Liberty men in their ninety-six depositions that there was only one possible conclusion—someone was committing perjury. Worse, the evidence advanced by the witnesses Adams and Quincy uncovered put the town of Boston in a most unholy light. For the first time the Loyalists had a weapon with which they could smite Samuel Adams hard. But Sam on his side retained the weapon he knew and handled best: the Boston mob.

Even with the packed jury, Preston's case was by no means a sure thing. The prosecution attacked vigorously, parading witness after witness to the stand for the better part of two days; all of them agreed that the Captain gave the order to fire—and, equally important, that there was no provocation for it beyond name-calling and a few snowballs from the crowd gathered in King Street.

The defense attorneys did little to dispute these assertions in their cross-examination. But they did shake the believability of many witnesses by pointing out strange confusions in their testimony. Some swore the Captain stood in front of the men; others said he stood behind them. Several said that the Captain had on a "cloth color" surtout (a kind of overcoat); almost as many said they distinctly saw him in his bright red regimentals.

After a prosecution summation by Samuel Quincy, in which he accused Preston of "murder with malice aforethought," the defense produced their witnesses. The first few disputed the prosecution's claim that the crowd was small and peaceful, but said nothing that would stir an already tired jury. (It was the first time in Massachusetts' memory that a murder trial had lasted more than a day.) Then John Adams produced a merchant named Richard Palmes, and the courtroom came to life. Mr. Palmes was the real reason for the separate trials. He had earlier given a lengthy deposition supposedly supporting the Liberty side of the story. Even a cursory reading of this told a lawyer as keen as John Adams that detaching Preston from his men converted Palmes into a witness for the Captain.

Palmes knew it, and had desperately tried to decamp from Boston. John Adams had kept him in town by court order. On the stand, the reluctant Palmes was forced to repeat his sworn deposition. He told of stepping up to Preston as he joined his soldiers and asking: "Sir, I hope you don't intend the soldiers shall fire on the inhabitants."

"He said, 'by no means.' The instant he spoke I saw something resembling snow or ice strike the grenadier on the Captain's right hand, being the only one then at his right. [The grenadier] instantly stepped one foot back and fired the first gun. . . . The gun scorched the nap of my surtout at the elbow."

Other witnesses substantiated Palmes' statement. As a good lawyer, Adams also brought in a few people who bolstered the self-defense side of Preston's plea. But in his summation, he made it clear that Palmes was his key witness. Coolly, he noted that the mortified merchant was "an inhabitant of the town and therefore not prejudiced in favor of the soldiers." Robert Auchmuty, summing up after Adams, declared that Palmes' evidence "may be opposed to all the Crown's evidence." He went on to give an impressive speech, citing a wealth of precedents in the common law which permitted soldiers or other persons to kill rioters or even individuals who attacked them and threatened them with serious injury. Auchmuty's knowledge of the law was considered weak, but he sounded formidable as he cited case after case from Coke and other great authorities on English law. Undoubtedly he was using John Adams' research. But he put it together with an enthusiasm and flair that surprised and delighted Preston and the Tories who had been doubting him. His performance can probably be explained by a letter General Gage wrote to Colonel Dalrymple, "I am sorry," the British commander in chief said, "you doubt Mr. Auchmuty's zeal or good intentions. . . . If you find it necessary, you should encourage him, for very particular reports are to be made of every circumstance of the tryal." Caught between the threat of royal censure and his dread of the Boston mob, Auchmuty followed his Loyalist leanings and performed brilliantly.

Robert Treat Paine valiantly tried to rescue the prosecution's case. But he could not explain away Palmes. He called him "their principal witness" and admitted he was "a gentleman who I can by no means suppose would be guilty of a known falsehood." Paine could only maintain that this staunch Son of Liberty was "certainly mistaken," and fumble to an emotional peroration, calling on the jury to "find such a verdict as the laws of God, of nature and your own conscience will ever approve."

Now came the judges' charges to the jury. There were four sitting—Chief Justice Lynde and Justices John Cushing, Peter Oliver, and Edmund Trowbridge. Trowbridge was considered the best legal mind in Massachusetts. Stately in their white wigs and long red (for a murder trial) robes, they proceeded to examine the evidence and the law. Trowbridge spoke first, pointing out the contradictory accounts given by the witnesses and declaring that it did not appear to him that the prisoner gave orders to fire. But even if the jury should think otherwise, they surely could not call his crime murder. The people assembled were "a riotous mob" who had murderously attacked the prisoner and his party. If Preston was guilty of any offense, it could only be excusable homicide. The other three judges concurred. Oliver added, "in a very nervous and pathetic manner," that he was resolved to do his duty to his God, his King, and his country, and despise both insults and threats.

The jury was then locked up for the night. Within three hours they voted to acquit Preston and so reported it to the assembled court the next morning. The Captain was immediately released from jail and rushed by boat to Castle William, where the guns of his regiment guaranteed his safety against possible revenge from the Boston mob. But Samuel Adams' obvious acquiescence in the choice of a packed jury made it clear that he had long since agreed to let Captain Preston go in peace. His men were another matter.

Thus far, John Adams, with Josiah Quincy's help, had maintained his perilous balancing act. At one point during the five days of Preston's trial, he had objected angrily when Auchmuty tried to advance more evidence of a Liberty conspiracy to incite a riot. The Tories on the bench had stressed mob violence in their remarks to the jury; yet the violent side of the evidence had played only a minor role in Preston's trial. It had to be the heart of the soldiers' case. That they had fired their guns was beyond debating; five men were dead to prove it.

There was another hint of the way the local wind was blowing: Auchmuty now withdrew from the soldiers' defense, and another attorney, Sampson Salter Blowers, was appointed in his place. Like Quincy, he was young and comparatively inexperienced. Thus almost full responsibility for the soldiers' fate, both in a public and a private sense, fell on the stocky shoulders of John Adams.

If he had any illusions about the tactics of the opposition, they vanished when he picked up the *Boston Gazette* on the Monday before the trial began. "Is it then a dream—murder on the 5th of March with the dogs greedily licking human blood in King Street? Some say that righteous heaven will avenge it. And what says the Law of God? *Whoso sheddeth Man's Blood, by Man shall his Blood be shed!*" And the *Gazette* quoted at length from a sermon preached by the Reverend Doctor Chauncy, senior minister of Boston, declaring that should the soldiers be convicted of murder, Governor Hutchinson would never dare grant them a reprieve: "Surely he would not suffer the town and land to lie under the defilement of blood! Surely he would not make himself a partaker in the guilt of murder by putting a stop to the shedding of their blood, who have murderously spilt the blood of others."

On the day the second trial began, the audience was a good barometer of the local atmosphere. At Preston's trial the benches had been filled by Tories and army officers. Now the courtroom was jammed to the windows with townspeople. Shorthand-writer John Hodgson, who recorded the trial, complained that he did not have room to move his elbow. Outside, snow was falling, and the bailiffs had to light candles against the gloom. People shivered in winter clothes; the two small stoves in the room seemed to have no effect whatsoever on the pervading chill.

The prisoners were brought to the bar. Their blazing red coats set off their faces, drawn and pale from almost nine months in jail. The clerk of the court read an enlarged indictment to them. It accused them of murdering, besides Crispus Attucks, Samuel Maverick, a seventeen-year-old apprentice boy; Samuel Gray, a former employee of (but no relation to) the owner of Gray's rope works; James Caldwell, a sailor from a Massachusetts coasting vessel; and one Patrick Carr, known as "the Irish teague."

The jury was now chosen, and Adams and Quincy challenged and rejected no less than thirty prospects, forcing the sheriff to summon eight talesmen. As in Preston's case, the accepted jurymen were all from neighboring towns—Roxbury, Dedham, Milton, Hingham—and one, Isaiah Thayer, was from Adams' home town of Braintree. But there is no evidence that any had Tory leanings.

The prosecution opened with a brief, low-keyed talk by Samuel Quincy. He declared that the trial involved the "most melancholy event that has yet taken place on the continent of America, and perhaps of the greatest expectation of any that has yet come before a tribunal of civil justice in this part of the British dominions." He vowed to make no appeal to partiality or prejudice but to conduct himself "with decency and candor," with one object—"simply that of truth."

Whereupon he began summoning witnesses by the dozen. The first several (one was Jonathan W. Austin, John Adams' clerk) simply identified various soldiers and reported seeing one or two of the victims fall. Things heated up when Edward Langford, a town watchman, took the stand. He testified that Samuel Gray was standing beside him in the front rank of the crowd in the most peaceable manner, without any weapon, not even a snowball: "His hands were in his bosom." According to Langford, Gray asked him what was going on. Langford replied he did not know, and almost immediately Matthew Killroy's gun went off and Samuel Gray fell, striking Langford's left foot. A parade of succeeding witnesses repeatedly identified Killroy as Gray's assassin.

Richard Palmes returned to testify, for the prosecution this time, and was obviously much more comfortable about it. He identified bald-headed Hugh Montgomery, one of the sentries, and testified that he had knocked Montgomery down—but only *after* the grenadier had fired his gun, and was attempting to run Palmes through with his bayonet.

Subsequent testimony, notably by Nicholas Ferreter, supplied interesting background information for the "massacre." Ferreter was a worker at Gray's rope works. He reported that on Friday, March 2, during the lunch hour at Gray's, Samuel Gray hailed a passing soldier and asked him if he wanted work. "Yes," said the poorly paid redcoat, "I do, faith." Well, said Gray in pure Anglo-Saxon, he could go clean his outhouse. The soldier's temper exploded. He took a swing at Gray, and other ropemakers rushed to Gray's assistance. Ferreter described how he "knocked up his [the soldier's] heels, his coat flew open and out dropped a naked cutlass which I took up and carried off with me." The soldier was soon back with a dozen of his fellows, among them Matthew Killroy. A battle royal ensued, until the ropewalk owner, John Gray, stopped it. That afternoon the soldiers returned in force, and this time the rope workers, in a furious brawl, drove them back to their barracks.

Ill feeling on the part of the British garrison toward the populace was thus well established. Another point in the prosecution's attack was the conduct of the soldiers on the night of the killing. There was, they argued, a plot afoot among the members of the 29th Regiment to attack anyone they caught on the street. Nathaniel Appleton told how a dozen soldiers with drawn bayonets had attacked him on the steps of his house and only fast footwork got him inside in time to bolt the door. John Appleton, "a young lad," told how he had been with his nine-year-old brother in King Street when twenty soldiers with cutlasses in their hands attacked him. He begged them to spare his life, he testified, and one said, "No, damn you, we will kill you all," and struck at his head with a sheathed cutlass. Thomas Marshall told how he saw "a party from the main guard, ten or twelve, come rushing out violently. I saw their arms glitter by the moonlight, hallooing, 'Damn them, where are they, by Jesus, let them come.'"

Finally, to certify the hideous and bloodthirsty character of the defendants, one Joseph Crosswell testified that the next morning he saw blood dried on five or six inches of Killroy's bayonet.

Samuel Quincy summed up the prosecution's evidence. He dwelt at length on testimony that accused Killroy of firing directly at Gray, and deduced that the private was guilty of murder with malice. He then deplored the conduct of the soldiers before the riot, maintaining that the church bells had rung because it was the soldiers who, rushing to the street, had cried the word "fire." "It is probable," declared Quincy darkly, "the word fire was the watchword. It appears to me that if we can believe the evidence, they had a design of attacking and slaughtering the inhabitants that night and they could have devised no better method to draw out the inhabitants unarmed than to cry fire!" Finally, he hammered again at Killroy, reminding the jury that it is "immaterial, where there are a number of persons concerned, who gave the mortal blow; all that are present are in the eye of the law principals. This is a rule settled by the judges of England upon solid argument."

To the bar now stepped young Josiah Quincy to open for the defense. After a vigorous speech, in which he reminded the jurors that a soldier's life was, from a legal standpoint, "as estimable as the life of any other citizen," he began summoning witnesses to bolster his assertion that the soldiers had fired in self-defense. This was the climax of the Adams-Quincy tightrope act. Could the defense prove a mob was at work without pricking the jury's civic pride and political animosity? One by one the witnesses paraded to the stand.

James Crawford told how on the way home he met "numbers of people" going downtown with sticks in their hands. The sticks were "not common walking canes but pretty large cudgels." Archibald Wilson told of sitting in a house near Dock Square when "a certain gentleman" came in and asked how "he came to be sitting there when there was such trouble betwixt the soldiers and inhabitants." Looking out the window, Wilson saw thirty or forty men from the North End make "two or three sundry attacks up that lane where the barracks which are called Murray's were."

"How were they armed that came from the North End?" Josiah Quincy asked.

"They had sticks or staves, I know not what they are called," Wilson said.

In Dock Square Wilson found some two hundred men gathered. They surged away as if on a signal giving "two or three cheers for [*i.e.*, challenging] the main guard." Wilson followed them and was in Royal Exchange Lane, leading into King Street, when the bells rang. He said he heard voices shouting fire and remarked it was "uncommon to go to a fire with bludgeons." Somebody told him, "they were uncommon bells."

William Hunter, the next witness, added another significant detail to the gathering in Dock Square. He told of seeing "a gentleman" with a red cloak around whom the crowd gathered. "He stood in the middle of them and they were all very quiet; he spoke to them a little while, and then he went off and they took off their hats and gave three cheers for the main guard."

"Was the man who spoke to these people a tall or short man?" Josiah Quincy asked.

"Pretty tall."

"How was he dressed?"

"He had a white wig and red cloak, and instantly after his talking a few minutes to them they made huzzas for the main guard."

It may well have been at this point that John Adams arose in distress to interrupt his colleague and declare that he would walk out of the case if Quincy insisted on cross-examining witnesses to such unnecessary lengths, thereby setting the town in a bad light. (The transcript of the trial does not show us exactly where this happened but we know it occurred.) William Gordon, the British historian of the Revolution, describes the incident but mistakenly places it in Preston's trial. We must be grateful to him, nonetheless, because in John Adams' personal copy of Gordon's book he wrote an explanatory marginal note: "Adams' motive is not here perceived. His clients' lives were hazarded by Quincy's too youthful ardor." Could anything sum up more graphically the terrible pressure under which Quincy and Adams worked? If Quincy persuaded a witness to identify the tall, red-cloaked speaker in Dock Square (Samuel Adams was short, but Will Molineux, his right-hand man, was tall), the Liberty boys in wrathful self-defense would have almost certainly unleashed the mob, jammed the courtroom, and created the kind of atmosphere that had convicted Richardson.

The evidence Adams did tolerate was bad enough, from the Liberty viewpoint. Witness after witness confirmed that there had been mobs of Bostonians surging through the streets, armed with clubs. Doctor Richard Hirons gave some details of a scene before the barracks. As early as seven o'clock some twenty or thirty townspeople appeared there, he said, led by "a little man" who lectured four or five officers of the 29th Regiment on the conduct of their soldiers in the streets. The man then began making a speech, shouting, "We did not send for you. We will not have you here. We will get rid of you." The officers insisted they were doing their best to keep the soldiers in their barracks and urged the speechmaker to use "his interest" to disperse the people.

Next came Benjamin Davis, Jr., who shattered the prosecution's claim that Samuel Gray was "in the King's peace" on the night he died. Young Davis told of meeting Gray, who asked where the fire was. "I said there was no fire, it was the soldiers fighting. He said, 'Damn it, I am glad of it. I will knock some of them on the head.' He ran off. I said to him, take heed you do not get killed . . . He said, 'Do not you fear, damn their bloods.'"

"Had he a stick in his hand?"

"He had one under his arm."

Now Quincy concentrated his fire on the scene in Dock Square. Patrick Keaton saw "a tall mulatto fellow, the same that was killed; he had two clubs in his hand and he said, 'Here take one of them.' I did so." Nathaniel Russell, chairmaker, said he saw trouble coming and "intended to retreat as fast as I could. I had not got three yards before the guns were fired."

"How many people do you imagine were then gathered around the party?"

"Fifty or sixty able-bodied men."

"Did they crowd near the soldiers?"

"So near, that I think you could not get your hat betwixt them and the bayonets."

"How many people do you think there might be in the whole?"

"About two hundred."

"Did the soldiers say anything to the people?"

"They never opened their lips; they stood in a trembling manner, as if they expected nothing but death."

This hit the prosecution so hard that they introduced a Crown witness, one John Cox, a bricklayer, who testified that he saw three soldiers threatening, earlier in the evening, to chop down or blow up Boston's sacred Liberty tree. They also threw in a future Revolutionary War general, Henry Knox, who said that Preston and his squad, while forcing their way through the crowd, behaved "in a very threatening" manner. "They said, 'Make way, damn you, make way,' and they pricked some of the people."

But the defense returned relentlessly to the evidence of riot. Benjamin Burdick admitted he stood in the front ranks of the crowd brandishing a highland broad-sword. Newton Prince, a free black, told of watching people with sticks striking the guns of the soldiers at the right wing of the squad. Andrew, the black servant of Oliver Wendell, placed special emphasis on the conduct of Crispus Attucks. He told of seeing Attucks knock Killroy's gun away and strike him over the head. "The blow came either on the soldier's cheek or hat." Holding Killroy's bayonet with his left hand, Attucks tried to tear the gun loose, crying, "Kill the dogs. Knock them over." But Killroy wrenched his gun free, and Andrew, sensing imminent bloodshed, "turned to go off." He had gotten away "only about the length of a gun" when the first man fired.

"Did the soldiers of that party or any of them," Quincy asked, "step or move out of the rank in which they stood to push the people?"

"No," Andrew replied, "and if they had they might have killed me and many others with their bayonets."

Finally John Adams played his trump card, Doctor John Jeffries. Though he later became a Loyalist exile, Jeffries was one of Boston's most respected physicians. When Adams was representing America in London in the 1780s, he retained him as his family doctor. Jeffries told how he had been called to attend Patrick Carr, who had been mortally wounded in the firing.

Carr lived nine days, and Jeffries conversed with him several times about the brawl. Carr told how he had been drawn from his boardinghouse by the ringing bells and had followed the crowd up Cornhill to King Street. Carr had not been in the front rank of the rioters. He was on the other side of the street circling the outer rim of the crowd when the guns began to fire, and obviously was hit by a wild bullet. Jeffries asked him whether he thought the soldiers would fire:

> He told me that he thought that the soldiers would have fired long before. I then asked him if he thought the soldiers would have been hurt if they had not fired. He said he really thought they would, for he had heard many voices cry out "Kill them." I asked him then, meaning to close all, whether he thought they fired in self-defense or on purpose to destroy the people. He said he really thought they did fire to defend themselves; that he did not blame the man, whoever he was, who shot him. . . . He told me also that he was a native of Ireland, that he had frequently seen mobs and soldiers called upon to quell them: whenever he mentioned that he always called himself a fool, that he might have known better, that he had seen soldiers often fire on the people in Ireland, but had never seen them bear half so much before they fired in his life.

All by himself, Jeffries blew up ninety per cent of the prosecution's case. Proof of their consternation was the sudden production of additional witnesses at the very end of the trial. They were not particularly effective, merely reiterating what had been said before.

Josiah Quincy summed up for the defense. In a long, emotional speech he reviewed the evidence, urging the jurors to ask themselves crucial questions. "Was the sentinel insulted and attacked? Did he call for assistance, and did the party go to assist him? Was it lawful for them so to do? Were the soldiers when thus lawfully assembled, assaulted by a great number of people assembled? Was this last assembly lawful?" He closed with a moving appeal to mercy, quoting Shakespeare on the subject, asking the jurors to guarantee themselves "an absolving conscience" when the "agitations of the day" had subsided.

John Adams now took the floor to close for the defense. Thus far he had spoken little; Quincy had handled the interrogation of the witnesses. But everyone, jurors included, knew that Adams was the heart and head of the defense. His words would have a finality that Quincy, for all his emotion, could not convey.

Adams began with a direct and simple statement of his professional role: "I am for the prisoners at the bar." He would apologize for it, he said, only in the words of Cesare Beccaria, the eminent Italian jurist of the period: "If I can but be the instrument of preserving one life, his blessing and tears of transport shall be a sufficient consolation to me, for the contempt of all mankind."

In a quiet, matter-of-fact voice Adams proceeded to explain the law of homicide to the jury, and then applied the legal principle of self-defense to the situation of the soldiers in King Street, "with all the bells ringing to call the town together . . . [and] they knew by that time that there was no fire; the people shouting, huzzaing, and making the mob whistle. . . , which when a boy makes it in the street is no formidable thing, but when made by a multitude is a most hideous shriek, almost as terrible as an Indian yell; the people crying, 'Kill them! Kill them! Knock them over!' heaving snowballs, oyster shells, clubs, white birch sticks . . . " Consider, he asked the jury, whether any reasonable man in the soldiers' situation would not have concluded the mob was going to kill him.

Next he cited the law on riot: "Wheresoever more than three persons use force or violence, for the accomplishment of any design whatever, all concerned are rioters." Were there
not more than three persons in Dock Square? Did they not agree to go to King Street and attack the main guard? Why hesitate then to call this so-called assembly a riot?

Perhaps at this point Adams saw the jurors' faces clouding. He swiftly led their emo-
tions in the opposite direction by distinguishing between rioters and rebels. "I do not
mean to apply the word rebel on this occasion: I have no reason to suppose that ever there
was one in Boston, at least among the natives of the country; but rioters are in the same
situation as far as my argument is concerned, and proper officers may suppress rioters and
so may even private persons."

From 11 A.M. to 5 P.M. Adams examined the law and the evidence, frequently reading directly from authorities to bolster his arguments. The next morning he continued his
summation, examining the testimony of various witnesses. He dismissed the Crown's attempt to prove Killroy's malice. "Admitting that this testimony is literally true and that he
had all the malice they would wish to prove, yet if he was assaulted that night and his life
in danger, he had a right to defend himself as well as another man."

The witnesses who had described Crispus Attucks' belligerent behavior were cited. Attucks
was, said Adams, "a stout mulatto fellow whose very looks was enough to terrify any person . . .
He had heartiness enough to fall in upon them [*i.e.*, the soldiers] and with one hand took hold
of the bayonet and with the other knocked the man down." It was to Attucks' "mad behavior,
in all probability, the dreadful carnage of that night is chiefly to be ascribed."

Proving he could play on the prejudices of the jurors as skillfully as he could cite the
law, Adams added: "And it is in this manner this town has been often treated; a Carr from
Ireland and an Attucks from Framingham, happening to be here, shall sally out upon their
thoughtless enterprises, at the head of such a rabble of negroes, etcetera, as they can collect
together, and then there are not wanting persons to ascribe all their doings to the good people of the town."

The law, Adams declared, was clear. The soldiers had a right to kill in their own defense.
If the attack on them was not so severe as to endanger their lives, yet if they were assaulted at
all, the law reduces their offense to manslaughter.

Finally came a soaring peroration.

> To your candor and justice I submit the prisoners and their cause. The law,
> in all vicissitudes of government, fluctuations of the passions, or flights of
> enthusiasm, will preserve a steady, undeviating course. It will not bend to the
> uncertain wishes, imaginations, and wanton tempers of men . . . On the one
> hand it is inexorable to the cries and lamentations of the prisoners; on the
> other it is deaf, deaf as an adder, to the clamors of the populace.

Once more Robert Treat Paine strove to rescue the prosecution's collapsing case. But he
was in retreat all the way. "I am sensible, gentlemen," he began, "I have got the severe side of
the question to conduct." He wasted time trying to justify the presence of so many armed citizens on the streets, renewing the argument that the soldiers had started the trouble first. He
had nothing whatsoever to say about Doctor Jeffries' report of Carr's words, insisting instead
on his witnesses' versions of the conduct of Attucks and Gray: "Attucks, fifteen feet off leaning
on his stick, Gray, twelve feet off with his hand in his bosom." He ended by concentrating his
fire on Killroy, calling his deliberate murder of Gray "beyond dispute." He all but gave up on
the other soldiers in his closing lines. "You must unavoidably find him [*i.e.*, Killroy] guilty of

murder. What your judgement should think of the rest, though the evidence is undoubtedly the fullest against him, yet it is full enough against the rest."

The next morning, Justice Trowbridge charged the jury. It was a long and careful examination of the evidence and the law, most of which had already been covered by John Adams. But Adams must have stirred uneasily when he heard Trowbridge couple the words "riot and rebellion," and add a remark that the law in regard to treason should be "more generally known here than it seems to be." Judge Peter Oliver went even farther down this risky path. He declared that the riot had been perpetrated "by villains." As for the tall man in the red cloak and white wig, "that tall man is guilty in the sight of God of the murder of the five persons mentioned in the indictment."

Thus instructed, the jury withdrew. Two hours and a half dragged slowly by while the defense attorneys undoubtedly sat there fearing the worst. Finally, a door behind the bench opened, the twelve countrymen filed into their places, and the foreman, Joseph Mayo of Roxbury, arose to give the verdict. "William Wemms, James Hartegan, William McCauley, Hugh White, William Warren, and John Carroll: *Not guilty.* . . . Matthew Killroy and Hugh Montgomery, *Not guilty* of murder but *guilty* of manslaughter."

John Adams rose instantly and asked the benefit of clergy for Killroy and Montgomery. The judges dismissed the six acquitted men and quickly granted Adams' plea. ("Benefit of clergy," by 1770, had been interpreted to include anyone who was literate; and the "clergyman's" penalty for manslaughter was branding on the thumb.)

On December 14, Killroy and Montgomery were brought back to court. They read a passage from the Bible to establish their literacy, and prepared for the shock of the glowing iron. Adams recalled later he "never pitied any men more . . . They were noble, fine-looking men; protested they had done nothing contrary to their duty as soldiers; and, when the sheriff approached to perform his office, they burst into tears."

For Preston and the soldiers, the ordeal was over. They went their various ways, and John Adams saw only one of them again. Years later, when he was ambassador of an independent America to the Court of St. James's, he recognized Preston as he passed by on a London street. For bearing his part of the ordeal with patience and dignity, Preston, retiring from the army almost immediately, received a pension of two hundred pounds a year from the King. The enlisted men, as was their lot in those days, received nothing.

In his diary and later letters, John Adams maintained that his "disinterested action" in defending the soldiers was "one of the best pieces of service I ever rendered my country." Samuel Adams did not think so, at least in public. Writing under the name *Vindex*, he denounced the jury's verdict and the defense arguments in a series of scathing articles in the *Boston Gazette*. But Samuel Adams was a very subtle man. Privately, his friendship with John became even more intimate; early in the following year, when John Adams took his family home to Braintree and became a commuter to his city law office, he frequently ate breakfast, lunch, and dinner at his "brother" Samuel's house.

Did Samuel Adams realize that without John at the defense table, the trials might well have sent him and other leaders of the Liberty party, such as the man in the red cloak, to London under arrest for treason? Did the trials enable John to convince his cousin that the Liberty policy of violence had come close to destroying the cause, and must be modified henceforth? Both conclusions seem almost inescapable. But two years later, patient Cousin Samuel revealed another reason for his friendship. He had organized an annual extravaganza to commemorate the death of the Massacre victims with prayers and fierce anti-British oratory. In 1772, Samuel asked John to make the principal address. It would have been a most satisfactory way of including him at last on the Boston side of the case. But John Adams was still his own man. He quietly declined, explaining that he felt "I should only expose myself to the lash of ignorant and malicious tongues on both sides of the question."

There the matter would have undoubtedly remained if Parliament had not foolishly reignited the quarrel with the colonies the following year. The dead rioters thereby became enshrined in American folklore as martyrs. And John Adams was able to stand beside his Cousin Samuel with a dear conscience in the struggle against British oppression. That John won the larger place in history should not be surprising to anyone who penetrates beyond the patriotic myth to the interior drama of this great but little-understood trial.

December 1966

VI

Triumph at Yorktown

Jack Rudolph

The brilliant luck of the last great battle for United States independence occurred just miles from where the English American experience began. In the following assessment of the various players in this great drama, Jack Rudolph explains the roles of British leaders, French allies, and America's generals in this pivotal victory.

Long after midnight, October 23, 1781, hoofbeats broke the silence of slumbering Philadelphia's empty streets. Reeling in the saddle from exhaustion and shaking with malarial chills, Lieutenant Colonel Tench Tilghman, aide to General George Washington, pulled up to ask an elderly German night watchman how to get to the home of Thomas McKean, president of the Continental Congress. Having pointed the way, the watch resumed his round, excitedly ringing his hand-bell and bellowing in fractured English: "Past dree o'clock und Corn-val-lis ist ta-gen! Past dree o'clock und Cornvallis ist tagen!"

Four days earlier at an obscure river hamlet on Virginia's Tidewater, Lieutenant General Charles Cornwallis, Earl Cornwallis, had surrendered a beleaguered British army to a Franco-American force under Washington.

The year now drawing to a close had not begun so auspiciously. It was, in fact, one of the blackest hours in the struggle for independence. In September, 1780, Benedict Arnold, one of Washington's ablest men, had defected, almost taking the vital Hudson River fortress of West Point with him. American finances were a shambles. Despite the presence of a French army and naval squadron in Rhode Island, the French Alliance was turning sour, and British arms seemed everywhere invincible.

A powerful army under Lieutenant General Sir Henry Clinton lay secure in New York City while Washington's half-clad Continentals watched hungrily from their cold camps along the Hudson. In North Carolina Nathanael Greene was running for his life before the relentless pursuit of that same Lord Cornwallis, and the Royal Navy had a lock on the coast from Canada to Spanish Florida.

On New Year's Day, 1781, six regiments of the Pennsylvania Continental Line mutinied, followed by part of the New Jersey Line. Order was restored, but the mutiny cost Washington half his Pennsylvanians, until then among the most reliable troops in the army. At the same time, Arnold, now a British brigadier general, landed in Virginia and swept unopposed to Richmond, burning and pillaging as he advanced.

But if the rebellious colonists had troubles, so did the British. Maintaining an army, in combat three thousand miles from England was a terrible strain on a nation with no friends in

Europe, which found itself at war with France, Spain, and Holland in addition to its erstwhile colonies. The command system was failing apart. Clinton, commander in chief in New York, was disgusted, feeling sorry for himself, and quarreling with everyone. Cornwallis, ostensibly his subordinate, was doing as he pleased in the Carolinas with the tacit approval of Lord George Germain in London, who, as Secretary of State for American Colonies, compounded the confusion by trying to run the war from home.

The navy was in poor shape. Keeping the long Atlantic supply line open, holding the American coastline, protecting the English Channel, Gibraltar, the Mediterranean, and far-off India were almost more than it could handle. Should England lose, even briefly, her tenuous superiority in American waters, the war would be in jeopardy.

The chain of events leading to Yorktown began early in 1781 with a series of uncoordinated maneuvers in widely separated areas—in New York, Virginia, New England, North Carolina, and the West Indies. Their convergence was a delicate balance of calculated risks, careful planning, execution, and luck on one side aided by mediocre leadership and insubordination on the other.

In late February, Washington acted to take some pressure off defenseless Virginia by sending his colorful inspector general, "Baron" Friedrich von Steuben, to teach green recruits how to become soldiers. Steuben set up shop in the Piedmont west of Richmond and began to whip some five hundred volunteers into Regulars, with his particular amalgam of enthusiasm, energy, and multilingual profanity.

Washington also dispatched the twenty-three-year-old Marie Joseph Paul Yves Roch Gilbert du Motier south with three battalions of light infantry to take care of Arnold. It was the Marquis de Lafayette's first independent command, but the ungainly and excitable youth measured up to the challenge.

First, he had to face another incipient mutiny. The troops didn't like the idea of going so far from home. Lafayette rounded up the principal agitators, executed one and pardoned another under the muzzles of a firing squad, then paraded the division and chewed it out. Anyone who objected, he announced, didn't have to go. All he had to do was step forward, get his dishonorable discharge, and go home.

Nobody called his hand. Near the end of April he reached Richmond with one thousand Continentals and two thousand militia, just in time to prevent the British from burning the town. Not ready for a showdown, the raiders withdrew to Portsmouth on the coast.

Meanwhile, deep in the North Carolina wilderness, one of the decisive battles of the war had been fought. Greene won the race for safety, crossing the Dan River into Virginia with Cornwallis' breath hot on the back of his neck. Having lost the quarry and outrun his supplies, the latter fell back toward Hillsboro, North Carolina. Greene promptly recrossed the Dan and became, in turn, the pursuer.

In mid-March Cornwallis turned and attacked Greene at Guilford Courthouse, a country crossroad just north of present day Greensboro. He won a tactical victory but took heavy casualties, which virtually wrecked his army. Three days after the, battle he began a two hundred-mile retreat to Wilmington on the coast. Greene let him go. In the opinion of many military analysts, the British won a battle at Guilford but lost the war. Thereafter it was all downhill for Cornwallis.

While restoring his muscle at Wilmington, Cornwallis indulged in some deep thought. His Carolina experience convinced him that a Southern campaign must be won in Virginia, but he couldn't sell Clinton, who wanted him to secure Georgia and the Carolinas. On April 25 Cornwallis took the bit in his teeth. In violation of orders and without prior notice to Clinton, he set out for Virginia, a march of two hundred and twenty miles. Clinton was appalled. Instead of ordering his ambitious subordinate back to the Carolinas, however, he made the best of what he considered a poor situation. He even sent reinforcements.

Earlier a contingent of two thousand men had reached Virginia, and Major General William Phillips replaced Arnold in command. When Cornwallis arrived at Petersburg on May 20, however, he found that Phillips had died of typhoid fever seven days before. Phillips, who had been captured with Burgoyne at Saratoga and exchanged, was one of Britain's best artillerymen. His loss would be felt keenly later.

The arrival of two more British regiments and two battalions of Germans raised Cornwallis' strength to seventy-two hundred, with a corresponding leap in his confidence. "The boy cannot escape me," he gloated as he took after Lafayette.

The boy was well aware of his predicament. He had already complained to Washington that he was "not strong enough even to get beaten." Lafayette withdrew to Fredericksburg over ground that the great-grandsons of his men, both North and South, would know with bitter intimacy eighty years later. His immediate concern was to avoid Cornwallis' clutches pending reinforcement by Anthony Wayne.

"Mad Anthony" left York, Pennsylvania, on May 26 with three regiments of the reorganized Pennsylvania Line and a six-gun artillery battery. The Pennsylvanians were still surly, but Wayne, who held an even lower opinion of mutiny than Lafayette, squelched them with ruthless efficiency. After shooting a couple of ringleaders, he locked all the ammunition in his supply wagons and pointed the cowed troops south with empty muskets. By the time they reached Virginia, he had marched the mutinous spirit out of them.

Three days after Wayne's arrival General William Campbell checked in with six hundred riflemen, and a week after that Steuben arrived with four hundred and fifty newly trained Continentals. His presence raised a potentially sticky question of command. Lafayette, the senior, was young and inexperienced; Steuben, twice his age, was a battlewise professional. The difficulty evaporated when Steuben came down with a convenient case of gout and took sick leave.

Now facing an American force of two thousand regulars, thirty-two hundred militia, and six hundred rifles. Cornwallis got another jolt when the jittery Clinton ordered him to return three thousand men to New York. Accordingly, he pulled back to Williamsburg. Lafayette followed cautiously.

Raiding columns under Lieutenant Colonels Banastre Tarleton and John Simcoe, meanwhile, were raising hell west of Richmond. While flushing the Virginia legislature out of its temporary refuge at Charlottesville, "Bloody Ban" narrowly missed collaring Governor Thomas Jefferson. Warned with only minutes to spare, the author of the Declaration of Independence hightailed it down one side of Monticello's mountain while Tarleton's dragoons were pounding up the other.

Falling back to Portsmouth after laying a trap for Lafayette at Green Spring that the marquis almost blundered into, Cornwallis found himself bombarded with a series of on-again-off-again orders from Clinton before being told to keep everything and establish a naval base in Virginia. The exasperated earl chose Yorktown. He landed there in early August and at his leisure began to fortify the place with the aid of some two thousand runaway slaves, among them some from Washington's Mount Vernon.

Although not easily, defended against a land attack, Yorktown was a good choice for an advance naval station, its deep anchorage big enough to accommodate a large fleet. Cornwallis knew its weakness but, having been promised more troops, was confident he could hold it as long as the navy controlled Chesapeake Bay. If the place got too hot, he could always escape by sea.

Settled in 1691 on a sixty-foot cliff above the York River—only half a mile wide at that point—Yorktown, then simply called York, had been a busy tobacco port with some three hundred houses and three thousand inhabitants clustered along a single main street and four cross streets. Extensive dockage lined the riverbank. After 1750, however, the town began to slip. By 1781 its dwindling population occupied about seventy houses, with many empty buildings falling into ruin.

The leading resident was Thomas Nelson III, a signer of the Declaration of Independence and one of Virginia's wealthiest men. A jovial fat man whose affability and fund of off-color stories hid an inner core of steel, Nelson shortly succeeded Jefferson as governor and set about reviving Virginia's war effort, stepping on a lot of toes and bankrupting himself in the process.

While Lafayette and Cornwallis shadowboxed in the Tidewater, the long threads of a victorious strategy were being drawn together five hundred miles to the north. On May 21 and 22 Washington and the Comte de Rochambeau, commander of the French army, met at Wethersfield, Connecticut. After deciding to join forces along the Hudson, they surveyed the strategic possibilities, including a move against Cornwallis.

Recapturing New York was an obsession with Washington. "Papa" Rochambeau, as he liked to call himself, wasn't enthusiastic, especially, after a good look at the British defenses. Jean Baptiste Donatien de Vimeur had been a soldier for forty of his fifty-six years and knew his trade. Nevertheless, he went along with Washington's wishes.

After the meeting, Washington wrote to various subordinate commanders and congressional leaders, going into some detail about his proposed attack. On June 15 the pouch containing his dispatches landed on Clinton's desk. To this day, nobody is sure whether the capture was a lucky break or a deliberate plant. Many on Clinton's staff suspected the latter, but Clinton was convinced, until too late, that he was the Franco-American objective.

The French joined the Americans on July 6 after a smartly conducted march of two hundred and twenty miles in eleven days over wretched, dust-choked roads in midsummer heat. They consisted of the royal Bourbonnais, Soissonnais, Saintonge, and Deux Ponts regiments plus artillery and the Duke of Lauzun's legion of light infantry and hussars. In their brilliant uniforms—pure white, with each regiment bearing its own color on collars and lapels, the sergeants wearing ostrich plumes in their caps, and the Duke of Lauzun's officers astride tiger-skin saddlecloths—they may have looked like comic opera soldiers but they were as tough as Scotland's "ladies from hell."

If the Americans were awed by the lavish equipment of their allies, the latter were equally amazed at how the former made do with almost nothing. Each recognized and respected the quality of the other. Except for minor dustups, the armies got along well.

Meanwhile, another loop in the snare to choke Cornwallis was taking shape. In early summer Admiral the Comte de Grasse brought a powerful French fleet to the West Indies. He was to cooperate with the Spanish there but had leeway to help Washington if the opportunity arose. Fortunately, the Spanish were not eager to start anything.

Rochambeau wrote de Grasse explaining the situation, imploring him to come soon with whatever reinforcements he could scrape together, as well as badly needed cash to pay the armies. He outlined both the New York and Virginia options, subtly emphasizing the latter and trusting the admiral to read between the lines. De Grasse didn't disappoint him.

A major miscalculation by the British naval commander in the Indies helped. Admiral Sir George Rodney, returning to England, didn't think the French would leave their sugar islands and merchant shipping unprotected with an enemy fleet at hand. He departed with six ships of the line, leaving Admiral Sir Samuel Hood with only fourteen to deal with the French, now reinforced to twenty-eight of the line.

It was one of the great strategic mistakes of the war. Instead of dispersing his fleet, Admiral François Joseph Paul de Grasse, Marquis de Grasse-Tilly and Comte de Grasse, concentrated it, borrowed three infantry regiments and General Claude Anne de St. Simon from the San Domingo garrison and raised 1,200,000 livres in silver by popular subscription in Havana. On August 5 he sailed north. No British admiral would have dared such a gamble.

On August 14 Washington learned that de Grasse was coming, that his destination was Chesapeake Bay, and that he could stay no later than October 15. Suspecting he'd been outflanked, Washington exploded. Everybody—most notably Rochambeau—kept out of his way until the storm had blown itself out. Despite his disappointment, Washington scrapped his cherished New York project and began to plan a southward move.

Leaving some four thousand men under Major General William Heath to watch Clinton, the Franco-American army moved to King's Ferry on the Hudson, where it crossed between August 20 and 25. Next day it began the historic four-hundred-and-fifty-mile march to Virginia. Security was so tight only Washington, Rochambeau, and a few key staff officers knew where they were going.

An elaborate cover plan was laid on to confuse the British. Wooden landing craft were conspicuously displayed among the columns, roads leading to Staten Island—logical jump-off for a shore-to-shore assault on Manhattan were repaired, and the French made a big gesture of building bake ovens. Clinton was completely duped. Not until the Americans were out of reach did it dawn on him that he'd been hoodwinked.

The feint having succeeded, the allies swung south through New Jersey, crossed the Delaware River at Trenton, and reached Philadelphia at the end of August. After parading through the capital the columns continued on to Head of Elk, an inlet at the top of the Chesapeake (now Elkton, Pennsylvania), where they arrived September 6.

In the West Indies, Admiral Hood had learned that de Grasse was going north, although it never occurred to him that the Frenchman was taking his whole armada. On August 10 Hood set sail for the Chesapeake with his fourteen ships. He arrived at the mouth of the bay on the twenty-fifth, found it empty, and continued on to New York. While the British were sailing up the coast, Vice Admiral Jacques-Melchoir St. Laurent, Comte de Barras, slipped out of Newport, Rhode Island, with eight battleships, four frigates, and sixteen supply vessels loaded with siege artillery, ammunition, and fifteen hundred barrels of salt beef. British Admiral Thomas Graves, his strength increased to nineteen of the line with the arrival of Hood, set sail from New York to intercept Barras.

Despite a calm front, Washington was worried. At Philadelphia he had expected to hear that the French fleet had reached the Chesapeake but all he learned was that Barras had put to sea and that Graves was on the prowl.

De Grasse was the key. Even without Barras the allies probably, could wrap up Cornwallis, though it would take longer and be more costing. But if anything happened to de Grasse—a scattering storm or defeat by the British, a distressing habit of French admirals—the game was up. French naval superiority in the Chesapeake was crucial.

Washington left Philadelphia on September 5 to catch up with the army while Rochambeau proceeded more leisurely by boat to Chester, Pennsylvania. A few miles beyond Chester a courier from the south met Washington on the road. The general took one look at the dispatches, whirled around, and headed back to Chester at a gallop. As Rochambeau's boat neared the landing, his party beheld the usually reserved Washington on the dock jumping up and down like a schoolboy, waving his hat in one hand and a handkerchief in the other. A few minutes later two normally dignified generals were happily whacking each other on the back.

De Grasse had reached the bay and was already, landing St. Simon's troops at Jamestown. Barring accidents, Cornwallis was doomed. As Virginia militia general "Joe Courd" (the ex-tavernkeeper's name was George but his men had hung the nick-name on him) Weedon wrote: "We have got him handsomely in a pudding bag."

His mind at ease, Washington ordered the march to continue, then set off on a bruising sixty-mile ride to Mount Vernon, his first homecoming in six years. There he relaxed for three days and entertained Rochambeau. As he was about to rejoin the army on September 12, however, he got disquieting news.

On the fifth the British fleet had appeared off the Virginia Capes, and de Grasse had sailed out to meet it. There had been a sea battle beyond the horizon, but nobody knew who won. After the sound of gunfire had died away, neither fleet had returned. Halting the army at Annapolis, Washington and Rochambeau rode hard for Williamsburg, arriving late in the afternoon of the fourteenth. Lafayette welcomed them warmly, but he didn't know where de Grasse was either. Twenty-four hours later the clouds lifted. De Grasse was back, Barras had come in and was off-loading the guns and stores at landings along the James. As soon as his transports were empty, he sent them up the bay to ferry the waiting troops to the final rendezvous.

The fleets had fought an indecisive, two-hour engagement known today as the Battle of the Virginia Capes. Graves surprised the French fleet at anchor in Lynnhaven Bay, short seventeen hundred seamen ferrying St. Simon upriver and with four big ships absent patrolling the mouths of the James and York rivers. Slipping his cables, de Grasse cleared hastily for action but came out in ragged formation.

The overcautious Graves let his chance get away. In the battle that followed, only a dozen of his ships got into action, and no more than eight of them took a significant part against fifteen French. If the battle had a hero, it was Commodore Louis Antoine de Bougainville, commanding the French van. Bougainville, who had already given his name to an exotic flowering shrub and a tropical Pacific island destined for sinister fame among a later generation of Americans, inflicted most of the damage. The affair wasn't conducted very brilliantly on either side, but it sufficed.

For three days the fleets jockeyed within sight of each other, moving farther away from the bay. Finally, at nightfall on the ninth, de Grasse turned back. Arriving the next morning, he found that Barras had slipped in while the battle was going on. Now faced with thirty-six ships of the line, double his own strength, Graves withdrew to New York. As one naval historian later put it: "He had lost no engagement, no ships. . . . He had merely lost America."

While the army was closing up around Williamsburg, Washington, Rochambeau, and their staffs visited de Grasse aboard his flagship, the 104-gun *Ville de Paris,* then the mightiest warship in the world. As Washington reached the deck, he was engulfed in a bear hug by the effusive Frenchman. Hearing their tall leader greeted as "My dear little general!" put a strain on the dignity of his staff, but all managed to keep a straight face except Henry Knox. The portly chief of artillery let out a loud guffaw.

More likely to bring a smile to Washington's stern features was a commitment by de Grasse to stay to the end of October. The admiral refused to bring his big ships close enough to participate in the bombardment of Yorktown but he offered several hundred marines to help out. The fleet took no further part in the actual investment, but its presence assured there'd be no escape for Cornwallis by sea.

On September 28 the reassembled army left Williamsburg for Yorktown, eleven miles away. It was organized in two "wings" (the term "army corps" hadn't yet been invented). In the absence of exact figures, overall strength has been variously estimated from sixteen to twenty thousand, with the Americans, including militia, slightly outnumbering the French. It may have had as many as one hundred twenty artillery pieces—Barras brought eighty from Newport—of which about one hundred eventually went into action. Most were 18- and 24-pounder guns, plus howitzers and siege mortars.

The American wing had three divisions, each made up of two brigades, commanded by Lafayette, von Steuben, and Major General Benjamin Lincoln, who was also Washington's deputy. Two brigades of Virginia militia were held in reserve under Governor Nelson, while General Weedon's brigade was sent across the York River to block any escape via Gloucester Point.

Rochambeau led the French wing of two divisions. One was made up of the four regiments that had marched from Rhode Island, the other of the three regiments brought by St. Simon from the West Indies. St. Simon, felled by malaria but determined to be on hand, rode at the head of his column in a litter. With no need for mounted troops in a trench battle, Lauzun's Legion followed Weedon to the other side of the river.

The march encountered no resistance. By late afternoon Yorktown was loosely encircled just out of artillery range. To prevent a surprise attack, Washington ordered everyone to "lay on their arms" for the night.

For Cornwallis, outnumbered at least two to one, Yorktown was not a strong place to stand. The foreground was clear and flat, with no dominating features. In the American sector facing the British left, a wooded stream bed called Wormley's Creek offered a covered approach to within easy range of his main line. The earl later insisted he would never have considered holding out had he not been promised relief.

His principal defensive position consisted of a continuous line of trenches, batteries, and redoubts about three hundred yards from the river encircling the village in an arc some one thousand yards long. The right flank was covered by a star-shaped fort called the Fusilier Redoubt because it was garrisoned by one of Cornwallis' best regiments, the 23rd Royal Welsh Fusiliers. Behind the redoubt a steep, heavily wooded and swampy ravine constituted a major obstacle to a direct assault. Two more advanced redoubts, Numbers Nine and Ten—the latter also known as the Rock Redoubt—guarded the left. In the center, facing an open area known as the Pigeon Quarter, a strongly manned salient, the Horn Work, discouraged frontal attack. Three outposts were placed farther forward in the open.

To deny Gloucester Point to an attacker as well as providing a jump-off for a possible breakout, Cornwallis built another line there. Eventually this position was occupied by twelve hundred men, including Tarleton's British Legion and Simcoe's Queen's Rangers.

Sixty-five artillery pieces were formed into fourteen batteries, four of which were sited on the beach below the bluff to fend off amphibious attacks. Most, however, were light field guns, the only heavies being short-range naval 18-pounders from the frigate H.M.S. *Charon*. A smaller frigate, *Guadaloupe*, was anchored near the Fusilier Redoubt. Rations were in fairly good supply but artillery ammunition was worrisome.

The army of approximately eight thousand men was a mixture of British and German regulars. Seven British infantry regiments plus a "brigade of guards" and one of light infantry constituted the backbone, bolstered by two battalions (regiments) of Anspachers and two Hessian Regiments, one of the latter commanded by a major with the stout but un-Teutonic name of O'Reilly. The "guards" weren't royal household troops but a composite of the grenadier companies of the line regiments, so designated because they were led by an officer of the Coldstreams, Brigader General Charles O'Hara. The light brigade consisted of the light companies of the same regiments.

While Washington spent the twenty-ninth, a Saturday, in a thorough survey of the British position preparatory to attacking the outposts, siege artillery and stores began moving from Trebell's Landing on the James River, a mile and a half above Carter's Grove Plantation (now part of Colonial Williamsburg). The going was glacial, however, in the absence of the artillery teams, still en route overland from Head of Elk. Some horses and oxen were rounded up, including Washington's personal baggage teams, but the unwieldy guns had to be manhandled six miles over soft, sandy roads.

That same day Cornwallis heard from Clinton that a relief force would leave New York on October 5. Confident he could hold out that long, the earl abandoned his outposts, which were promptly occupied by the allies. He was later criticized for giving them up without a fight, but with the information and strength he had, he was probably right.

The only fighting took place on the left, where St. Simon launched a probing attack against the Fusilier Redoubt. It was beaten off, but the French established a trench line and batteries close enough to reach the anchorage behind the bluff as well as into the town itself. For the next week the front was quiet as both sides dug in. The British kept up a steady but ineffective long-range fire to which the Americans made no reply. One of the batteries had a bulldog mascot which, whenever a gun was fired, took off across no man's land in pursuit of the shell. The Americans wanted to catch and send him back with an insulting message tied to his tail, but be looked so mean that nobody would volunteer to be dogcatcher.

Having decided to take Yorktown by siege rather than by a quicker but more costly frontal assault, the allies exchanged muskets for axes, picks, and shovels. Thousands of men cut saplings from which they made and stockpiled gabions (bottomless wicker baskets to be filled with earth to strengthen gun emplacements) and big bundles of sticks called "fascines." Others set up and filled supply and ammunition dumps and aid stations.

Since the ravine and open ground ruled out the left and center, respectively, the main approach was to be made in the right, or American, sector. The siege was to be conducted with all the formalities of European practice, although, except for Steuben, none of the Americans had ever even seen one. Rochambeau, however, was a veteran of fourteen, and he quietly, took charge. Washington signed the voluminous and detailed orders, but French officers wrote them, after which Lieutenant Colonel John Laurens of his staff translated them into English.

The first step was to build a line of redoubts and batteries with connecting trenches parallel to and within effective artillery range of the defensive position. From there, while siege guns battered the defenders, zig-zag approaches would go forward to a second, closer parallel, the process being repeated until the besiegers were near enough for a final rush.

The only break in the fighting lull occurred across the river. Washington sent eight hundred marines loaned by de Grasse to reinforce Weedon and put French Brigadier Claude Gabriel de Choisy in command. Cornwallis countered Tarleton, Simcoe, and their mounted outfits. On October 3 Choisy, advancing toward Gloucester Point, collided with a foraging party under Tarleton. A brisk skirmish flared, during which Lauzun and Bloody Ban almost crossed swords in a mounted saber duel before the British withdrew.

Meanwhile, Washington, Rochambeau, and the division commanders roamed the front. On one occasion the American general, with an army chaplain tagging along out of curiosity, was fired on, and the shot landed close enough to shower them with dirt. As the shaken minister examined his spattered hat, the general smiled and said, "Mr. Evans, you'd better carry that home and show it to your wife and children."

By October 6 the allies were ready to open the first parallel. That night, forty-three hundred men from the divisions of Lincoln and the Baron de Viomenil spread out in rain and darkness across the front from the Horn work to the river, a line about two thousand

yards long between seven hundred and eight hundred wards from the British entrench-
ments. While most of the troops formed a protective screen, fifteen hundred men were detailed to dig.

Out of the darkness in the middle of the American sector appeared a tall Continental officer. General George Washington was handed a pick, took a couple of symbolic stripes at the
ground, and the digging began. By morning the trench was deep enough to protect the laborers despite heavy shelling and minor damage.

By late afternoon of the seventh the parallel was ready for occupancy. Lafayette's Light
Division drew the honors, marching in with flags flying and drums beating. After the colors
were planted, Lieutenant Colonel Alexander Hamilton added a defiant twist by ordering his
battalion to mount the parapet, face the enemy, and execute the manual of arms. The startled
defenders let the insult pass without firing a shot.

Not until October 9 were sufficient batteries in place to begin the bombardment. First
honors went to the French gunners on the far left, who opened about 3:00 P.M. and soon
drove the *Guadaloupe* from its anchorage to the Gloucester shore. Washington was present
when the first American battery let fly two hours later and he personally touched off the first
round. Tradition has it that his shot landed in the dining room of a Yorktown house where
British officers were just sitting down to dinner, killing one and wounding others.

Next morning four more batteries were ready, including a French Grand Battery of ten
18- and 24-pounders and six mortars. As one of the American batteries prepared to open fire,
Governor Nelson, who was present, was invited to select the first target. Without hesitation
he pointed to a large brick house on a slight rise in the middle of the village. "There," he said.
"That's my house, the best in town. Lord Cornwallis is probably using it for his headquarters." When the gunners seemed reluctant to zero in on his handsome home, Nelson offered
five guineas for the first hit. Subsequent damage apparently wasn't great: the house is still
there, still occupied, with cannonballs imbedded in the walls. Before the day was out, at least
forty-six big guns were pouring destruction into the hapless town. Steadily and inexorably the
British fortifications began to disintegrate under unceasing day-and-night bombardment.
Feeding the troops in the lines became increasingly difficult for all but the Germans. They
feasted on chocolate taken from a Dutch merchant.

Cornwallis was driven from his town billet to cover under the cliff. A story is still told in
Yorktown that he lived in a "grotto" there, and a shallow cave is so identified, although it is
more likely that he pitched a tent close to the cliff.

The night of the tenth, hot shot from St. Simon's guns set fire to the *Charon,* which broke
its moorings and collided with a couple of transports. All went up in flames, after which
Cornwallis scuttled most of the remaining vessels.

The allies were getting cocky, and touches of professional rivalry surfaced. Viomenil, in
command of the French section of the parallel, took it upon himself to warn Steuben of the
danger of a British sortie and offered the use of eight hundred men if he got in trouble.
Steuben loftily informed the messenger that he not only needed no help but was prepared to
send eight hundred to bail out Viomenil. After the messenger left, Anthony Wayne reminded
Steuben that he had only one thousand men in the whole division.

Steuben grinned. "Ja, I know Wayne . . . but if I boasted a little it was only for the honor
of your country." Wayne solemnly shook hands, then turned to a group of eavesdroppers and
reminded them they'd heard what the man said and that it was up to them to make good. He
was cheerfully reassured.

A few days later Wayne and Steuben were up front when a shell landed in the redoubt.
Both hit the dirt, Wayne landing on top of Steuben. As they dusted themselves off after the

explosion, the Prussian chuckled: "Ah, ah, Wayne. You cover your general's retreat in the best manner possible."

Henry Knox took a different view of a similar situation with Alexander Hamilton. They were casually discussing a recent order about shouted warnings of approaching shells. Hamilton scorned the regulation as "unsoldierly," but Knox thought it a good idea. Suddenly, the cry went up: "A shell! A shell!" Both dove for cover as two shells landed in the emplacement. Hamilton hid behind the bulky Knox, who threw him off toward the sputtering projectiles. Fortunately, Washington's future Secretary of the Treasury scrambled back before they went off. The danger past, Knox rounded on Hamilton. "Now what do you think, Mr. Hamilton, about crying, ' Shell'? But let me tell you not to make a breastwork of me again." That's how the exchange came out in the language of late-eighteenth-century memoirs; the actual remark was probably more pungently informal.

Under cover of the bombardment, approach trenches pushed forward. The night of October 11 the digging of the second parallel began, unhindered by the defenders, who were shooting at the first. By morning troops were in the new position and wheeling additional guns into place. The parallel couldn't be extended to the river, however until Redoubts Nine and Ten were eliminated.

Soon after dark on October 14 they were stormed in quick, smartly executed bayonet attacks. Four hundred American volunteers swarmed into the Rock Redoubt while the French took the other. American casualties were light, among them Sargeant William Brown of the 5th Connecticut. For his courage and coolness as a member of the "forlorn hope" advance party, Brown was awarded the Badge of Merit, one of the few known recipients of the first United States combat decoration, now the Purple Heart.

During the attack Washington and his staff moved into the open between the parallels to observe as best they could in the darkness. When random shells began to drop uncomfortably close, Lieutenant Colonel David Cobb became concerned for the safety of his chief. "Sir," he said, "you are too much exposed here. Hadn't you better step back a little?"

Washington froze him with a glance and in an icy tone replied, "Colonel Cobb, if you are afraid, you have the liberty to step back." Poor Cobb subsided but didn't accept the invitation. When cheers from the front signaled success, the general quietly expressed satisfaction, called for his horse, and rode calmly back to headquarters.

By morning the parallel had been extended to include the captured redoubts, and more guns wrestled into position. The besiegers could now sweep the British works from end to end at almost point-blank range. With at least one hundred guns combing the lines, British gunners couldn't serve their pieces, which in any event were almost out of ammunition. Casualties and sickness were further reducing their capacity to take much more.

After enduring the pounding for nearly a week, Cornwallis threw his first—and only—counterpunch. A sortie struck an unfinished battery emplacement on the hinge between the French and Americans, penetrated briefly, and spiked several guns before being driven out. The spiking was done hurriedly, however, and all were soon back at their deadly task.

In New York, meanwhile, General Clinton was frantically convening councils of war and tearing his hair trying to get Admiral Graves off the farthing and complete repairs to his damaged warships. He had concocted a scheme to move south with the fleet and five thousand troops, lure de Grasse out to sea, and slip into Chesapeake Bay à la Barras, but his subordinates weren't overwhelmed. In the unlikely event they could fight their way through to Cornwallis they might well find themselves in the same trap.

Despite reinforcements raising his strength to twenty-five ships of the line, Graves was in no rush to tangle with de Grasse's thirty-six and he kept stalling. Although the newly arrived

Admiral Robert Digby ranked Graves, he had no intention of taking a failure rap and declined to assume command. Not until October 17 was the expedition ready to sail, only to be delayed two more days by contrary winds. By then it was too late.

With his defenses crumbling around him and casualties mounting, Cornwallis finally yielded to subordinates' pleas to break out. By abandoning artillery, heavy baggage, and the sick and wounded, he might be able to cross the river, brush Choisy aside, and flee north. If he got a couple of days head start, there was a fighting chance he could evade pursuit long enough to link up with a relief column.

During the night of October 16 he began ferrying his infantry to Gloucester. One wave got across before a severe squall swept in, scattered the boats, and forced cancellation of the gamble. There was only one decision left, and Cornwallis, a decent man with great concern for his troops, bit the bullet.

About 10:00 A.M. on October 17, with the bombardment at its height, a red-coated drummer boy appeared on the parapet of the Horn work. He couldn't be heard over the thunder of the guns, but everybody knew what it meant. He was beating the internationally recognized call for a parley.

A British officer with a white flag joined the drummer as the firing ceased and started toward the allied lines. An American ran out, blindfolded the man, and led him in. He carried a message from Cornwallis to Washington proposing a halt in hostilities to discuss surrender terms. The earl asked for twenty-four hours. Washington, suspecting a stall until help arrived, gave him two.

For the rest of the day, while messengers shuttled back and forth, an almost eerie silence settled over the peninsula that for days had trembled to the shock of the massive cannonade. The opposing parapets were soon crowded with soldiers staring at each other across shot-scarred ground where, not long before, they would have courted death by raising their heads.

Four years earlier, to the day, Gentleman Johnny Burgoyne had surrendered at Saratoga.

The next day John Laurens and the Vicomte de Noailles, Lafayette's brother-in-law, met two British officers in the home of Augustine Moore near the river (the restored house is now a stop on the National Park Service's tour of the battlefield) to arrange terms. Haggling continued well into the night before agreement was reached. At 11:00 A.M., October 19, the papers, signed by Cornwallis, were delivered to Washington at the Rock Redoubt. He added a line: "Done in the trenches before Yorktown in Virginia, October 19, 1781," then signed. Rochambeau and Admiral de Barras, representing de Grasse, who was too ill to come ashore, added their signatures. Far to the north the British rescue fleet was just clearing New York harbor.

Washington's conditions were generous, with one exception. Remembering General Benjamin Lincoln's humiliation at Charleston the year before, he decreed the same for the British army. It must march out with colors cased and bands playing only British tunes instead of the traditional "honors of war," which permitted the vanquished to come out with flags flying—oddly enough to a tune of the victor's (either as an acknowledgment of the courtesy or as a last gesture of defiance). The British representatives demurred but reluctantly agreed when Laurens, a fiery South Carolinian who had been taken at Charleston, declared the article would remain or he ceased to be a commissioner.

Friday, the nineteenth, was a warm, bright October day. Very early the allied bivouacs were bustling with activity as the troops spruced up for the final scene of the drama. Shortly before noon long columns poured out of the French and American camps to positions in double ranks on both sides of the main road from Yorktown. The fields behind them soon began to fill with civilians who converged from all over the peninsula on foot, in carriages, and on horseback to watch the curtain fall.

The formation extended for more than a mile from the second allied parallel to a large, grassy meadow, now preserved as the "Surrender Field" by the Park Service. The French in dress whites, bright regimental facings, shiny black gaiters, plumes, and silk battle flags, were a colorful contrast to the drab Continentals and the militia behind them, who paraded in the only clothes they possessed.

When the units were in place, detachments of American and French infantry made a symbolic occupation of the battered Yorktown defenses. As Ensign Ebenezer Denny of the 2nd Pennsylvania Continentals prepared to raise the unit colors on the parapet, he was forestalled by Steuben, who snatched them away and planted them himself. The impulsive act so outraged pudgy Colonel "Dickie" Butler, commander of the Pennsylvanians, that after the ceremony he blew off steam with a stinging letter of protest. Steuben took it as an insult, and a duel was only avoided by the personal intervention of Washington and Rochambeau.

Although Denny lost his moment of triumph, eighteen-year-old Ensign Wilson had his. As part of the surrender ritual a detail of British and German captains was to turn over the cased colors. When they found a like number of American sergeants lined up to take them, the rank-conscious English officers balked. Hamilton solved the contretemps by designating Wilson, the youngest officer in the Continental Army, to receive the flags. Wilson accepted them one by one and transferred them to the NCOs.

Shortly before two o'clock, drums rattled and the waiting lines snapped to attention as Washington, Rochambeau, and their staffs in full dress trotted up the road to the head of the line. As they took their places, Admiral de Barras provided the only light moment to the solemnity of the occasion. Barras, who could stand solidly on the pitching quarter-deck of a man-of-war in the wildest storm at sea, had no such security on the back of a horse. When his mount stretched to relieve itself, the admiral let out a yelp of alarm: "HELP. My horse is sinking!" A snicker, quickly suppressed, rippled through the staffs.

Minutes later the sally-port gate of the Horn Work swung open and a mounted group led by a handsome officer resplendent in the dress uniform of a general of the Coldstream Guards emerged. It wasn't Lord Cornwallis. The earl, unable to face the humiliation of it all, was too "ill" to appear and had sent Brigadier General O'Hara as his deputy. Ignoring the American party, O'Hara rode up to Rochambeau to surrender Cornwallis' sword. The French commander stonily pointed across the road to the American commander in chief. As O'Hara, muttering an apology for his "mistake" and an explanation of Cornwallis' nonappearance, offered the sword to Washington, the general waved him aside to General Lincoln. The latter reached out, touched the hilt, and told O'Hara to keep it.

The story is still often told that Washington's gesture was in revenge for Lincoln's humiliation at Charleston. Not so. If Cornwallis had sent a deputy, he would have to deal with his deputy, who happened to be Lincoln—although both American generals undoubtedly took great satisfaction from the coincidence.

Behind General O'Hara the defeated army, began its passage "under the woke" between the silent allied ranks. The blue-and-green-clad Germans came first, stepping out smartly to the Surrender Field, which was ringed by Lauzun's mounted hussars, jaunty in light blue uniforms and fur-trimmed pelisses. There they stacked arms briskly and made way for the British. They had served faithfully and well, but it wasn't their war, and they were happy to escape with whole skins from a fight in which they had no stake.

With the British it was different. Proud, combat-tested regiments, the 17th Leicestershires, 23rd Royal Welsh Fusiliers, 33rd West Ridings, 43rd Oxfordshires, 71st Fraser Highlanders, 76th Highlanders, and 80th Royal Edidburgh Volunteers had repeatedly faced and driven these same Continentals from the field, albeit with increasing difficulty. The Fusiliers had covered the retreat from Lexington, stormed the Bunker Hill ramparts with the 17th, and had charged at Long Island, Brandywine, Germantown, Camden, Guilford Courthouse—and it had all come to this!

On they came, slowly and reluctantly, to the lugubrious beat of a tune called "The World Turned Upside Down." Although most of them wore new uniforms, their demeanor didn't match their haberdashery. Alignments were sloppy, they didn't bother to keep in step, and many were unsteady on their feet after a final go at the rum kegs before their enemies got there. Some faces were stained with tears, all wore defiant scowls. Englishmen, as their enemies from William the Conqueror to Adolf Hitler have discovered, do not surrender graciously. At the Surrender Field they flung their muskets on the growing piles, disgustedly ripped off cartridge belts, and sullenly returned to Yorktown.

Washington didn't linger for the entire ceremony. Returning to headquarters, he wrote a laconic dispatch to the Continental Congress announcing the triumph. Before dark, Colonel Tilghman was on his way to Philadelphia.

While the victorious allies, with the reluctant help of their prisoners, tidied up the battlefield, the British fleet drew nearer. A couple of days out, news of the surrender reached Clinton and Graves and they turned back. Everybody sensed that the long, bloody ordeal was drawing to a close.

Five years earlier thirteen mutually suspicious but angry colonies had proclaimed their independence. At Yorktown, with the help of France, they made it stick. The war dragged on for two more years, but with the surrender of Cornwallis American independence was assured.

October 1981

VII

BUSINESS OF THE HIGHEST MAGNITUDE

Robert C. Alberts

The Constitution of the United States holds a place of such homage in American lore, that frequently the intense political origin of its acceptance is overlooked. The Constitutional ratification debates produced many fascinating political tales. Perhaps none, more so, than in Benjamin Franklin's Philadelphia. In the following account Robert C. Alberts explains some of the maneuvering that made Pennsylvania the second state to ratify the proposed new government.

Dr. Benjamin Rush believed the hand of God must have been involved in the noble work. John Adams, writing from Grosvenor Square, London, called it the greatest single effort of national deliberation, and perhaps the greatest exertion of human understanding, the world had ever seen. A great many people, however, held a contrary view, and in the fall of 1787 their opposition made it seem likely that the proposed Constitution of the United States would not be forwarded to the states by the Continental Congress, or, if forwarded, would not be ratified by the American people.

Opposition was especially intense in Pennsylvania, the only state with a well-developed, statewide two-party system. The Pennsylvania Democrats (Anti-federalists) were efficiently organized; they controlled the state militia and the mobs in most cities; and they were led by a group of uncompromising idealogues who were determined that their state would not ratify the new Constitution. Both the Democrats and the pro-Constitution Federalists knew that Pennsylvania was the pivotal state and that the fight there would be an influential and perhaps decisive factor in the larger national contest. The struggle that ensued has not often been equalled in this country for bitterness, violence, vehemence of debate, or political high comedy.

The Constitutional Convention completed its work on September 17, after sixteen weeks of almost daily sessions. The engrossed Constitution, signed by thirty-nine delegates from twelve states, was sent forthwith to the Congress in New York City. With it went a covering letter from General George Washington, written, it is thought, by Gouverneur Morris of Pennsylvania. A resolution of the Convention asked the Congress to submit the Constitution for ratification, not, as expected, to the state legislatures, but to a convention of delegates popularly chosen in each state, and convened solely for that purpose.

The next day Benjamin Franklin led the Pennsylvania delegation to the second floor of the State House in Philadelphia to appear before the Pennsylvania House of Assembly. General Thomas Mifflin, Speaker and one of the delegates, read the Constitution aloud.

When he finished, the citizens standing in the rear of the chamber broke into applause. On Wednesday the Constitution was printed in full in the *Packet*, the *Journal*, and the *Independent Gazetteer or Chronicle of Freedom*, and thereafter in others of the country's eighty-odd news-papers. It was distributed in Pennsylvania as a pamphlet, with five hundred copies in the German language for the benefit of the state's large German-speaking population.

The first public response seemed to be favorable, but the Democrats were bursting with protest. Speaking "for the present and future ages—the cause of liberty and mankind," they went to work with handbills and pamphlets, with squibs and speeches, with articles and letters in the papers, in meetings and in exchanges in the boarding houses and taverns. To Democrats the new Constitution was the product of "as deep and wicked a conspiracy as ever was invented in the darkest ages against the liberties of a free people," and it "would surely result in a monarchy or a tyrannical aristocracy," and perhaps in civil war. They voiced these major objections:

1. Congress had instructed the Convention delegates to recommend possible amendments to the Articles of Confederation and Perpetual Union. Instead, meeting behind locked doors in a "dark conclave," they had willfully written a plan for an entirely new form of government.

2. Their Constitution would annihilate the present confederation of coequal states, where the sovereign power should properly reside, and substitute for it a consolidated national government. The authority of the states would be grievously curbed if not obliterated. The ability of the new Congress to impose internal taxes and duties at its pleasure would undercut the taxing powers of the individual state legislatures.

3. Unprotected by their state governments, the citizens would be at the mercy of the central government. There was no bill of rights; liberty of the press, habeas corpus, and religious toleration were not assured; trial by jury was abolished in civil cases; and there was no prohibition of a standing army in time of peace.

4. The government of three branches, this "triple-headed monster," was unworkable. The President was too powerful, the Vice President "a needless and dangerous officer," the Senate too aristocratic, the House too small to represent the people, the jurisdiction of the Supreme Court too extensive. The country was too large to be ruled under the principles of liberty by a consolidated government.

5. The whole proposition was extravagant and would bankrupt the nation.

The more zealous Pennsylvania Democrats pounded hard on those objections and added several others of their own. For one thing, none of the eight Pennsylvania delegates to the Convention had been Democrats, and none had come from the six counties beyond the western mountains, where, among Scotch-Irish and German immigrant farmer-frontiersmen, the chief opposition to the Constitution lay. For another, the Democrats would lose jobs, power, and their control over the Pennsylvania militia. For a third, they would probably see the repeal of their ultrademocratic (and unworkable) state constitution. Without having bothered with the formality of a popular vote, they had imposed this constitution on the state in the turmoil of 1776, and they held it to be a model for other states and nations to follow. (Much of it was written by James Cannon, a mathematics professor at the College of Philadelphia who seems to have been somewhat ahead of his time. He tried but failed to include an article reading, "That an enormous proportion of property vested in a few individuals is dangerous to the rights, and destructive of the common happiness, of mankind; and therefore every free state hath a right by its laws to discourage the possession of such property.")

In New York, the Continental Congress had been unable to muster a quorum of seven states throughout the summer, but on Thursday, September 20, attendance picked up and the members took under consideration the new frame of government that had been placed before them. The assent of nine of the thirteen states was required for approval.

Pennsylvania's Federalist congressmen, under the leadership of William Bingham, a wealthy Philadelphia merchant and banker, pushed hard through a week-long debate to forward the Constitution with an affirmative and unanimous endorsement. Richard Henry Lee of Virginia, leading a strong minority, spoke of "essential alterations" and of the need to call another constitutional convention. He moved that a bill of rights and a long list of amendments be added, and he proposed a resolution stating that the new plan of government be submitted to the existing state legislatures rather than to state conventions assembled solely for that purpose. The minority then offered to forward the plan to the states for consideration, but with the warning that the Convention had acted improperly in producing it and with a reprimand to the delegates. The two sides worked for a suitable compromise.

Back in Philadelphia, without waiting for formal word from the Continental Congress, Democrats and Federalists prepared for a mighty struggle in the House of Assembly. The Democratic minority planned a delaying action. The House had resolved to adjourn sine die on Saturday, September 29. Delay would carry the issue over to a new Assembly to be elected five weeks later. Democrats might win a majority in that body and thus have the votes to defeat a call for a state convention—if the Congress really did send the Constitution forward. Or they might elect a majority of anti-Constitution delegates in the convention—if one had to be called. Defeat of the Constitution in Pennsylvania, or delay in calling a state convention, would strengthen the anti-Constitution forces in the twelve other states.

The Federalists not only wanted the Constitution to be ratified in Pennsylvania; they also wanted their state to be the first to act. That would strengthen the movement in the other states. It would take advantage of the early wave of sentiment in favor of the Constitution and give the western farmers less time to find fault with it. It would allow the Democratic leaders the least opportunity to return to their inland counties and organize the opposition. And early ratification would give Pennsylvania a leg up on placing the new seat of government near Philadelphia, where it obviously belonged.

The Federalists drew up a plan designed to take their opponents by surprise. They would make a motion for a state convention on Friday morning, one day before adjournment, and attempt to rush it through before the Democrats could recover. The procedure was irregular, perhaps, since the Congress had not yet *asked* for a convention, but the issue was vital and the cause was just.

William Bingham arranged to send news from New York by dispatch riders who would change horses at frequent posts along the ninety-mile route.

On Friday morning, September 28, every Federalist member was in his seat. After the House attended to some routine business, George Clymer, merchant of Philadelphia, signer of the Declaration of Independence and one of the framers of the new federal Constitution, rose in place. The members, he said suavely, could not have forgotten a business of the highest magnitude that had been recommended to their attention by the federal Convention. He was persuaded that they would readily concur in taking the necessary measures, and therefore he had prepared a resolution to that end.

His resolution was promptly seconded by Gerardus Wynkoop, who sat for Bucks County.

Robert Whitehill, member from Cumberland County, one of the authors of the ultrademocratic Pennsylvania constitution, rose to object. The members, he said, ought to have
time to consider the subject. He moved, therefore, to postpone consideration until the afternoon session.

Thomas Fitzsimons (City of Philadelphia), one of the signers of the federal Constitution, declared that the business was of the highest consequence. The only object of consideration was not the merits of the new Constitution, but solely whether the election of
delegates should be held. It was the general wish of the people that the House should go
forward in the matter.

William Findley (Westmoreland County), Ulster-born, former weaver and teacher, now a
farmer and Democratic leader, agreed that the subject was important. It was so important, indeed, that the House should go into it with deliberation. It was so important that the members
should not be surprised into it.

Daniel Clymer (Berks County), cousin of George, said (in extract): "I have heard, Sir,
that only four or five leading party-men in this city are against it, whose names I should be
glad to know, that their characters might be examined; for I am confident they will be hereafter ashamed to show their faces among the good people whose future prosperity they wish to
blast in the bud. Let them be careful, lest they draw upon themselves the odium of that people
who have long indulged their rioting upon public favor."

Findley: "The gentleman from Berks has spoken warmly against opposing the present
measure in a manner as if intended to prevent men from speaking their minds. He has
charged some leading characters in this city with giving opposition; if he means me as one
of them—"

Daniel Clymer (addressing the Speaker): "No, Sir, upon my honor, I did not mean him."

Findley: "Well, then, I don't consider that part of his speech as addressed to the House,
but merely to the gallery."

Daniel Clymer: "The measure will be adopted; for it is too generally agreeable, and too
highly recommended, to be assassinated by the hand of intrigue and cabal."

Whitehill: "The gentlemen that have brought forward this motion must have some design. Why not allow time to consider it? I believe if time is allowed, we shall be able to show
that this is not the proper time for calling a convention; and I don't know any reason there can
be for driving it down our throats, without an hour's preparation."

George Clymer: "To hesitate upon this proposition will give a very unfavorable aspect to
a measure on which our future happiness, nay, I may also say, our future existence, as a nation, depends."

Hugh Henry Brackenridge of Westmoreland County, Princeton graduate, former
schoolteacher and chaplain in the Revolutionary Army, now a lawyer, author, and wit, was
the only member from the western counties and the only Democrat to support the Constitution actively. He rose to express the view that, "from its magnitude and importance," the
members surely must have reflected for some days on the matter. In his opinion they were
as well prepared now to determine upon the principle as they would be after having eaten
their dinner.

Whitehill: "Congress ought to send forward the plan before we do anything at all in this
matter. For of what use was sending it forward to them, unless we meant to wait their determination? Now as these measures are not recommended by Congress, why should we take
them up? Why should we take up a thing which does not exist? Is it not better to go safely on
the business, and let it lie over till the next House? When we have adjourned, let our constitu-

ents think of it, and instruct their representatives to consider of the plan proper to be pursued. Will not the next House be able to determine as we are?"

Daniel Clymer: "The Constitution lately presented to you [was] framed by the collective wisdom of a continent, centered in a venerable band of patriots, worthies, heroes, legislators and philosophers—the admiration of a world. No longer shall thirty thousand [Philadelphians] engage all our attention—all our efforts to procure happiness. No!—The extended embrace of fraternal love shall enclose three millions, and ere fifty years are elapsed, thirty millions, as a band of brothers!

"As this subject is now before us, let us not hesitate, but eagerly embrace the glorious opportunity of being foremost in its adoption. Let us not hesitate, because it is damping the ardor with which it should be pursued. Sir, it is throwing cold water on the flame that warms the breast of every friend of liberty, and every patriot who wishes this country to acquire that respect to which she is justly entitled."

The question was put: Would the House agree to postpone consideration of the matter? It was defeated.

George Clymer spoke to the real Federalist concern. "If this House order a convention," he said, "it may be deliberated and decided some time in November, [1787], and the Constitution may be acted under by December. But if it is left over to the next House, it will inevitably be procrastinated until December, 1788."

The Federalists began to cry, "Question! Question!" and a vote was taken on the resolution: Would the House agree to elect delegates and call a state convention? It was carried 43 to 19.

Whitehill then moved that the session adjourn until four o'clock that afternoon, at which time, he said, they might decide the lesser issues of time and place of the election of delegates and the holding of the convention.

Undoubtedly, congratulations were exchanged, and there was much joking at the Federalists' luncheon tables at how smoothly everything had been managed and how clearly the victory had been won. But when the session resumed at four o'clock, the Federalists were astounded to find not one of the nineteen Democratic members in his seat. With forty-four members present, the House was two votes short of a quorum—which meant that no business could be conducted.

Mr. Wynkoop observed that the missing members were those who had given opposition that morning, and he suspected that they had conspired to absent themselves. He moved that the sergeant at arms be ordered to fetch them. The sergeant accordingly was dispatched. When he returned, he was examined at the bar of the House.

Speaker: "Well, Sergeant, have you seen the absent members?"

The sergeant replied that he had seen seventeen members at Major Boyd's boarding house on Sixth Street.

Speaker: "What did you say to them?"
Sergeant: "I told the gentlemen that the Speaker and the House had sent for them, and says they, 'There is no House.'"
Speaker: "Did you let them know they were desired to attend?"
Sergeant: "Yes, Sir, but they told me they could not attend this afternoon, for they had not made up their minds yet."
Daniel Clymer: "How is that?"

Sergeant: "They had not made up their minds this afternoon to wait on you."
Speaker: "Who told you this?"
Sergeant: "Mr. Whitehill told me first."
Clymer: "Who told you afterward?"
Sergeant: "Mr. Clarke said they must go *electioneering* now."
Clymer: "Was there no private citizens there?"
Sergeant: "No, Sir."
Clymer: "There was none then, but men in public offices?"
Sergeant: "No."
Clymer: "Did you hear of any one willing to come?"
Sergeant: "No, Sir."

The Federalists, outwitted, baffled, and angry at this breach of trust, debated what to do next. If no business could be conducted, the Assembly would be forced to adjourn the next day without naming a date for selecting delegates or for holding the convention. Mr. Wynkoop declared, "I would be glad to know, if there is no way to compel men, who deserted from the duty they owed their country, to a performance of it, when they were within reach of the House. If there is not, then *God be merciful to us!!!*"

A search of the books revealed no regulation compelling an absent member to attend, the only penalty being loss of one third of a day's pay for each absence. The Speaker declared a recess until nine thirty the following morning.

Federalists discussed the affair in homes and taverns throughout the evening, with liberal abuse for the nineteen recalcitrant members and much speculation about what the minority would do when the Assembly reconvened. The Democratic leaders worked through the night behind locked doors at Major Boyd's; they were preparing an address to their constituents in which they set forth their objections to the new plan of government.

When General Mifflin took the chair on Saturday morning, the minority members were again absent and again no quorum could be declared.

George Clymer presented to the House a packet of documents he had received from New York in the early morning. It contained, he said, a resolution of Congress, passed unanimously, requesting the legislature of each state to put the proposed Constitution to a vote of a popularly elected convention. This had been signed the day before, and Mr. William Bingham had forwarded it to him by express rider, "having chosen this mode in preference to the ordinary conveyance by post." The resolution was read aloud.

Fortified by this new evidence of regularity, the Speaker again sent the sergeant at arms to find the missing members and request their attendance, this time accompanied by the assistant clerk carrying the resolution of Congress. They returned to report that they had seen a dozen of the members in various places and had delivered the message and shown them the resolution. Mr. Findley had "mended his pace" and escaped; others had declared they would not attend; one said he would consider the matter and do what he thought just.

In the meantime word had spread around the city that the Democrats had "absconded" from their duties at the Assembly. A crowd of men gathered, and as time passed they grew impatient. They marched off in search of any two absent members, and the path led straight to Major Boyd's boarding house. There they found two Democrats: James McCalmont of Franklin County and Jacob Miley of Dauphin. Both men had been militia officers in the Revolution. McCalmont, fifty, a major, had a distinguished record as a frontier scout and fighter of Native American warriors; he had been famous for his speed in running and his ability to reload a musket or rifle while in full flight or pursuit.

Several of the crowd entered and read the congressional resolution aloud. McCalmont and Miley refused to budge. When that information was conveyed to those waiting outside, they shouted imprecations, smashed windows with stones, broke down the front door, and stormed into the house. McCalmont and Miley were collared, dragged from the premises, and pushed and pulled through the streets to the State House. General Mifflin, hearing a commotion outside and suspecting the reason, discreetly absented himself for a while from the chamber. The two men, their clothes dirtied and torn, their faces white with anger, were thrust onto the floor of the House and escorted to their seats. The clerk wrote in his minutes, in what must be considered something of an understatement, "The Speaker left the chair, and in a few minutes Mr. James McCalmont and Mr. Jacob Miley entered the House. The Speaker resumed the chair, and the roll was called." Both men answered to their names or were declared present by others. With forty-six members on the floor the Speaker declared a quorum.

McCalmont rose to protest that he had been brought into the Assembly room by force, contrary to his wishes, by a number of citizens he did not know. He asked to be dismissed from the House.

Fitzsimons replied that he would be glad to know if any member of the House had been guilty of forcing the gentleman from his determination to absent himself. If so, the House should mark such conduct with its disapprobation, he said.

Brackenridge added: "If the member has been conducted by the citizens of Philadelphia to his seat in the legislature, and they have not treated him with the respect and veneration he deserves, it must lie with him to obtain satisfaction, but not with us. How he came here can form no part of our enquiry. Whether his friends brought him (and I should think they could not be his enemies who would compel him to do his duty and avoid wrong), I say, Sir, whether his friends brought him, or by the influence of good advice persuaded him to come, and he did come; or whether to ease his difficulty in walking to this room they brought him in a sedan chair, or by whatever ways or means he introduced himself among us, all we are to know is that he is here, and it only remains for us to decide whether he shall have leave of absence."

McCalmont: "I desire that the rules may be read, and I will agree to stand by the decision of the House."

The rules were read, and they were found to state that "every member who did not answer on calling the roll should pay two shillings and six pence, or, if there was not a quorum without him, five shillings."

McCalmont rose, took some loose silver from his pocket, held it out, and said, "Well, Sir, here is your five shillings to let me go."

The crowd gathered behind the railing roared with laughter. The Speaker declared that the person appointed to receive fines was not in his place, and that even if he had been, the member should not pay a fine. McCalmont had not broken the rule, the Speaker said. He had appeared and answered to his name and therefore could keep his money.

Mr. Robinson of Philadelphia County, though a Federalist, had some uneasy qualms of conscience. He opined that the House had no authority to detain the member as though he were in prison. Mr. Wynkoop expressed his amazement at this solicitude for a member who had absconded "from his duty at the bar of the House." Mr. McCalmont declared that he had to answer for his conduct at a more important bar than that of the House.

Fitzsimons was stern. He declared that he was a true friend to good order and decorum, but that he believed the gentleman's complaint was not to be   redressed by the House of Assembly. The member himself had trespassed, Fitzsimons said; McCalmont had perhaps offered the greatest indignity to the legislature of Pennsylvania that could be offered. He had tendered a pittance, a fine of five shillings, in order to be permitted to destroy the business, if not the good government, of the state. The member was now present, Fitzsimons said, and should stay, not only on constitutional grounds, but from the law of nature that would not suffer any body to destroy its own existence prematurely.

Robinson: "Suppose the House determine that he shall not leave, and yet he should attempt to withdraw. Certainly you will not lock your doors."

Fitzsimons: "Yes, Sir, if no other method could retain him."

A moment later McCalmont rose and made a dash for the door. The crowd yelled, "Stop him!" and those about the door barred his way. McCalmont returned to his seat.

The Speaker put the question: "Shall Mr. McCalmont have leave of absence?" It was voted "almost unanimously in the negative."

Brackenridge then moved that the delegates to the state convention be elected on the first Tuesday in November. McCalmont objected that this was much too early and moved the last Tuesday in December. His motion failed. He moved the third Tuesday in December, then the second Tuesday, with the same result. He moved that the site of the convention be moved from Philadelphia to Carlisle, but he was not upheld. He moved that the change be made to Lancaster and was enthusiastically supported by the member from Lancaster. Fifteen members voted for Lancaster in a defeated motion.

The formal resolution was now put: That the election of delegates be held on November 6, 1787, and that the convention meet in the State House in Philadelphia on the third Tuesday in November. It was passed by a vote of 44 to 2. The Federalists had won their victory. The Assembly adjourned. McCalmont and Miley were released.

In the campaign that followed for election of delegates, Democrats and Federalists attacked one another with arguments and invective and sometimes with clubs, stones, and fists.

October 5, 1787: The first of twenty-four letters of "Centinel" (sentinel of the people's liberties) appeared in the *Gazetteer.* These papers, running through the next fourteen months, still of undetermined authorship, were the Democratic counterpart of the eighty-five papers *(The Federalist)* produced by "Publius" in New York. Centinel attacked Publius on many points and brilliantly set forth the Democratic case against the constitution, the "harpies of power," and "the wealthy and ambitious, who in every community think they have a right to lord it over their fellow creatures." The treatment accorded McCalmont and Miley, Centinel said, showed what would happen to free citizens under the Federalist Constitution.

October 6: At a public meeting in the State House yard, James Wilson cogently answered the Democratic arguments point by point, and in so doing assumed the role of the country's most effective proponent of the Constitution in debate. His speech was widely distributed, reprinted, copied, and quoted. The Democrats attacked it as a "train of pitiful sophistries and evasions," compared Wilson (unfavorably) with Tiberius, Caligula, and Nero, and charged that he was "strongly tainted with the spirit *of high aristocracy.*"

November 6: The Federalists scored an overwhelming victory in the election of delegates, losing only the six western counties. Their majority was 2 to 1, or 46 convention votes to 23. Elated at their victory, several dozen Federalists gathered on election night before Major Boyd's, reviled the "damned rascals" housed therein, flung stones through the newly repaired windows, and broke the door with large rocks.

November 21: The convention convened in the State House. The delegates spent the first week arguing about procedure. James Wilson distinguished himself with five powerful, if somewhat florid, speeches. Robert Whitehill, the Democrat from Cumberland County, submitted fifteen proposed amendments to the Constitution as a bill of rights. They were ignored. On a number of occasions the members were close to physical assault on one another.

December 7: Delaware ratified the Constitution, won over by the compromise that gave the small states equal representation in the Senate (the Constitution's only irrevocable article). John Smilie of Fayette County, who with Whitehill and Findley was leading the fight against ratification in the Pennsylvania convention, sneered that Delaware had "reaped the honor of having first surrendered the liberties of the people."

December 12: Pennsylvania became the second state—and the first large state—"to assent to and ratify" the Constitution. The vote was, predictably, 46 to 23. A transcript of the convention proceedings was made for publication, but the Federalists persuaded the court printer to release only the Federalist speeches.

December 13: The delegates marched in procession to the Court House at Market and Second streets, accompanied by members of the new Assembly, state and city officials, and other local dignitaries. The ratification was read from a balcony to a great gathering of citizens. The city bells rang out, and thirteen cannons fired salvos.

December 18: The defeated Democratic delegates issued a pamphlet titled *Reasons for Dissent* and mailed a copy to every printer in the country. No copies were delivered. Democrats charged that they were destroyed by "the sons of power" who controlled the Pennsylvania post-office system.

December 27: Federalists in Carlisle, a Scotch-Irish town of three hundred houses in the Cumberland Valley some 120 miles west of Philadelphia, staged a public celebration in honor of the ratification. They procured James Wilson for an oration, dragged a cannon to the public square, and heaped up a great stack of barrels for a bonfire. Antifederalists charged the crowd, upset the barrels, spiked the cannon, burned a copy of the Constitution, and began to beat Wilson with bludgeons. An old soldier saved his life by throwing himself over the body and taking the blows until help came.

Two days of riots followed. John Montgomery, venerable Federalist, one of the founders of Dickinson College in Carlisle five years earlier, wrote to a friend, "They are violent on both sides. . . . We [Federalists] are in a very disagreeable unhapey situation in this place nothing ever happned so bad amongst us neaghbours pass each other without speaking."

June 21, 1788: The Constitution became law and the United States a new nation with ratification by New Hampshire, the ninth state.

July 4: Philadelphia mounted an all-day celebration to mark the day of Independence and the forming of the new Union. Some five thousand marched or rode in a Federal Procession a mile and a half long. All the trades, crafts, and professions were represented, many of them with elaborate floats, in a spectacle such as no American had ever seen before. High point of the procession was a structure called the "New Roof or Grand Foederal Ediface," 36 feet high, drawn by ten white horses. Benjamin Rush called the Ediface "truly sublime" and observed approvingly that of the thousands who took part in the ceremonies that day, very few engaged in quarrels and almost no one was intoxicated.

On an open field at the parade's end, James Wilson, standing on the Grand Ediface, delivered the Fourth of July oration. Some of his passages were drowned out by the ill-timed firing of thirteen cannons on vessels anchored in the Delaware, but his soaring closing words were loud and clear: "PEACE walks *serene* and *unalarmed* over all the unmolested regions—while LIBERTY, VIRTUE, and RELIGION go hand in hand harmoniously *protecting, enlivening,* and *exalting* all! HAPPY COUNTRY, MAY THY HAPPINESS BE PERPETUAL!"

The Pennsylvania Democrats made their peace with the new form of government. Within two years they got the Bill of Rights they had fought for: ten amendments to the Constitution that were remarkably like the amendments Robert Whitehill had vainly offered to the Pennsylvania state convention. James McCalmont became a judge, and Jacob Miley a representative, under the new Pennsylvania constitution. Robert Whitehill served four terms and John Smilie served eight terms in the House of Representatives of the United States. William Findley served eleven terms, and in one of them, in 1795, he moved the creation of the first standing congressional committee—a body of honest representatives called the Ways and Means Committee, formed to keep a sharp eye on the financial operations of a Federalist administration.

February 1971

VIII

LIBERTÉ, EGALITÉ, ANIMOSITÉ

Garry Wills

The French Revolution began in the great hope of establishing a free and democratic France much like the new United States. But, soon events turned violent and the hoped for results eluded the revolutionaries. As one faction removed another, American opinions likewise began to divide. The resulting antagonism accelerated political divisions between Hamiltonian Federalists and Democrat-Republican Jeffersonians. Garry Wills weaves the exciting narrative of French intrigue and American reactions together in this piece.

There were two great revolutions against European monarchs in the late eighteenth century. In the first, the French nation helped Americans achieve their independence from George III. Without that help our revolution could not have succeeded. Yet when the French rebelled against Louis XVI, Americans hailed their action, then hesitated over it, and finally recoiled from it, causing bitterness in France and among some Americans. Why had the "sister republics" not embraced each other when they had the opportunity? Instead of marching together, the revolutions, so similar in their ideals, roots, and principles, passed each other at shouting distance. What began in mutual encouragement ended in mutual misapprehension.

The root of the trouble lay in the equivocal nature of the aid France extended to America in the 1770s. The American Revolution wore two different faces in France, and each was one of the many faces of Benjamin Franklin. On the one hand, Louis XVI was using British colonists to discommode his rival, George III, and Franklin was the courtier who pointed out the advantages of such a course to Louis's ministers. A famous contemporary image of Franklin is the porcelain statuette group by Lemire, in which Franklin bows to the French king, who presents him with the Treaty of 1778, which allied us to France (a document that would be the subject of heated controversy just over a decade later).

A more complex picture of the diplomatic forces at work is the allegorical print by Étienne Pallière, which shows Franklin helping unleash the French Hercules, who bashes with his club Britannia and her cowering lion. On the right side of the print, Neptune dispatches the French navy, carrying cannon forged by Vulcan. All the gods of neoclassicism move to accomplish the will of Louis XVI's government. One king rebukes another in the balance of imperial politics. (Although the Declaration of Independence had been specifically crafted to bring France into the conflict, Louis responded only after the first substantial defeat of an English army at Saratoga.)

But to the philosophes of the French Enlightenment, Franklin bore quite another face—himself a neoclassical god now, Prometheus, the tamer of lightning and the scourge of tyrants, the scientist and the philosopher of freedom. That's the way Fragonard drew Franklin and Marguerite Gérard engraved him, adding the heroic hexameter of Turgot, *Eripuit coelo fulmen, sceptrumque tyrannis* ("He tore from heaven lightning, and the scepter from kings"). Turgot, the reforming economist, had to circulate his line of poetry anonymously, since the plural for *kings (tyrannis)* showed that French thinkers hoped the American Revolution would effect changes in their own society, weakening the hold of Louis XVI's establishment, which had censored their works. Franklin encouraged this view of America's meaning for the future, joining the Paris-based Masonic lodge of the Nine Sisters, where hopes of a revolution in France were harbored.

Some of the officers who went to serve in the American Revolution—notably Lafayette, Rochambeau, Chastellux, and Admiral d'Estaing—were enlightened critics of their own government as well as supporters of American aspirations, but George Washington never forgot that the motive of King Louis in sending these auxiliaries was not any devotion to anti-monarchical principle but a maneuver to regain some of the holdings in the New World he had lost to England after the Seven Years' War.

Washington alone took the measure of French aid in both its aspects. He was a champion of the Enlightenment in areas like his opposition to established churches, but he also had an eye to the practical conditions for exercising freedom. (In the recent debates in Congress over Central America, he would definitely agree with those who think free elections mean little to people who cannot feed their own children.) He meant to keep America free from dependence on France as well as from submission to England.

When Lafayette, for example, tried to organize an army to recapture Canada, Washington expressed to Congress his vigorous objections. He wanted to use France, not be used by it. The independence of America could only be maintained by keeping it nonaligned between the great powers. The historian Edmund S. Morgan has convincingly traced Washington's neutrality policy back to the touchiness he felt about accepting French help from a king with his own designs in mind. Washington's caution was justified years later, at the end of the war over the American colonies, when it came out that Louis was negotiating with George III to grant Spain all American territory across the Alleghenies.

But this was a secret war of wills between Washington and King Louis that went on under a surface of amity. Washington did not even confide his misgivings to Lafayette, despite their friendship. After the war diplomatic relations between the two countries, though strained somewhat by French commercial losses in the war, were cordial as a result of Alexander Hamilton's efforts to repay on a regular basis the debts incurred to France. Meanwhile, the leading thinkers in the two countries seemed to form a single community of rational discourse. French visitors to America—Crèvecoeur and Brissot de Warville—found models for French social reform in American institutions. American visitors to France—Thomas Jefferson and Joel Barlow—saw the stirrings of discontent with the established church and state as natural consequences of the example America had set in its state and federal constitutions. Thomas Paine, having argued for common-sense government in America, went to France to vindicate the rights of man. The French officers who had served with Washington were the only men at Louis XVI's court allowed to wear a foreign decoration—the Order of the Cincinnati eagle, designed by a Frenchman, Pierre Charles L'Enfant.

When the Bastille fell in 1789, Lafayette—recognizing the indebtedness of the French Revolution to Americans, who had shown the way—sent the key of that prison to Washington. Lafayette's face became the first of many that the French Revolution would turn toward America—and a more welcome appearance could not be wished. Jefferson, who had recently returned from France to become Secretary of State—Lafayette was at his farewell dinner in

Paris—was actually more enthusiastic about the French Revolution than was France's minister to America, Jean Baptiste de Ternant. Jefferson thought the French experiment would not only confirm the American one but spread irresistibly to all the other enlightened parts of Europe. When the National Assembly in France, conscious of the model offered by the Declaration of Independence, issued a Declaration of the Rights of Man, it was designed to be adaptable to any country.

Hamilton, the Secretary of the Treasury, thought, like Jefferson, that French republicanism would spread to other countries—a prospect he feared as destabilizing. He reminded Washington that all treaties had been made with the regime of Louis XVI and that any new government in France would not have the same claim upon America as had the one that actually supplied help to America in its time of crisis. This was Hamilton's way of turning the revolutionary assistance France had given to America against that country's own revolutionary effort. The equivocal nature of Louis XVI's actions was coming back to haunt Franco-American relations.

Jefferson was not convinced. He argued heatedly in cabinet debate that treaties are made with the people who make up a nation and that any people can alter its form of government without forfeiting prior claims upon other nations. Washington agreed with Jefferson that treaty obligations must be met—that, for instance, payments on the war debt should be continued—but he was no more ready to commit America's fortunes to the giant republic of France than to the giant monarchy of France.

While the cabinet debate was going on in private, an international propaganda war broke out in 1790 over the future of the French Revolution. Thomas Paine was at the center of a triangular debate in England, France, and America. The mob's invasion of Versailles, menacing the queen—an attack repulsed by Lafayette—had ruffled the great parliamentarian Edmund Burke's deep sense of historical decorum. Burke wrote his impassioned *Reflections on the Revolution in France* to defend ancient establishments. Paine responded from France with *The Rights of Man,* saying Burke "pities the plumage, but forgets the dying bird" of the French nation. Thomas Jefferson indiscreetly recommended Paine's book to its American publisher as an answer to "heresies" that had arisen in America over the French Revolution—an allusion to John Adams's *Discourses on Davila* (1790), in which Adams denounced French experiments with freedom. When Jefferson's letter was published, he had to apologize for this attack by one member of Washington's administration on the Vice-President of the United States.

There was great misunderstanding on all sides because events were moving rapidly in France, though reports of them came slowly to America. In 1792, when news arrived that France had declared war on the alliance of kings that was taking shape in response to the Revolution, Hamilton argued that America's guarantee of French rights in the West Indies was framed in case a *defensive* war should arise, and France had now taken the offensive. Jefferson replied that France was forced to take pre-emptive steps.

But Jefferson's words were being undermined without his knowledge. Lafayette, leading French troops (with Rochambeau) against the Austrians, concluded in 1792 that his home government had reeled out of control. He defected from the army and was soon writing Washington from an Austrian jail, posing delicate problems for the President, who wanted to help his old ally without committing America to either of the two sides Lafayette had already taken. The French Revolution no longer wore a face familiar from America's own fighting days.

Jefferson's hopes shifted to Brissot de Warville, the rising leader of the Girondin faction, a friend of America who spoke of "our" revolutions and republics (Washington deleted a similar "our" from one of Jefferson's documents addressed to France). The summary execution of aristocrats by popular tribunals in France led to some nervous arguments in America over the need to break eggs when making revolutionary omelets. Jefferson had written to Lafayette, before his defection, that "we are not to expect to be translated from despotism to liberty in a feather-bed." After Lafayette's imprisonment Jefferson wrote to his former secretary, William Short: "My own affections have been deeply wounded by some of the martyrs to the cause, but rather than it should have failed, I would have seen half the earth desolated. Were there but an Adam & an Eve left in every country, & left free, it would be better than as it now is."

Jefferson did not know, when he wrote those words, that Louis XVI had been executed on January 21, 1793. Jefferson later wrote that he would have voted, if he were in the French government, for removing the king but not for killing him. That was also Thomas Paine's attitude at the time, and Paine was in a position to do something for the king. Ironically, he tried to arrange to have Louis conducted into exile in America, under the safe-conduct of the new minister about to depart for Philadelphia, Edmond Charles Edouard Genêt. Despite Paine's arguments, Citizen Louis Capet was condemned, and Americans began to realize that revolution meant one thing in a home country deposing its ruler and another in colonies seceding from an empire. There had been no regicide involved in the American Revolution—not even any executions of Loyalists. The death of the king raised the stakes of this second revolution, for its sympathizers as well as its participants.

"Republicans" in America had to rationalize the violence by a harsher definition of what revolution means. As French philosophes had used the American Revolution to change their society, so Jeffersonians out of government argued that the French Revolution, by its logic of anti-aristocratic purity, showed that changes were still to be made in American society. If the French Revolution was different from the American, that only meant that the American Revolution should be made to resemble the French more closely. Democratic-Republican Societies were formed not only to support the French Revolution but to import some of its practices. Some Americans began to address each other as "Citizen" and to wear the liberty cap. Bostonians even decided that the proper term for a woman was "Citess."

The aim of all this activity was to push America into open support of France. To prevent this, Washington decided to proclaim the neutrality he had been observing all along. Jefferson argued that he had no power to do this—that only Congress can declare war and that the state of peace when no such declaration has occurred does not need to be proclaimed by the Executive, the department of government that lacks war powers. But Americans were organizing support for a foreign belligerent, and Washington wanted to prevent that. Jefferson at least succeeded in keeping the actual word *neutrality* out of the so-called neutrality proclamation of 1793.

At the very time Washington was proclaiming neutrality in Philadelphia, the new French minister arrived in Charleston. With him, the French Revolution acquired a particular face in America that would prove fatal to hopes for Franco-American unity—the face of Citizen Genêt. Genêt, a young aristocrat popular with the Girondins, made it his open aim to rally the American citizenry against its own government's stated policy. This was a bracing prospect for people like James Madison, who deplored the President's neutrality in a letter to Jefferson: "The proclamation was in truth a most unfortunate error. It wounds the national honor, by seeming to disregard the stipulated duties to France. It wounds the popular feelings by a seeming indifference to the cause of liberty. . . . If France triumphs, the ill-fated proclamation will be a millstone which would sink any other character [but Washington's] and will force a struggle even on his."

Unfortunately for Genêt, he listened to similar talk from "true Americans," who felt that he must save the President from his own advisers. Hamilton had argued against receiving

Genêt at all. Washington overruled him, but Genêt made matters sticky by not bothering to seek a diplomatic reception before he began rallying opinion and money for the French cause. He made a public tour that brought him in a leisurely fashion to the seat of government in Philadelphia.

Jefferson, for as long as he could, nurtured great hopes for the Genêt mission. He was glad to see Ternant, the royal minister, removed, since he thought that remnant of the old regime had been an obstacle to the natural sympathy that would be expressed between the two republics once they understood each other. Jefferson assured his friends that Genêt "offers everything and asks nothing." Genêt had brought with him a personal letter to Jefferson from his old friend Condorcet, which urged that "our republic, founded like yours on reason, on the rights of nature, on equality, ought to be your true ally . . . [that] we ought in some sort to form one people."

This was Jefferson's hope too, but Genêt took the idea of one people so literally that he acted as a citizen of the world talking to Americans as one of them. The Girondin stage of the French Revolution was the most optimistically proselytizing one, and Genêt felt he could speak to all free men without regard for the ceremonies of established governments. He had replaced his own title with the universal "Citizen." He expected American officials to set aside their titles too.

When they did not, Genêt treated them as betrayers of their own revolution. He threatened to appeal over the head of Washington to the people the President claimed to represent. He even attacked Jefferson for the State Department's implementation of the neutrality policy. Jefferson, in his turn, came to realize that Genêt was doing far more damage to the French cause than Ternant ever had. By July 1793 he was writing Madison: "Never in my opinion was so calamitous an ointment made, as that of the present Minister of F[rance] here. Hotheaded, all imagination, no judgment, passionate, disrespectful and even indecent towards the P[resident] in his written as well as verbal communications, talking of appeals from him to Congress, from them to the people, urging the most unreasonable & groundless propositions, & in the most dictatorial style. . . . He renders my position immensely difficult."

Jefferson's only hope of preventing a public reaction against Genêt (and through him against France) was to keep the insulting record of his dealings from publication. But that was made impossible when Genêt went from propagandizing to active war making: he was in touch with Western leaders like George Rogers Clark, who wanted to seize Louisiana from the Spanish. Genêt, an adjutant general of the French army, offered the support of his nation to such a "filibustering" movement. This was all the more embarrassing for Jefferson since Genêt had extracted a letter of recommendation from him introducing Genêt's emissary in this matter to the governor of Kentucky. Genêt, at first a nuisance, had become a disaster.

Yet by the time his recall was demanded, Genêt had to request asylum in this country (where, indeed, he lived out the rest of his long life). During his absence the Jacobins had replaced the Girondins and instituted the Terror. Friends of America like d'Estaing were sent to the guillotine—to which Genêt would undoubtedly have been conducted had he returned to France. Paine, imprisoned by Robespierre, lived in the shadow of the guillotine until its blade fell on Robespierre himself. The Revolution was devouring its own.

America was now a "sister republic" to France only in its own bitter divisions. The ideal accepted by all sides at the beginning of the Washington administration had been a factionless society, in which partisan appeals were to be submitted to impartial consideration. Early divisions had occurred, in the cabinet and in Congress, over matters like the establishment of a federal banking system. But these had not become matters of widespread popular agitation until Genêt made his appeals to the people and Democratic-Republican Societies began staging rallies in imitation of the Parisian mobs. John Adams was no doubt exaggerating when he remembered, late in his life, a time "when ten thousand people in the streets of Philadelphia, day after day threatened to drag Washington out of his house." But there was tumult and disorder of the sort not seen since the demonstrations against George III.

When Washington criticized the Democratic-Republican Societies for introducing faction into American life, he was assailed for suppressing free speech. When Paine published his *Age of Reason* in 1794, it was made the occasion for attacks on the "atheism" of the French Revolution. Jefferson, suffering guilt by association with Paine, would be branded an atheist by his political enemies for the rest of his career. Not only were there public factions now, but one side saw behind the other a despotic foreign conspiracy and the other side saw an anarchic foreign atheism. Each looked through the other at a European specter. Monarchy had had its own odious image before 1789. But after 1794 even republicanism had a horrid aspect when one looked at a France reeling from the Terror.

John Adams's early prediction that force alone would put down the French disruption seemed confirmed by the ascent of Napoleon. The American statesman Stephen Higginson rightly assessed it as something that "drew a red-hot plough-share through the history of America as well as through that of France. It not merely divided parties, but molded them; gave them their demarcations, their watchwords and their bitterness. The home issues were for a time subordinate, collateral; the real party lines were established on the other side of the Atlantic."

Despite the American Revolution's priority in time, the French Revolution became the revolution for all later ages. It is the model, the measure by which other uprisings are judged—the one used, retrospectively, to belittle or enlarge our own earlier rebellion. The Russian Revolution of 1917 was criticized according to its proximity to or departure from the French Revolution—not by its detractors and defenders only, but even by its participants, who were conscious, despite their emphasis on the future, that they were reenacting various stages of that primordial overturn and who looked among themselves for people to play the roles of Danton, Robespierre, and others.

The French Revolution ideologized the modern world. Its period even gave us the term ideology, when followers of the philosopher Condillac's theory of knowledge became known as *idéologues*. It made the champions of unarticulated loyalties, people like Burke, paradoxically articulate a rationale for such loyalties, laying the basis for conservatism to this very day. Burke did not describe himself as a conservative, since the terms *liberal* and *conservative* were not yet in political use as polar terms. But the Revolution gave us the first lasting expression of such a polarity: the use of *left* and *right* in a political sense—taken from the pro-Revolutionary and anti-Revolutionary parties sitting to the left and right of the speaker in the National Constituent Assembly.

A wave of émigrés fleeing the French Revolution brought the establishment (especially the churchly) view of the Revolution to this country, to find allies or enemies for that view. So deeply did reactions to the French Revolution enter into our own attitudes that such a "vernacular" masterpiece as *The Adventures of Huckleberry Finn* draws heavily on the picture of the Revolution established in the English-speaking, world by Carlyle and Dickens. Even the most isolated and parochial reaches of American society reacted to the cardinal event of modern history.

Jefferson, looking back years later on the French Revolution, wrote Adams as one old man to another: "Your prophecies to Dr. Price proved truer than mine; and yet fell short of the fact, for instead of a million, the destruction of 8. or 10. millions of human beings has probably been the effect of these convulsions. I did not, in 89, believe they would have lasted so long nor have cost so much blood. But altho' your prophecy has proved true so far, I hope it does not preclude a better final result."

Jefferson sadly concluded that the French people were not yet "Virtuous" enough to accept a sudden republicanism after so many years of superstition and despotism; this was the fear that made him want to limit immigration to America from lands where established churches had corrupted men's outlook. The Girondin hope for an early liberation of mankind was obliterated. For Jefferson, the past was destroying the Revolution. For Burke, the Revolution was destroying the past. Each was, in his own way, right. In the end the "twin republics" of the eighteenth century could claim only a bitter sisterhood in disillusionment.

July 1989

TIMID PRESIDENT? FUTILE WAR?

Irving Brant

James Madison has often been portrayed as a tortured philosopher forced to be a warrior. This slight, bookworm seemed totally unfit to make military decisions and lead the country in war. But, Irving Brant, Madison's great biographer, makes a powerful case that Madison rose to the occasion and made the critical and correct determinations that achieved a satisfactory end to this war nobody wanted.

Of all the major events in American history, the War of 1812 is least known to the most people. Its naval glories are exploited in popular narrative. Its military failures, formerly glossed over, are emphasized by more objective historians with something akin to pleasure. Least known of all is the part taken by President Madison, who by virtue of the Constitution was commander in chief of the Armed Forces, charged with the duty of "making" the war that Congress "declared."

Through the years, however, a picture of James Madison has been built up by the brushes or palette knives of historians and popular word-artists. He appears as a pacifistic little man overshadowed by the ample figure of his wife, Dolley; a great political philosopher overwhelmed by the responsibilities of a war into which he was projected, at the age of sixty-one, against his will and with no capacity for executive leadership.

The purpose of this article is to appraise, not to acquit or indict. But in the case of Madison, the adverse preconceptions are embedded so deeply that they stand in the way of a fair appraisal. Historians have rejected the Federalist charge that he carried the United States into war to help Napoleon master the Old World. But with few exceptions they have treated him as the dupe of the French Emperor, tricked into war with England by the apparent repeal by the French of the Berlin and Milan Decrees at a time when both countries were despoiling American commerce. As for his conduct of the war Madison has received little credit for victories and plenty of blame for misfortunes. Finally, the Treaty of Ghent satisfied none of the grievances cited in the declaration of war, and the one decisive military victory—that of General Andrew Jackson at New Orleans—was won two weeks after the signing of the peace treaty. It all adds up to the picture of a useless and costly conflict, saved by mere luck from being a disaster, and coming to an inconclusive end.

"Everybody knew" in 1812, just as everybody "knows" today, that Madison was timid, hesitant, ruled by stronger men. Everybody knew it, that is, except the foreign diplomats who were sent to overawe him. "Curt, spiteful, passionate," France's Louis Turreau called him. "Madison is now as obstinate as a mule," wrote England's "Copenhagen" Jackson (the Francis

James Jackson who in 1807 had burned Denmark's capital) just before the President kicked him out of the country. Turreau's friendlier successor, Louis Sérurier, heard that the Chief of State was ruled by his Cabinet. He waited several months before he wrote to Paris: "Mr. Madison governs by himself."

Expelling an obnoxious minister was a civilian job. But how could Madison be anything of a war leader when "everybody knew" that he had been kicked into the war by Clay, Calhoun, Grundy, and other congressional War Hawks? There were certain things that "everybody" did not know. They did not know that in March, 1809, two weeks after he became President, Madison authorized British Minister David M. Erskine to inform his government that if she would relax her Orders in Council, he would ask Congress "to enter upon immediate measures of hostility against France."

They did not know of a simultaneous notice to France that if she ceased her commercial aggressions and Great Britain did not, "the President of States will advise to an immediate war with the latter." Neither Congress nor the public ever learned that when President Madison proclaimed nonintercourse with England on November 2, 1810, he informed General Turreau that continued interference with American trade by England "will necessarily lead to war"—as it did. The 1809 offer to join England against France brought gasps of astonishment in Congress when Madison revealed it in asking for the declaration of war against England. It brought no gasps of any sort from writers of history. It didn't fit their conception of Madison, so they disposed of it by silence.

England first, then France, was Madison's schedule of redress. In August, 1812, the moment he was notified that England had repealed her Orders in Council, he offered to settle the one remaining issue—impressment of seamen—by informal agreement. At the same time he wrote to his minister in Paris that if England made peace and France failed to repair American wrongs, war would be declared against France as soon as Congress convened, and that if England did not make peace he might even recommend a double war. Joel Barlow was directed to show that letter to the French government. As a result, Barlow was called to Poland to confer with Napoleon in the field and complete a treaty, but Napoleon's defeat at Berezina intervened, and Barlow died of pneumonia near Cracow on his way back to Paris. Madison's letter has been in print for nearly a hundred years, ignored even by historians who knew that it was described in the French foreign office as an ultimatum of war.

The same Federalist editors who jeered at "poor Madison" in 1812 denounced him as a dictator in 1814. They were free to do so. Open sedition and silent resistance forced the United States to fight the war with one arm—New England—tied behind her back. That was more crippling than incompetent generals, raw militia, and an empty treasury. Yet the President rejected every counsel that would have narrowed the constitutional liberties of those who gave vocal aid to the enemy. They would hang themselves, he said, and they did. Among all the words of praise addressed to him when he left office, he may have felt keenest pride in those of the Citizens' Committee of Washington:

> Power and national glory, sir, have often before been acquired by the sword;
> but rarely without the sacrifice of civil or political liberty. When we reflect
> that this sword was drawn under your guidance, we cannot resist offering
> you our own as well as a nation's thanks for the vigilance . . . the
> energy . . . and the safety with which you have wielded an armed force of
> 50,000 men . . . without infringing a political, civil or religious right.

It takes time, of course, for people to accept a portrait after a hundred years of caricature. At the risk of being abrupt, let us turn to Madison's actions as war leader. Expecting hostilities with England, why did he not call for adequate preparations? He did, but in Congress a vote for taxes was looked on as political suicide. Madison's first action in national defense was to lay up most of President Jefferson's little gunboats as wasteful of men and money in proportion to gunpower and to order laid-up frigates refitted. Congress cut the requested appropriation and stopped the work. In September, 1811, Sérurier told his government that the President was stimulating a nationwide debate on the question of whether it suited the Republic to have a navy, and if so, should it not be "such as can make the American flag respected"? The proposition had to be presented "in this questioning and deferential form," said the Minister, to avoid exciting state jealousy of federal power.

At the ensuing session of Congress the administration asked for twelve seventy-four-gun ships and ten new frigates, and the repair or reconstruction of six of the ten existing frigates. The new construction was voted down and the reconditioning limited to three ships.

To prepare for the land war, which would have to be fought either on American or Canadian soil, the President wanted a quick build-up of military forces. Then, if the expected bad news came from England, the troops would be ready to march on weakly defended Montreal and Quebec before reinforcements could cross the ocean.

With an authorized personnel of ten thousand, the Army had only about four thousand. The President asked that the old regiments be filled up, that ten thousand additional regulars be recruited, and that provision be made for fifty thousand volunteers. Senator William Branch Giles of Virginia, leader of the anti-Madison Democrats, shook the roof as he decried these puny measures. He demanded thirty-five thousand regulars and five-year enlistments, making it necessary to build a large and costly officer corps before men could be recruited. "The efforts of General [Senator Samuel] Smith and of Mr. Giles of Virginia," British Minister Augustus J. Foster reported, "have been added to those of the Federalists as a means to overthrow Mr. Madison and his administration." Congress talked most of the winter and Giles won. The bill for fifty thousand volunteers occasioned a lengthy constitutional harangue and a decision for state-appointed officers. The result, many believed, would be a militia that could refuse to go onto foreign soil. Skeptically, Madison signed the bills for the regulars and the volunteers.

His skepticism had warrant. On June 8 the number of recruits was estimated at five thousand, and there were few unbalky volunteers except in the West.

With England unyielding, the President on March 31 notified the House Committee on Foreign Relations that he was ready to ask for a shipping embargo—a prelude to war. But "the Executive will not take upon itself the responsibility of declaring that we are prepared for war." Congress must make the final decision with its eyes open. Four days later it did so, the embargo taking effect on April 4.

By that time, military and naval decisions were crowding in upon the Executive. In those fields, two stories are told which carry the suggestion that Madison was stupid, or at least indecisive. The fact that they are still in circulation proves that some writers have been a trifle credulous. One story says that the President decided to make an untrained civilian, Henry Clay, supreme military commander but was dissuaded by his Cabinet. The other is that Madison made up his mind to keep the American Navy tied up for harbor defense, but reversed himself on the pleas of Navy Captains Charles Stewart and William Bainbridge.

The story of the abortive appointment of Henry Clay reached full and rounded form in Calvin Colton's 1857 biography of Clay. It can be traced backward in print and manuscript, diminishing as it recedes—back to Colonel Isaac Cole's recollection, in 1838, of what he once heard from General John Mason, back to Mason's memory of what he was told by his brother-in-law, General Ben Howard. And that was: a group of Clay's friends suggested Clay's appointment to President Madison, who "assented to their opinion of [Clay's] fitness, etc., but said he could not be spared out of Congress." That was the molehill out of which the mountain grew.

The naval history was no third-hand, dry-land scuttlebutt. It came from Captain Stewart himself. As Stewart published the story in 1845, he and Captain Bainbridge went to the Navy Department on June 21, 1812, three days after the declaration of war, to solicit commands at sea. They were told by Secretary Paul Hamilton that the President and Cabinet had decided to keep the ships tied up. They protested, and the argument was continued before the President, who agreed with the captains but gave way to the Cabinet at a special meeting called that evening. Bainbridge and Stewart thereupon drafted a joint letter to the President, who overruled the Cabinet and ordered the Navy into action. Capping Stewart's story was his account of a great naval ball in the following December to which a courier brought news of Captain Stephen Decatur's victory over the frigate *Macedonian*. Whereupon President Madison told the assembled guests that if it had not been for Bainbridge and Stewart, the warships never would have gone to sea.

All rather convincing, unless you happen to know that Madison did not attend that December ball, that on June 23 Bainbridge wrote from Boston (he was not in Washington at all at the time) asking for a fighting command, and that all major warships ready for action were ordered to sea on the day war was declared. Stewart did not invent his 1845 story. It arose out of his muddled recollection and grandiose enlargement of a discussion held at the White House in February, 1812, some months before the declaration of war, in which the President sided with the captains against the Secretary of the Navy. Congress had just rejected the administration's request for twenty-two new war ships. The captains, arguing with Hamilton, conceded that even if an American vessel were victorious it might, without reinforcements, be overwhelmed and captured by the enemy. To which Madison replied: "It is victories we want; if you give us them and lose your ships afterwards, they can be replaced by others."

The February discussion between the captains and the President was prophetic. For when Madison made his next request for greater sea power, in the closing weeks of 1812, it was dramatized by the *Constitution's* victory over the *Guerrière* in August, the capture of the *Macedonian* by the *United States* in October, and especially by the gallant exploit of the sloop *Wasp*, which ran into exactly the kind of trouble Stewart and Bainbridge had predicted. Victorious over the *Frolic*, the *Wasp* was unable to hoist a sail when a lumbering British seventy-four came along and took both victor and prize to Bermuda. Captain Stewart, in this campaign for funds, furnished Secretary Hamilton with the technical arguments that helped persuade Congress to authorize four ships of the line, four heavy frigates, and as many sloops of war.

In one critical area the issue of naval power could not wait until the war began. In March, 1812, Stewart was called to Washington and offered a yet-uncreated command on the Great Lakes, controlled then by a few British armed vessels. The President intended to ask Congress for money to build a fleet; in the meantime enough would be scraped up for an eighteen-gun brig. Stewart refused; he was a deep-sea man.

The matter was given a new turn just then by Governor William Hull of Michigan Territory, a veteran of the Revolution. Offered a commission as brigadier general, he urged the building of lake squadrons. But with Stewart rejecting the command and Congress hostile to naval construction, Hull assured the President that he could lead an army across the Detroit River and down the north shore of Lake Erie to the Niagara River. That would restrain the northwestern Native Americans, deliver much of upper Canada into American hands, and win control of the lakes in less time and at less cost than the building of a fleet would require.

A Detroit campaign was being forced on the government anyway. Early operations against Montreal were made impossible by the dearth of regulars and the refusal of New England governors to furnish militia for federal service. On the other hand, western volunteers were so eager to break up the British-Native American alliance, Clay and others reported, that inaction might chill their spirit. Madison accepted Hull's promise of lake control by land action and thereby made the biggest strategic error of the war.

The appointment of Hull was a major blunder, but hardly a foreseeable one. Thirty years of peace with the Army almost nonexistent forced the President to choose his generals either from aging Revolutionary veterans with fighting experience and reputation, or from young regimental officers who had never seen action. Among the veterans called back, Hull had an unsurpassed Revolutionary record. Even Federalist editors applauded Madison's selection.

Hull commanded twenty-five hundred confident Kentuckians, Ohioans, regulars, and Michigan territorials. He crossed into Canada on July 12, 1812, skirmished with the vastly outnumbered enemy, and retreated to Fort Detroit. There, on August 16, without firing a shot, without consulting his officers, he surrendered his entire army to General Isaac Brock, who was advancing at the head of 330 British regulars and 400 Canadian militiamen, with several hundred Native Americans whooping in the woods.

Hull's claim that he was short of supplies was categorically denied by his officers but avidly accepted by the Federalist press, with a resultant impact on historians. His most startling assertion was that he had only one day's supply of powder. When he made the same remark to Sir George Prevost, the British commander handed him "the return of the large supply found in the fort; it did not create a blush." Those were the words of British Adjutant General Edward Baynes. Hull's actions, wrote another member of Prevost's staff, "stamp him either for a coward or a traitor." With such comments coming from the captors, it seems just a trifle severe to blame the surrender on either the President or the War Department.

Suppose, instead, we find out how the President reacted to the disaster. New land forces, he said, could be counted on to redeem the country's honor. The immediate necessity was to speed up the building of warships to gain control of the lakes—a method that would have been adopted at the outset "if the easy conquest of them by land held out to us [by Hull] had not misled our calculations." The strength of his feeling was recorded by Richard Rush, who wrote to John Adams the following June: "I know the President to be so convinced upon this subject that I heard him say last fall if the British build thirty frigates upon [the lakes] we ought to build forty."

Madison's insistence produced the warships with which Commodore Perry defeated and captured the British squadron on Lake Erie in September, 1813, changing the whole complexion of the war. He ordered the building of ship after ship on Lake Ontario. Superiority swung back and forth on that lake like reversing winds, but neither side could force a decision because each had protected bases—the British at York (now Toronto) and Kingston, the Americans at Sackets Harbor—to retire to when the other was ahead.

Far more important and more critical was the state of affairs in 1814 on Lake Champlain, the great sluice that opened a supply route northward to Montreal and southward to the Hudson River valley. By summer, more than twenty thousand seasoned veterans of the Peninsular War, released for transatlantic service by Napoleon's downfall, were crowding onto British transports bound for Canada, Chesapeake Bay, and New Orleans. On Lake Champlain, the American ship *Saratoga* was launched thirty-five days after the laying of her keel. Sailors were in short supply both there and on Lake Ontario. Madison ordered the crews filled up with soldiers and told the protesting Secretary of War that naval efficiency was essential even for land operations.

Then came news that the enemy was building a new vessel on Lake Champlain, the *Confiance*, far more powerful than the twenty-six-gun *Saratoga*. Loss of the lake might still be averted, Captain Thomas Macdonough believed, by the swifter building of a light brig. Navy Secretary William Jones, though far more vigorous and capable than his predecessor, said the limit of available funds had been reached.

Madison ordered the ship built anyhow: Its keel had been laid when Jones again drew back. "God knows where the money is to come from," he wrote. The President reaffirmed the order and obtained a pledge of the utmost speed. On July 15 the timbers of the twenty-gun *Eagle* were still standing in the forest. The vessel was launched on August 11 and furnished the margin of power that changed sure defeat into a victory which resounded from Washington to Ghent.

"The battle of Lake Champlain, more than any other incident of the War of 1812, merits the epithet 'decisive,'" wrote the distinguished naval historian Alfred Thayer Mahan many years later. Within earshot of the battle, many of them within sight, nearly fourteen thousand of Wellington's battle-hardened soldiers waited for the Royal Navy to open the way to Albany and New York. When the British fleet surrendered, the army of invasion marched back to Canada and never returned.

In naval affairs, Madison could rely on officers unsurpassed anywhere in the world for knowledge and ability. In army matters he had to learn by hard experience. His first Secretary of War, William Eustis, was a Massachusetts medical man of bustling energy who bore a tremendous load of work in a War Department consisting of himself and eight clerks. Eustis, even in the opinion of some congressmen who wanted him fired, outperformed what anybody had a right to expect in equipping the Army as war approached. But he had no more than a civilian's knowledge of military operations, did little to systematize the nation's defenses, and seemed unable to recognize incompetence in field officers before it was demonstrated in battle. The President shared this last fault. When Adjutant General Baynes visited Major General Henry Dearborn under a flag of truce, he saw at a glance that the American commander lacked energy. Neither Madison nor Eustis sensed this, and the President couldn't see the deficiencies of Eustis. His resignation, after failures on the Niagara front followed the Hull catastrophe, was a concession to public opinion.

Brigadier General John Armstrong, who succeeded Eustis, was notorious for political intrigue but had enough of a military reputation to warrant his selection. The President chose him reluctantly, after Secretary of State James Monroe and Senator William Harris Crawford had refused the place.

During the next year and a half, until the burning of Washington forced him to resign, Armstrong performed his work with one eye on the war and the other on the 1816 presidential race. His good and bad traits showed up at once but not in equal measure. He drove the competent Andrew Jackson to fury and disobedience with a brusque, unappreciative dismissal of his temporary Tennessee volunteers in a distant wilderness. He removed the incompetent General Dearborn with a note even more callous. Both men wrote to the President, Jackson boiling with indignation, Dearborn heartbroken. Madison forced Armstrong to make amends to Jackson. He himself consoled Dearborn but affirmed the removal.

Armstrong's strategy to gain the presidential nomination paralleled that of his rival, James Monroe. Each hoped to be made a lieutenant general and win the war. Monroe's chance vanished when Armstrong took the War Department. Armstrong's opportunity seemed to open when the President, in June of 1813, was stricken with an almost fatal illness followed by several months' convalescence in Virginia. Freed of effective presidential supervision,

Armstrong went north under the pretense of making an inspection trip and did not come back until Christmas. During the interval he assumed personal direction of a two-pronged campaign against Montreal, failed to co-ordinate the mishandled offensive movements, and ducked away to Albany to watch the approaching double fiasco as a detached observer.

Personal ambition and laziness turned Armstrong's strategic ideas, even when sound, into flashy gambits, without the preparation or drive required to follow through. Two weeks before the event that drove him out of office, he received a written rebuke from Madison that would have pierced the hide of a rhinoceros—though it did not penetrate his—for secretly exercising powers delegated by Congress to the President, ordering military operations without consultation, suppressing letters intended for the President, accepting the resignation of General William Henry Harrison without authority, and posing to Harrison's successor as the bestower of the appointment.

Nevertheless, Armstrong possessed capabilities that, combined with Madison's ability to thwart their misuse, gave a new look to the American Army. Both men recognized youthful talent, and Armstrong was ruthless enough to get rid of old incompetents.

Zebulon Pike, promoted to brigadier general, was killed in winning his first victory. Jacob Brown and George Izard, lately raised to the same rank, stood out in the Montreal campaign in contrast to their soon-to-be-ousted commanders, Major Generals James Wilkinson and Wade Hampton. Shining talents were displayed by Colonels E. P. Gaines and Winfield Scott; solid performance by Alexander Macomb, T. A. Smith, E. W. Ripley. Every one of these eight men was recommended by Armstrong for promotion, with the exception of Brown. He advised the President that for major generals, not a moment should be lost in promoting Brigadiers Izard and Thomas Flournoy.

Flournoy, a nobody at New Orleans! His promotion, by making Andrew Jackson his subordinate instead of his superior, would have knocked Jackson straight out of the military service—if not into apoplexy. But it also would have barricaded the upward path of Brown— the man most likely to stand in Armstrong's way if Armstrong succeeded in establishing the grade of lieutenant general—by filling all the major-generalships allowed by law.

The President nominated Izard—*and Brown*. It could almost be said that at that moment the Battle of New Orleans was won, although Jackson's appointment as major general still awaited a future vacancy. Also, the leadership was established that retrieved American prestige in the 1814 battles of the Niagara peninsula and helped persuade England that the time was ripe for peace.

The location of that Niagara campaign, illogical because of its limited objective, resulted from troop movements made by Armstrong without consulting the President. To remedy that feature, the Secretary sent a proposal to Madison at Montpelier that Brown's army bypass the peninsula and swing around Lake Ontario to Burlington and York. Madison imposed the same restriction that was to be recognized a hundred years later by Admiral Mahan: control of the lake must first be won to prevent the landing of an army in the American rear. The civilian commander in chief was learning the art of war. By a succession of decisions affecting strength, strategy, and leadership on Lake Champlain, at New Orleans, and on the Niagara front—overruling his subordinates in every instance—Madison went far to determine the outcome.

In spite of their conflicts over appointments, Armstrong and the President worked effectively together in a fundamental regeneration of the military command. On the day war was declared the United States Army had eight generals, most of them just appointed. Their average age was sixty years. Two years later all of them were out of service or assigned to quiescence. In the first half of 1814 nine generals were appointed or promoted—their average age was thirty-six—and these men turned raw American recruits into disciplined soldiers. When the war ended they had just begun to fight.

These redeeming events of 1814 are obscured in popular narrative and even in histories by the burning of Washington and the miserable failure of its defenders. For that occurrence President Madison bore an inescapable responsibility: constitutionally, he was commander in chief; physically, he was in Washington when the enemy approached. Why did he not foresee the attack, or, if he did, why didn't he guard against it?

The answer to the first question accentuates the second. On May 24, after reading a British proclamation calling for a general uprising of southern slaves, the President wrote to Armstrong that this presaged a campaign of ruthless devastation in which the national capital could not fail to be "a favorite target." On July 1, without dissent but with skepticism concerning the danger (so wrote Navy Secretary William Jones), the Cabinet approved Madison's proposal that ten thousand militiamen be drawn out to help guard the Washington-Baltimore area. When Brigadier General William H. Winder wished to summon them, Secretary Armstrong (the chief skeptic) made the fatal reply that the best mode of using militia "was upon the spur of the occasion." Nevertheless, the power and responsibility belonged to the President, and his own recorded foresight called for vigorous defensive measures. He intervened again and again, to overcome Armstrong's sloth and skepticism, but never forced action on a large enough scale.

Almost in another world is the popular word-picture of the Madisons at this time. It is a composite of Dolley saving the portrait of George Washington as the enemy approached, and of the President—as depicted by the scurrilous (and anonymous) versifier of "The Bladensburg Races"—galloping in terrified flight forty miles into Maryland.

The rhapsodic glee with which the versifier danced in the ashes of the Capitol and White House may not impeach his veracity, but his figurative observation post hardly matched the physical one of Sérurier, who had a panoramic view from the unmenaced Octagon House. The President, Sérurier wrote to Talleyrand two days before the battle, "has just gone to the camp to encourage, by his presence, the army to defend the capital." Madison returned to the White House from the actual battlefield (where Congreve rockets fell near him) after Dolley left the house. He remained there, the French minister said, until after the Georgetown and Washington militia streamed by in confused flight toward Frederick. The manner of his departure as described by Sérurier would be of little moment except that it emphasizes still further how different Madison's character was from the one history has bestowed on him:

> It was then, my lord, that the President, who, in the midst of all this
> disorder, had displayed to stop it a firmness and constancy worthy of a better
> success . . . coolly mounted his horse, accompanied by some friends, and
> slowly gained the bridge that separates Washington from Virginia.

By the time the news of the burning of Washington reached London, the bellicosity and bad temper that had given rise to Admiral Alexander Cochrane's "treat 'em rough" instructions were things of the past. War weariness in England, fresh dangers emerging in chaotic Europe, and the sharp improvement in the American position, strength, and morale in the north, all helped produce a sudden reversal of British policy at Ghent. Peace was signed the day before Christmas, and the fighting ended on January 8, 1815, when two thousand British soldiers—a third of the entire assaulting army—fell dead or wounded at New Orleans.

The Treaty of Ghent left things as they were. Did the war itself leave them unchanged? Impressment and the Orders in Council both vanished before the treaty was signed. European peace removed them as immediate future hazards. If the war had lifted American prestige, no treaty was needed to abolish them forever. By that measurement the New Orleans victory was climax, not epilogue. In 1815, Justice Joseph Story weighed the results of the war and found them massive:

> Never did a country occupy more lofty ground; we have stood the contest, single-handed, against the conqueror of Europe; and we are at peace, with all our blushing victories thick crowding on us. If I do not much mistake, we shall attain to a very high character abroad as well as crush domestic faction.

Domestic faction was crushed in the next election. Those who would fix the time at which the country attained international stature might ask themselves: Could there have been a Monroe Doctrine in 1823 without the War of 1812? It was under the quiet guiding hand of President James Madison that the struggling young republic won an equal position among the free nations of the world, and began its long climb to leadership.

October 1959

CHILDREN OF DARKNESS

Stephen B. Oates

The name Nat Turner struck fear into the hearts of mid nineteenth century southerners. How did this meek, mild mannered slave preacher achieve such a sinister reputation? Stephen B. Oates describes with insight and clarity the role, intentions and results of the only Ante-bellum slave rebel to strike dead some of the white masters.

Until August, 1831, most Americans had never heard of Virginia's Southampton County, an isolated, impoverished neighborhood located along the border in the southeastern part of the state. It was mostly a small farming area, with cotton fields and apple orchards dotting the flat, wooded landscape. The farmers were singularly fond of their apple crops: from them they made a potent apple brandy, one of the major sources of pleasure in this hardscrabble region. The county seat, or "county town," was Jerusalem, a lethargic little community where pigs rooted in the streets and old-timers spat tobacco juice in the shade of the courthouse. Jerusalem lay on the bank of the Nottoway River some seventy miles south of Richmond. There had never been any large plantations in Southampton County, for the soil had always been too poor for extensive tobacco or cotton cultivation. Although one gentleman did own eighty slaves in 1830, the average was around three or four per family. A number of whites had moved on to new cotton lands in Georgia and Alabama, so that Southampton now had a population that was nearly 60 percent black. While most of the blacks were still enslaved, an unusual number—some seventeen hundred, in fact—were "free persons of color."

By southern white standards, enlightened benevolence did exist in Southampton County—and it existed in the rest of the state, too. Virginia whites allowed a few slave schools to operate—then a crime by state law—and almost without complaint permitted slaves to hold illegal religious meetings. Indeed, Virginians liked to boast that slavery was not so harsh in their "enlightened" state as it was in the brutal cotton plantations in the Deep South. Still, this was a dark time for southern whites—a time of sporadic insurrection panics, especially in South Carolina, and of rising abolitionist militancy in the North—and Virginians were taking no chances. Even though their slaves, they contended, were too happy and too submissive to strike back, Virginia was nevertheless almost a military garrison, with a militia force of some hundred thousand men to guard against insurrection.

Southampton whites, of course, were caught in the same paradox: most of the white males over twenty-one voluntarily belonged to the militia and turned out for the annual drills, yet none of them thought a slave revolt would happen here. *Their* blacks, they told themselves, had never been more content, more docile. True, they did get a bit carried away in their religious meetings these days, with much too much singing and clapping. And true, there were white preachers who punctuated their sermons with what a local observer called "ranting cant about equality" and who might inspire black exhorters to retail that doctrine to their congregations. But generally things were quiet and unchanged in this remote tidewater county, where time seemed to stand as still as a windless summer day.

It happened with shattering suddenness, an explosion of black rage that rocked Southampton County to its foundations. On August 22, 1831, a band of insurgent slaves, led by a black mystic called Nat Turner, rose up with axes and plunged southeastern Virginia— and much of the rest of the South—into convulsions of fear and racial violence. It turned out to be the bloodiest slave insurrection in southern history, one that was to have a profound and irrevocable impact on the destinies of southern whites and blacks alike.

Afterward, white authorities described him as a small man with "distinct African features." Though his shoulders were broad from work in the fields, he was short, slender, and a little knock-kneed, with thin hair, a complexion like black pearl, and large, deep-set eyes. He wore a mustache and cultivated a tuft of whiskers under his lower lip. Before that fateful August day, whites who knew Nat Turner thought him harmless, even though he was intelligent and did gabble on about strange religious powers. Among the slaves, though, he enjoyed a powerful influence as an exhorter and self-proclaimed prophet.

He was born in 1800, the property of Benjamin Turner of Southampton County and the son of two strong-minded parents. Tradition has it that his African-born mother threatened to kill him rather than see him grow up in bondage. His father eventually escaped to the North, but not before he had helped inculcate an enormous sense of self-importance in his son. Both parents praised Nat for his brilliance and extraordinary imagination; his mother even claimed that he could recall episodes that happened before his birth—a power that others insisted only the Almighty could have given him. His mother and father both told him that he was intended for some great purpose, that he would surely become a prophet. Nat was also influenced by his grandmother, who along with his white masters taught him to pray and to take pride in his superior intelligence. He learned to read and write with great ease, prompting those who knew him to remark that he had too much sense to be raised in bondage—he "would never be of any service to any one as a slave," one of them said.

In 1810 Benjamin Turner died, and Nat became the property of Turner's oldest son Samuel. Under Samuel Turner's permissive supervision Nat exploited every opportunity to improve his knowledge: he studied white children's school books and experimented in making paper and gunpowder. But it was religion that interested him the most. He attended black religious meetings, where the slaves cried out in ecstasy and sang hymns that expressed their longing for a better life. He listened transfixed as black exhorters preached from the Bible with stabbing gestures, singing out in a rhythmic language that was charged with emotion and vivid imagery. He studied the Bible, too, practically memorizing the books of the Old Testament, and grew to manhood with the words of the prophets roaring in his ears.

Evidently Nat came of age a bit confused if not resentful. Both whites and blacks had said he was too intelligent to be raised a slave; yet here he was, fully grown and still in bondage. Obviously he felt betrayed by false hopes. Obviously he thought he should be liberated like the large number of free blacks who lived in Southampton County and who were not nearly so gifted as he. Still enslaved as a man, he zealously cultivated his image as a prophet, aloof, austere, and mystical. As he said later in an oral autobiographical sketch, "Having soon discovered to be great, I must appear so, and therefore studiously avoided mixing in society, and wrapped myself in mystery, devoting myself to fasting and prayer."

Remote, introspective, Turner had religious fantasies in which the Holy Spirit seemed to speak to him as it had to the prophets of old. "Seek ye the kingdom of Heaven," the Spirit told him, "and all things shall be added unto you." Convinced that he "was ordained for some great purpose in the hands of the Almighty," Turner told his fellow slaves about his communion with the Spirit. "And they believed," Turner recalled, "and said my wisdom came from God." Pleased with their response, he began to prepare them for some unnamed mission. He also started preaching at black religious gatherings and soon rose to prominence as a leading exhorter in the slave church. Although never ordained and never officially a member of any church, he was accepted as a Baptist preacher in the slave community, and once he even baptized a white man in a swampy pond. There can be little doubt that the slave church nourished Turner's self-esteem and his desire for independence, for it was not only a center for underground slave plottings against the master class, but a focal point for an entire alternate culture—a subterranean culture that the slaves sought to construct beyond the white man's control. Moreover, Turner's status as a slave preacher gave him considerable freedom of movement, so that he came to know most of Southampton County intimately.

Sometime around 1821 Turner disappeared. His master had put him under an overseer, who may have whipped him, and he fled for his freedom as his father had done. But thirty days later he voluntarily returned. The other slaves were astonished. No fugitive ever came back on his own. "And the negroes found fault, and murmured against me," Turner recounted later, "saying that if they had my sense they would not serve any master in the world." But in his mind Turner did not serve any earthly master. His master was Jehovah—the angry and vengeful God of ancient Israel—and it was Jehovah, he insisted, who had chastened him and brought him back to bondage.

At about this time Nat married. Evidently his wife was a young slave named Cherry who lived on Samuel Turner's place. But in 1822 Samuel Turner died, and they were sold to different masters—Cherry to Giles Reese and Nat to Thomas Moore. Although they were not far apart and still saw each other from time to time, their separation was nevertheless a painful example of the wretched privations that slavery placed on black people, even here in mellowed Southampton County.

As a perceptive man with a prodigious knowledge of the Bible, Turner was more than aware of the hypocrisies and contradictions loose in this Christian area, where whites gloried in the teachings of Jesus and yet discriminated against the "free coloreds" and kept the other blacks in chains. Here slave owners bragged about their benevolence (in Virginia they took care of their "niggers") and yet broke up families, sold blacks off to whip-happy slave traders when money was scarce, and denied intelligent and skilled blacks something even the most debauched and useless poor whites enjoyed: freedom. Increasingly embittered about his condition and that of his people, his imagination fired to incandescence by prolonged fasting and Old Testament prayers, Turner began to have apocalyptic visions and bloody fantasies in the fields and woods southwest of Jerusalem. "I saw white spirits and black spirits engaged in battle," he declared later, "and the sun was darkened—the thunder rolled in the heavens, and blood flowed in streams—and I heard a voice saying, 'Such is your luck, such you are called to see, and let it come rough or smooth, you must surely bare it.'" He was awestruck, he recalled, but what did the voice mean? What must he bare? He withdrew from his fellow slaves and prayed for a revelation; and one day when he was plowing in the field, he thought the Spirit called out, "Behold me as I stand in the Heavens," and Turner looked up and saw forms of men there in a variety of attitudes, "and there were lights in the sky to which the children of darkness gave other names than what they really were—for they were the lights of the Saviour's hands, stretched forth from east to west, even as they extended on the cross on Calvary for the redemption of sinners."

Certain that Judgment Day was fast approaching, Turner strove to attain "true holiness" and "the true knowledge of faith." And once he had them, once he was "made perfect," then the Spirit showed him other miracles. While working in the field, he said, he discovered drops of blood on the corn. In the woods he found leaves with hieroglyphic characters and numbers etched on them; other leaves contained forms of men—some drawn in blood—like the figures in the sky. He told his fellow slaves about these signs—they were simply astounded—and claimed that the Spirit had endowed him with a special knowledge of the seasons, the rotation of the planets, and the operation of the tides. He acquired an even greater reputation among the county's slaves, many of whom thought he could control the weather and heal disease. He told his followers that clearly, something large was about to happen, that he was soon to fulfill "the great promise that had been made to me."

But he still did not know what his mission was. Then on May 12, 1828, "I heard a loud noise in the heavens," Turner remembered, "and the Spirit instantly appeared to me and said the Serpent was loosened, and Christ had laid down the yoke he had borne for the sins of men, and that I should take it on and fight against the Serpent." Now at last it was clear. By signs in the heavens Jehovah would show him when to commence the great work, whereupon "I should arise and prepare myself, and slay my enemies with their own weapons." Until then he should keep his lips sealed.

But his work was too momentous for him to remain entirely silent. He announced to Thomas Moore that the slaves ought to be free and would be "one day or other." Moore, of course, regarded this as dangerous talk from a slave and gave Turner a thrashing.

In 1829 a convention met in Virginia to draft a new state constitution, and there was talk among the slaves—who communicated along a slave grapevine—that they might be liberated. Their hopes were crushed, though, when the convention emphatically rejected emancipation and restricted suffrage to whites only. There was also a strong backlash against antislavery publications thought to be infiltrating from the North, one of which—David Walker's *Appeal*—actually called on the slaves to revolt. In reaction the Virginia legislature enacted a law against teaching slaves to read and write. True, it was not yet rigorously enforced, but from the blacks' viewpoint slavery seemed more entrenched in "enlightened" Virginia than ever.

There is no evidence that Turner ever read antislavery publications, but he was certainly sensitive to the despair of his people. Still, Jehovah gave him no further signs, and he was carried along in the ebb and flow of ordinary life. Moore had died in 1828, and Turner had become the legal property of Moore's nine-year-old son—something that must have humiliated him. In 1829 a local wheelwright, Joseph Travis, married Moore's widow and soon moved into her house near the Cross Keys, a village located southwest of Jerusalem. Still known as Nat Turner even though he had changed owners several times, Nat considered Travis "a kind master" and later said that Travis "placed the greatest confidence in me."

In February, 1831, there was an eclipse of the sun. The sign Turner had been waiting for—could there be any doubt? Removing the seal from his lips, he gathered around him four slaves in whom he had complete trust—Hark, Henry, Nelson, and Sam—and confided what he was called to do. They would commence "the work of death" on July 4, whose connotation Turner clearly understood. But they formed and rejected so many plans that his mind was affected. He was seized with dread. He fell sick, and Independence Day came and passed.

On August 13 there was another sign. Because of some atmospheric disturbance the sun grew so dim that it could be looked at directly. Then it seemed to change colors—now pale green, now blue, now white—and there was much excitement and consternation in many parts of the eastern United States. By afternoon the sun was like an immense ball of polished silver, and the air was moist and hazy. Then a black spot could be seen, apparently on the sun's surface—a phenomenon that greatly aroused the slaves in southeastern Virginia. For Turner, the black spot was unmistakable proof that God wanted him to move. With awakened resolution he told his men that "as the black spot passed over the sun, so shall the blacks pass over the earth."

It was Sunday, August 21, deep in the woods near the Travis house at a place called Cabin Pond. Around a crackling fire Turner's confederates feasted on roast pig and apple brandy. With them were two new recruits—Jack, one of Hark's cronies, and Will, a powerful man who intended to gain his freedom or die in the attempt. Around mid afternoon Turner himself made a dramatic appearance, and in the glare of pine-knot torches they finally made their plans. They would rise that night and "kill all the white people." It was a propitious time to begin, because many whites of the militia were away at a camp meeting. The revolt would be so swift and so terrible that the whites would be too panic-stricken to fight back. Until they had sufficient recruits and equipment, the insurgents would annihilate everybody in their path—women and children included. When one of the slaves complained about their small number (there were only seven of them, after all), Turner was quick to reassure him. He had deliberately avoided an extensive plot involving a lot of slaves. He knew that blacks had "frequently attempted similar things," but their plans had "leaked out." Turner intended for his revolt to happen completely without warning. The "march of destruction," he explained, "should be the first news of the insurrection," whereupon slaves and free blacks alike would rise up and join him. He did not say what their ultimate objective was, but possibly he wanted to fight his way into the Great Dismal Swamp some twenty miles to the east. This immense, snake-filled quagmire had long been a haven for fugitives, and Turner may have planned to establish a slave stronghold there from which to launch punitive raids against Virginia and North Carolina. On the other hand, he may well have had nothing in mind beyond the extermination of every white on the ten-mile route to Jerusalem. There are indications that he thought God would guide him after the revolt began, just as He had directed Gideon against the Midianites. Certainly Turner's command of unremitting carnage was that of the Almighty, who had said through his prophet Ezekiel: "Slay utterly old and young, both maids and little children, and women. . . . "

The slaves talked and schemed through the evening. Night came on. Around two in the morning of August 22 they left the woods, by-passed Giles Reese's farm, where Cherry lived, and headed for the Travis homestead, the first target in their crusade.

All was still at the Travis house. In the darkness the insurgents gathered about the cider press, and all drank except Turner, who never touched liquor. Then they moved across the yard with their axes. Hark placed a ladder against the house, and Turner, armed with a hatchet, climbed up and disappeared through a second-story window. In a moment he unbarred the door, and the slaves spread through the house without a sound. The others wanted Turner the prophet, Turner the black messiah, to strike the first blow and kill Joseph Travis. With Will close behind, Turner entered Travis' bedroom and made his way to the white man's bed. Turner swung his hatchet—a wild blow that glanced off Travis' head and brought him out of bed yelling for his wife. But with a sure killer's instinct Will moved in and hacked Travis to death with his axe. In minutes Will and the others had slaughtered the four whites they found in the house, including Mrs. Travis and young Putnam Moore, Turner's legal owner. With Putnam's death Turner felt that at last, after thirty years in bondage, he was free.

The rebels gathered up a handful of old muskets and followed "General Nat" out to the barn. There Turner paraded his men about, leading them through every military maneuver he knew. Not all of them, however, were proud of their work. Jack sank to his knees with his head in his hands and said he was sick. But Hark made him get up and forced him along as they set out across the field to the next farm. Along the way somebody remembered the Travis baby. Will and Henry returned and killed it in its cradle.

And so it went throughout that malignant night, as the rebels took farm after farm by surprise. They used no firearms, in order not to arouse the countryside, instead stabbing and decapitating their victims. Although they confiscated horses, weapons, and brandy, they took only what was necessary to continue the struggle, and they committed no rapes. They even spared a few homesteads, one because Turner believed the poor white inhabitants "thought no better of themselves than they did of negroes." By dawn on Monday there were fifteen insurgents—nine on horses—and they were armed with a motley assortment of guns, clubs, swords, and axes. Turner himself now carried a light dress sword, but for some mysterious reason (a fatal irresolution? the dread again?) he had killed nobody yet.

At Elizabeth Turner's place, which the slaves stormed at sunrise, the prophet tried once again to kill. They broke into the house, and there, in the middle of the room, too frightened to move or cry out, stood Mrs. Turner and a neighbor named Mrs. Newsome. Nat knew Elizabeth Turner very well, for she was the widow of his second master, Samuel Turner. While Will attacked her with his axe the prophet took Mrs. Newsome's hand and hit her over the head with his sword. But evidently he could not bring himself to kill her. Finally Will moved him aside and chopped her to death as methodically as though he were cutting wood.

With the sun low in the east, Turner sent a group on foot to another farm while he and Will led the horsemen at a gallop to Caty Whitehead's place. They surrounded the house in a rush, but not before several people fled into the garden. Turner chased after somebody, but it turned out to be a slave girl, as terrified as the whites, and he let her go. All around him, all over the Whitehead farm, there were scenes of unspeakable violence. He saw Will drag Mrs. Whitehead kicking and screaming out of the house and almost sever her head from her body. Running around the house, Turner came upon young Margaret Whitehead hiding under a cellar cap between two chimneys. She ran crying for her life, and Turner set out after her—a wild chase against the hot August sun. He overtook the girl in a field and hit her again and again with his sword, but she would not die. In desperation he picked up a fence rail and beat her to death. Finally he had killed someone. He was to kill no one else.

After the Whitehead massacre the insurgents united briefly and then divided again, those on foot moving in one direction and Turner and the mounted slaves in another. The riders moved across the fields, kicking their horses and mules faster and faster, until at last they raced down the lane to Richard Porter's house, scattering dogs and chickens as they went. But the Porters had fled—forewarned by their own slaves that a revolt was under way. Turner knew that the alarm was spreading now, knew that the militia would soon be mobilizing, so he set out alone to retrieve the other column. While he was gone Will took the cavalry and raided Nathaniel Francis' homestead. Young Francis was Will's owner, but he could not have been a harsh master: several free blacks voluntarily lived on his farm. Francis was not home, and his pregnant young wife survived Will's onslaught only because a slave concealed her in the attic. After killing the overseer and Francis' two nephews Will and his men raced on to another farm, and another, and then overran John Barrow's place on the Barrow Road. Old man Barrow fought back manfully while his wife escaped in the woods, but the insurgents overwhelmed him and slit his throat. As a tribute to his courage they wrapped his body in a quilt and left a plug of tobacco on his chest.

Meanwhile Turner rode chaotically around the countryside, chasing after one column and then the other, almost always reaching the farms after his scattered troops had done the killing and gone. Eventually he found both columns waiting for him at another pillaged homestead, took charge again, and sent them down the Barrow Road, which intersected the main highway to Jerusalem. They were forty strong now and all mounted. Many of the new recruits had joined up eager "to kill all the white people." But others had been forced to come along as though they were hostages. A black later testified that several slaves—among them three teenage boys "were constantly guarded by negroes with guns who were ordered to shoot them if they attempted to escape."

On the Barrow Road, Turner's strategy was to put his twenty most dependable men in front and send them galloping down on the homesteads before anybody could escape. But the cry of insurrection had preceded them, and many families had already escaped to nearby Jerusalem, throwing the village into pandemonium. By midmorning church bells were tolling the terrible news—*insurrection, insurrection*—and shouting men were riding through the countryside in a desperate effort to get the militia together before the slaves overran Jerusalem itself.

As Turner's column moved relentlessly toward Jerusalem one Levi Waller, having heard that the blacks had risen, summoned his children from a nearby schoolhouse (some of the other children came running too) and tried to load his guns. But before he could do so, Turner's advance horsemen swept into his yard, a whirlwind of axes and swords, and chased Waller into some tall weeds. Waller managed to escape, but not before he saw the blacks cut down his wife and children. One small girl also escaped by crawling up a dirt chimney, scarcely daring to breathe as the insurgents decapitated the other children—ten in all—and threw their bodies in a pile.

Turner had stationed himself at the rear of his little army and did not participate in these or any other killings along the Barrow Road. He never explained why. He had been fasting for several days and may well have been too weak to try any more killing himself. Or maybe as God's prophet he preferred to let Will and the eight or nine other lieutenants do the slaughtering. All he said about it afterward was that he "sometimes got in sight in time to see the work of death completed" and that he paused to view the bodies "in silent satisfaction" before riding on.

Around noon on Monday the insurgents reached the Jerusalem highway, and Turner soon joined them. Behind them lay a zigzag path of unredeemable destruction: some fifteen homesteads sacked and approximately sixty whites slain. By now the rebels amounted to fifty or sixty—including three or four free blacks. But even at its zenith Turner's army showed signs of disintegration. A few reluctant slaves had already escaped or deserted. And many others were roaring drunk, so drunk they could scarcely ride their horses, let alone do any fighting. To make matters worse, many of the confiscated muskets were broken or too rusty to fire.

Turner resolved to march on Jerusalem at once and seize all the guns and powder he could find there. But a half mile up the road he stopped at the Parker farm, because some of his men had relatives and friends there. When the insurgents did not return, Turner went after them—and found his men not in the slave quarters but down in Parker's brandy cellar. He ordered them back to the highway at once.

On the way back they met a party of armed men—whites. There were about eighteen of them, as far as Turner could make out. They had already routed his small guard at the gate and were now advancing toward the Parker house. With renewed zeal Turner rallied his remaining troops and ordered an attack. Yelling at the top of their lungs, wielding axes, clubs, and gun butts, the blacks drove the whites back into Parker's cornfield. But their advantage was short-lived. White reinforcements arrived, and more were on the way from nearby Jerusalem. Regrouping in the cornfield, the whites counterattacked, throwing the rebels back in confusion. In the fighting some of Turner's best men fell wounded, though none of them died. Several insurgents, too drunk to fight any more, fled pell-mell into the woods.

If Turner had often seemed irresolute earlier in the revolt, he was now undaunted. Even though his force was considerably reduced, he still wanted to storm Jerusalem. He led his men away from the main highway, which was blocked with militia, and took them along a back road, planning to cross the Cypress Bridge and strike the village from the rear. But the bridge was crawling with armed whites. In desperation the blacks set out to find reinforcements: they fell back to the south and then veered north again, picking up new recruits as they moved. They raided a few more farms, too, only to find them deserted, and finally encamped for the night near the slave quarters on Ridley's plantation.

All Monday night news of the revolt spread beyond Southampton County as express riders carried the alarm up to Petersburg and from there to the capitol in Richmond. Governor John Floyd, fearing a statewide uprising, alerted the militia and sent cavalry, infantry, and artillery units to the stricken county. Federal troops from Fortress Monroe were on the way, too, and other volunteers and militia outfits were marching from contiguous counties in Virginia and North Carolina. Soon over three thousand armed whites were in Southampton County, and hundreds more were mobilizing.

With whites swarming the countryside, Turner and his lieutenants did not know what to do. During the night an alarm had stampeded their new recruits, so that by Tuesday morning they had only twenty men left. Frantically they set out for Dr. Simon Blunt's farm to get volunteers—and rode straight into an ambush. Whites barricaded in the house opened fire on them at pointblank range, killing one or more insurgents and capturing several others—among them Hark Travis. Blunt's own slaves, armed with farm tools, helped in the defense and captured a few rebels themselves.

Repulsed at Blunt's farm, Turner led a handful of the faithful back toward the Cross Keys, still hoping to gather reinforcements. But the signs were truly ominous, for armed whites were everywhere. At last the militia overtook Turner's little band and in a final, desperate skirmish killed Will and scattered the rest. Turner himself, alone and in deep anguish, escaped to the vicinity of the Travis farm and hid in a hole under some fence rails.

By Tuesday evening a full-scale manhunt was under way in southeastern Virginia and North Carolina as armed whites prowled the woods and swamps in search of fugitive rebels and alleged collaborators. They chased the blacks down with howling dogs, killing those who resisted—and many of them resisted zealously—and dragging others back to Jerusalem to stand trial in the county court. One free black insurgent committed suicide rather than be taken by white men. Within a week nearly all the bona fide rebels except Turner had either been executed or imprisoned, but not before white vigilantes—and some militiamen—had perpetrated barbarities on more than a score of innocent blacks. Outraged by the atrocities committed on whites, vigilantes rounded up blacks in the Cross Keys and decapitated them. Another vigilante gang in North Carolina not only beheaded several blacks but placed their skulls on poles, where they remained for days. In all directions whites took blacks from their shacks and tortured, shot, and burned them to death and then mutilated their corpses in ways that witnesses refused to describe. No one knows how many innocent blacks died in this reign of terror—at least a hundred twenty, probably more. Finally the militia commander of Southampton County issued a proclamation that any further outrages would be dealt with according to the articles of war. Many whites publicly regretted these atrocities but argued that they were the inevitable results of slave insurrection. Another revolt, they said, would end with the extermination of every black in the region.

Although Turner's uprising ended on Tuesday, August 24, reports of additional insurrections swept over the South long afterward, and dozens of communities from Virginia to Alabama were seized with hysteria. In North Carolina rumors flew that slave armies had been seen on the highways, that one—maybe led by Turner himself—had burned Wilmington, butchered all the inhabitants, and was now marching on the state capital. The hysteria was even worse in Virginia, where reports of concerted slave rebellions and demands for men and guns swamped the governor's office. For a time it seemed that thousands of slaves had risen, that Virginia and perhaps the entire South would soon be ablaze. But Governor Floyd kept his head, examined the reports carefully, and concluded that no such widespread insurrection had taken place. Actually no additional uprisings had happened anywhere. Out of blind panic whites in many parts of the South had mobilized the militia, chased after imaginary insurgents, and jailed or executed still more innocent blacks. Working in cooperation with other political and military authorities in Virginia and North Carolina, Floyd did all he could to quell the excitement, to reassure the public that the slaves were quiet now. Still, the governor did not think the Turner revolt was the work of a solitary fanatic. Behind it, he believed, was a conspiracy of Yankee agitators and black preachers—especially black preachers. "The whole of that massacre in Southampton is the work of these Preachers," he declared, and demanded that they be suppressed.

Meanwhile the "great bandit chieftain," as the newspapers called him, was still at large. For more than two months Turner managed to elude white patrols, hiding out most of the time near Cabin Pond where the revolt had begun. Hunted by a host of aroused whites (there were various rewards totalling eleven hundred dollars on his head), Turner considered giving himself up and once got within two miles of Jerusalem before turning back. Finally on Sunday, October 30, a white named Benjamin Phelps accidentally discovered him in another hideout near Cabin Pond. Since the man had a loaded shotgun, Turner had no choice but to throw down his sword.

The next day, with lynch mobs crying for his head, a white guard hurried Turner up to Jerusalem to stand trial. By now he was resigned to his fate as the will of Almighty God and was entirely fearless and unrepentant. When a couple of court justices examined him that day, he stated emphatically that *he* had conceived and directed the slaughter of all those white people (even though he had killed only Margaret Whitehead) and announced that God had endowed him with extraordinary powers. The justices ordered this "fanatic" locked up in the same small wooden jail where the other captured rebels had been incarcerated.

On November 1 one Thomas Gray, an elderly Jerusalem lawyer and slaveholder, came to interrogate Turner as he lay in his cell "clothed with rags and covered with chains." In Gray's opinion the public was anxious to learn the facts about the insurrection—for whites in Southampton could not fathom why their slaves would revolt. What Gray wanted was to take down and publish a confession from Turner that would tell the public the truth about why the rebellion had happened. It appears that Gray had already gathered a wealth of information about the outbreak from other prisoners, some of whom he had defended as a court-appointed counsel. Evidently he had also written unsigned newspaper accounts of the affair, reporting in one that whites had located Turner's wife and lashed her until she surrendered his papers (remarkable papers, papers with hieroglyphics on them and sketches of the Crucifixion and the sun). According to Gray and to other sources as well, Turner over a period of three days gave him a voluntary and authentic confession about the genesis and execution of the revolt, recounting his religious visions in graphic detail and contending again that he was a prophet of Almighty God. "Do you not find yourself mistaken now?" Gray asked. Turner replied testily, "Was not Christ crucified?" Turner insisted that the uprising was local in origin but warned that other slaves might see signs and act as he had done. By the end of the confession Turner was in high spirits, perfectly "willing to suffer the fate that awaits me." Although Gray considered him "a gloomy fanatic," he thought Turner was one of the most articulate men he had ever met. And Turner could be frightening. When, in a burst of enthusiasm, he spoke of the killings and raised his manacled hands toward heaven, "I looked on him," Gray said, "and my blood curdled in my veins."

On November 5, with William C. Parker acting as his counsel, Turner came to trial in Jerusalem. The court, of course, found him guilty of committing insurrection and sentenced him to hang. Turner, though, insisted that he was not guilty because he did not feel so. On November 11 he went to his death in resolute silence. In addition to Turner, the county court tried some forty-eight other blacks on various charges of conspiracy, insurrection, and treason. In all, eighteen blacks—including one woman—were convicted and hanged. Ten others were convicted and "transported"—presumably out of the United States.

But the consequences of the Turner revolt did not end with public hangings in Jerusalem. For southern whites the uprising seemed a monstrous climax to a whole decade of ominous events, a decade of abominable tariffs and economic panics, of obstreperous antislavery activities, and of growing slave unrest and insurrection plots, beginning with the Denmark Vesey conspiracy in Charleston in 1822 and culminating now in the worst insurrection Southerners had ever known. Desperately needing to blame somebody besides themselves for Nat Turner, Southerners linked the revolt to some sinister Yankee-abolitionist plot to destroy their cherished way of life. Southern zealots declared that the antislavery movement, gathering momentum in the North throughout the 1820s, had now burst into a full-blown crusade against the South. In January, 1831, William Lloyd Garrison had started publishing *The Liberator* in Boston, demanding in bold, strident language that the slaves be immediately and unconditionally emancipated. If Garrison's rhetoric shocked Southerners, even more disturbing was the fact that about eight months after the appearance of *The Liberator* Nat Turner embarked on his bloody crusade—something southern politicians and newspapers refused to accept as mere coincidence. They charged that Garrison was behind the insurrection, that it was his "bloodthirsty" invective that had incited Turner to violence. Never mind that there was no evidence that Turner had ever heard of *The Liberator;* never mind that Garrison categorically denied any connection with the revolt, saying that he and his abolitionist followers were Christian pacifists who wanted to free the slaves through moral suasion. From 1831 on, northern abolitionism and slave rebellion were inextricably associated in the southern mind.

But if Virginians blamed the insurrection on northern abolitionism, many of them defended emancipation itself as the only way to prevent further violence. In fact, for several months in late 1831 and early 1832 Virginians engaged in a momentous public debate over the feasibility of manumission. Out of the western part of the state, where antislavery and anti-black sentiment had long been smoldering, came petitions demanding that Virginia eradicate the "accursed," "evil" slave system and colonize all blacks at state expense. Only by removing the entire black population, the petitions argued, could future revolts be avoided. Newspapers also discussed the idea of emancipation and colonization, prompting one to announce that "Nat Turner and the blood of his innocent victims have conquered the silence of fifty years." The debate moved into the Virginia legislature, too, and early in 1832 proslavery and antislavery orators harangued one another in an unprecedented legislative struggle over emancipation. In the end most delegates concluded that colonization was too costly and too complicated to carry out. And since they were not about to manumit the blacks and leave them as free men in a white man's country, they rejected emancipation. Indeed, they went on to revise and implement the slave codes in order to restrict blacks so stringently that they could never mount another revolt. The modified codes not only strengthened the patrol and militia systems, but sharply curtailed the rights of free blacks and all but eliminated slave schools, slave religious meetings, and slave preachers. For Turner had taught white Virginians a hard lesson about what might happen if they gave slaves enough education and religion to think for themselves.

In the wake of the Turner revolt, the rise of the abolitionists, and the Virginia debates over slavery, the other southern states also expanded their patrol and militia systems and increased the severity of their slave codes. What followed was the Great Reaction of the 1830s and 1840s, during which the South, threatened it seemed by internal and external enemies, became a closed, martial society determined to preserve its slave-based civilization at whatever cost. If Southerners had once apologized for slavery as a necessary evil, they now trumpeted that institution as a positive good—"the greatest of all the great blessings," as James H. Hammond phrased it, "which a kind providence has bestowed." Southern postmasters set about confiscating abolitionist literature, lest these "incendiary" tracts invite the slaves to violence. Some states actually passed sedition laws and other restrictive measures that prohibited blacks and whites alike from criticizing slavery. And slave owners all across the South tightened up slave discipline, refusing to let blacks visit other plantations and threatening to hang any slave who even looked rebellious. By the 1840s the Old South had devised such an oppressive slave system that organized insurrection was all but impossible.

Even so, southern whites in the antebellum period never escaped the haunting fear that somewhere, maybe even in their own slave quarters, another Nat Turner was plotting to rise up and slit their throats. They never forgot him. His name became for them a symbol of terror and violent retribution.

But for antebellum blacks—and for their descendants—the name of Nat Turner took on a profoundly different connotation. He became a legendary black hero who broke his chains and murdered white people because slavery had murdered blacks. Turner, said an elderly black man in Southampton County only a few years ago, was "God's man. He was a man for war, and for legal rights, and for freedom."

October 1973

XI

PENTECOST IN THE BACKWOODS

Bernard A. Weisberger

The Second Great Awakening began in numerous frontier camp meetings long before it emerged in the fast growing nineteenth century urban centers. In this article Bernard Weisberger graphically details the rural origins of this significant religious movement. It was on these rural foundations that the new revivalism thrived.

The Great Revival in the West, or the Kentucky Revival of 1800, as it was sometimes called, was a landmark in American history. It was not some accidental outburst of religious hysteria that crackled through the clearings. Rather, it was one of many answers to a question on which America's destiny hung during Thomas Jefferson's Presidency. Which way would the West go? It was filling up fast in 1800, and yet it still remained isolated behind the mountain barriers, only thinly linked to the nation by a cranky, awkward, and dangerous transportation "system" of trails and rivers. Could it be held within the bounds of American institutions as they had developed over 175 colonial years? Would its raw energies pull it into some new orbit—say, an independent confederation? Or, if it stayed in the Union, would it send representatives swarming back eastward to crush old patterns under the weight of numbers?

No group asked this question more anxiously than eastern clergymen. For, in 1800, they saw that their particular pattern was being abandoned on the frontier. From Kentucky, Tennessee, the western Carolinas, and Virginia, reports came back of a world that was shaggy, vicious, and churchless. The hard-living men and women of the forest clearings were not raising temples to God. Their morals (to eastern eyes) were parlous. Corn liquor flowed freely; marriages were celebrated long after children had arrived; gun and rope settled far too many legal disputes. The West was crowded with Sabbath-breakers and profane swearers, thieves, murderers, and blasphemers, with neither courts of law nor public opinion to raise a rebuke. The whole region seemed "hair-hung and breeze-shaken" over Hell's vault. And this was a matter of life-or-death seriousness to the churches. It was clear even then that America's future lay beyond the mountains. And if the West grew up Godless, then the entire nation would one day turn from His ways, to its destruction. It was no wonder that pious folk of the seaboard dug into their pocketbooks to scrape up funds for "home missionary" societies aimed at paying the way of parsons traveling westward. Or that church assemblies warned of crises ahead and called for special days of fasting, humiliation, and prayer for the West.

Yet, for a fact, the easterners were wrong. They misjudged their pioneers. Western people wanted and needed the church just as badly as the church needed their support for survival. Religion had a part to play in the hard-driven lives of the frontier settlers. It was more than a mere foundation for morality. It offered the hope of a bright future, shining beyond the dirt-floored, hog-and-hominy present. It offered an emotional outlet for lives ringed with inhibition. It was a social thing, too, furnishing occasions on which to lay aside axe and gun and skillet and gather with neighbors, to sing, to weep, to pray, or simply to talk with others. The West had to have religion—but religion of its own special kind. The West was not "lost" in 1800, but on the verge of being saved. Only it was going to be saved the same way it did everything else: on its own individualistic terms.

The East found this hard to understand. The East had trouble taking stock of such a man as the father of the western revival, James McGready. McGready was an angular, black-eyed Scotch-Irishman, born on the Pennsylvania frontier. He came of a hard-working and pious stock that had filled the western stretches of the Colonies in the sixty years before the Revolution. McGready was true to the spirit of his Highland Calvinistic ancestors, who worked, prayed, and fought heartily. He grew to adolescence without becoming a swearer, drinker, or Sabbath-breaker, which made him something of a God-fearing rarity among frontier youth. So his family sent him to a private school conducted by a minister, where he wrestled with Scripture in the morning and did farm chores in the afternoon for his "tuition." In 1788, he was licensed to preach, and came down to western North Carolina's Guilford County, where his family had moved. Thus, McGready was a product of western Presbyterianism.

That was important. In the 1790s, the religious picture in the United States already showed considerable (and characteristic) variety. Episcopalianism was solidly rooted among the landed gentry of the South. The Dutch Reformed Church carried on the heritage established when the flag of Holland flapped over New York. Various shoots of Lutheranism pushed up out of the soil of German settlements. Baptism and Methodism were small but growing faiths. There were little wedges in the pie of church membership labeled "Quaker," "Catholic," and "Jewish." A few bold souls called themselves Deists. A few more were on the way to becoming Unitarians. American worship wore a coat of many colors. But in New England and the mid-Atlantic states, the Presbyterian and Congregational bodies were unquestionably in the forefront. Both were rooted in the preceding century's Puritanism. Both officially believed in "predestination" and "limited election"—God had chosen a few individuals to be saved from general damnation, and the list, made up from the beginning of eternity, was unchangeable. These chosen "saints" were born in sin, but in His own way God would convert them to holiness during their lifetimes. Meanwhile, the laws of God must be interpreted and explained to mankind. In order to do this, the Presbyterians and Congregationalists had raised up colleges to train their ministers, the most famous among them by 1800 being Harvard, Yale, and Princeton. Graduates of these schools thundered of Jehovah's wrath to their congregations in two-hour sermons rich with samples of their learning. During the week they warmed their study chairs ten hours a day, writing black-bound volumes of theology.

Religion of this sort lacked appeal for the Scotch-Irish migrants pushing into the frontier regions. They were Presbyterians in name. But their wild surroundings did something to them. They came to resent authority—whether exercised by excise collectors, land speculators, lawyers, or, finally, ministers. What was more, they wanted a little stronger assurance of salvation than a strict reading of limited election gave them. There was a need, in this fur-capped, bewhiskered Christian world, for more promise in life, and more passion too. Learned pulpit lectures might do for townspeople, but not for pioneers.

Among common folk, both East *and* West, a ferment of resentment against the "aristocratic" notion of election was at work. In the 1740s it had exploded in a revival called the Great Awakening. Baptist, Presbyterian, Congregationalist, Anglican, and Dutch-Reformed Christians were caught up in a common whirlwind of handclapping, shouting, and hosannaing. A good many new leaders, and a number of unpleasant schisms, had risen out of this storm. And in western Pennsylvania, revival-minded Presbyterians had founded a number of little academies to train their preachers. Derisively dubbed "log colleges" by the learned, they took the name proudly. Their graduates were short on Greek and exegesis but long on zeal. When the Great Awakening sputtered out before the Revolution, these colleges remained, helping to keep the sparks alive. Now, with the new nation established, the fire was ready to blaze again. McGready, himself a log-college graduate, was one of the first to blow on it.

McGready got to grips with the powers of darkness in North Carolina without wasting any time. He began to preach against the "formality and deadness" of the local churches. Besides that, he demanded some concrete testimony of good living from his flock, and the particular evidence he asked for was highly exacting. The new preacher insisted that strong drink was a slippery path to Hell. In Guilford County this did not sit well. Frontiersmen saw no harm in lightening a hard life with a dram or two, and they wanted no lectures on the subject from men of the cloth. In point of fact, there was no cloth. Pioneer ministers wore buckskin, and took their turn with the next man at hoeing corn or splitting kindling. McGready got nowhere—at least nowhere in North Carolina. After a futile battle, he left to seek a more promising future in Kentucky—some said by request of the congregation.

In Kentucky, circumstances were riper for him. Despite eastern concern, a new Christian community was taking shape in that rugged, bear-and-savage-haunted wilderness province, where crude living went along with high dreaming. It was a community ready to be stirred into life, and McGready was the man to seize the stick. In Logan County, in the southwestern part of the state—a region well-known for unregenerate doings—he had three small congregations: at Red River, Gasper River, and Muddy River. He began to preach to these congregations, and he did not deal with such recondite matters as the doctrines contained in Matthew, or their applications. Instead he would "so describe Heaven" that his listeners would "see its glories and long to be there." Then he went on to "array hell and its horrors" so that the wicked would "tremble and quake, imagining a lake of fire and brimstone yawning to overwhelm them." With that brimstone smoking away in the background, McGready struck for bedrock. The whole point of Christianity, for him, was in the conversion of sinners to saints assured of eternal bliss. His question of questions was dagger-sharp: "If I were converted, would I feel it and know it?" A McGready parishioner was not going to be allowed to rest in self-satisfaction merely because he attended worship and avoided the grosser forms of indecency.

Under such spurring, results began to show among the faithful. In 1799, during a service at Gasper River, many fell to the ground and lay "powerless, groaning, praying and crying for mercy." Women began to scream. Big, tough men sobbed like hysterical children. What could explain this? Simply the fact that belly-deep fear was taking over. For it is well to remember that in those days conversion was the only token of salvation. No matter how young one was, no matter how blameless a life he had led, until the moment of transformation one was a sinner, bound for torment. If death stepped in before conversion was completed, babes and grandsires alike sank screaming into a lake of burning pitch—a lake that was not metaphorical, not symbolical, but *real* and eternal. And death on the frontier was always around the corner—in the unexpected arrow, the milk sickness, the carelessly felled tree, the leap of the wounded grizzly. Frontiersmen bottled up their fear of these things usually. It was the price of sanity and survival. But when a religious service provided an acceptable excuse for breaking down the barriers, it was no wonder that men shivered and wept.

After shaking up the dry bones of the Gasper River settlement, McGready moved on in June of 1800 to Red River. He meant to hold a sacramental service, at the end of which church members would take the Lord's Supper together. What he got was something more uncontrolled. In a meetinghouse of undressed logs McGready shared his pulpit with three other Presbyterian ministers. A Methodist preacher was also present. That was not unusual. Frontier preachers were a small band. They knew each other well. A service was a social occasion, and therefore a treat, and several ministers often took part in order to draw it out.

The Presbyterian shepherds did their preaching, and what they said has not come down to us, but they must have dragged a harrow through the congregation's feelings. When John McGee, the Methodist, arose, an awesome hush had fallen on the house. McGee faced a problem. The Methodists were relative newcomers to America, officially on the scene only since 1766. They were frowned on by more established groups, mainly because they gave emotion free rein in their worship. It was not unusual at a Methodist meeting for women to faint, men to shout in strange tongues, and the minister himself to windmill his arms and bawl himself red-faced. For the more formal Presbyterians, such conduct was out of bounds. McGee knew this, and wanted to mind his ecclesiastical manners. But he knew a ripe audience when he saw one, too, and after an apparent debate with himself, he made his move. Rising, he shouted that everyone in the house should submit to "the Lord Omnipotent." Then he began to bounce from backless bench to backless bench, pleading, crying, shouting, shaking, and exhorting, "with all possible energy and ecstasy."

That broke the dam. The sinners of Red River had spent a lonely winter with pent-up terrors gnawing at them. McGee's appeal was irresistible. In a moment the floor was "covered with the slain; their screams for mercy pierced the heavens." Cursers, duelers, whiskey-swillers, and card-players lay next to little children of ten and eleven, rolling and crying in "agonies of distress" for salvation. It was a remarkable performance for a region "destitute of religion." When it was through, a new harvest of souls had been gathered for the Lord.

Word of the Red River meeting whisked through the territory. When McGready got to Muddy River, his next congregation, new scenes of excitement were enacted. During the meeting, sinners prayed and cried for mercy once again, and some of them, overwhelmed by feeling, bolted from the house and rushed in agony into the woods. Their cries and sobs could be heard ringing through the surrounding trees. And when this meeting had yielded up its quota of saved, the Kentucky Revival was not only a fact, but a well-known one. McGready announced another sacramental meeting for Gasper River, and before long, dozens, perhaps hundreds, of Kentuckians who did not belong to his district were threading the trails on their way to the service. Some came as far as a hundred miles, a hard week's trip in the back country. In wagons, on horseback, and on foot came the leather-shirted men, rifles balanced on their shoulders, and their pinched-looking, tired women, all looking for blessed assurance and a washing away of their sins.

At Gasper River, history was made. The cabins of the neighborhood could not hold the influx of visitors, so the newcomers came prepared to camp out. They brought tents—some of them—and cold pork, roasted hens, slabs of corn bread, and perhaps a little whiskey to hold them up through the rigors of a long vigil. The Gasper River meetinghouse was too small for the crowd, so the men got out their educated axes, and in a while the clop-clop of tree-felling formed an overture to the services. Split-log benches were dragged into place outdoors, and the worshipers adjourned to God's first temple. What was taking place was an outdoor religious exercise, meant to last two or three days, among people who camped on the spot. This was the camp meeting. Some claimed that Gasper River sheltered the very first of them. That claim has been challenged in the court of historical inquiry. But whether it stands up or not, the Gasper River meeting was something new in worship. It took its form from its western surroundings. Outsiders were a long time in understanding it, because they saw its crude outside and not its passionate heart.

The outside was raw enough. Once again McGready exhorted, and once again sinners fell prostrate to the ground. Night came on; inside the meetinghouse, candlelight threw grotesque, waving shadows on the walls. Outside, the darkness deepened the sense of mystery and of eternity's nearness. Preachers grew hoarse and exhausted, but insatiable worshipers gathered in knots to pray together, and to relieve their feelings by telling each other of "the sweet wonders which they saw in Christ." Hour followed hour, into dawn. For people who had to rise (and generally retire) with the sun each day of their lives, this alone was enough to make the meeting memorable for the rest of their lives. Lightheaded and hollow-eyed, the "mourners," or unconverted, listened alternately to threats of sulphur and promises of bliss, from Saturday until Monday. On Tuesday, after three throbbing days, they broke it up. Forty-five had professed salvation. Satan had gotten a thorough gouging.

Now the tide of camp-meeting revivalism began to roll northward. One of the visitors at the Logan County meetings was a young Presbyterian clergyman whose life was something of a copy of McGready's. Barton Warren Stone too had learned on the frontier to revere God Almighty and to farm well. He too had studied religion in a log college. But more than this, he was one of McGready's own converts, having fallen under the power of the older man's oratory in North Carolina. Stone liked what he observed in Logan County, and he took McGready's preaching methods and the camp-meeting idea back to his own congregations in Bourbon County, well to the north and east. Soon he too had imitators, among them Richard McNemar, who had small Presbyterian charges across the river in Ohio.

But it was Stone himself who touched off the monster camp meeting of the region's history. He set a sacramental service for August 6, 1801, at Cane Ridge, not far from the city of Lexington. Some undefinable current of excitement running from cabin to cabin brought out every Kentuckian who could drop his earthly concerns and move, by horseflesh or shoe leather, towards the campground. Later on, some people estimated that 25,000 were on hand, but that figure is almost too fantastic for belief. In 1800, Kentucky had only a quarter of a million residents, and Lexington, the largest town, numbered under two thousand. But even a crowd of three or four thousand would have overwhelmed anything in the previous experience of the settlers.

Whatever the actual number, there was a sight to dazzle the eyes of the ministers who had come. Technically the meeting was Presbyterian, but Baptist and Methodist parsons had come along, and there was room for them, because no one man could hope to reach such a mob. Preaching stands built of logs were set up outdoors. One man remembered a typical scene—a crowd spilling out of the doors of the one meetinghouse, where two Presbyterian ministers were alternately holding forth, and three other groups scattered within a radius of a hundred yards. One cluster of sinners was gathered at the feet of a Presbyterian preacher, another gave ear to a Methodist exhorter, and lastly, a knot of African Americans were attending on the words of some orator of their own race. All over the campground, individual speakers had gathered little audiences to hear of *their* experiences. One observer said that there were as many as three hundred of these laymen "testifying."

So Cane Ridge was not really a meeting, but a series of meetings that gathered and broke up without any recognizable order. One Methodist brother who could not find a free preaching-stand ventured up the slanting trunk of a partly fallen tree. He found a flat spot, fifteen feet off the ground, and he spoke from this vantage point while a friend on the ground held up an umbrella on a long pole to shelter him from the weather. Within a few moments, this clergyman claimed, he had gathered an audience of thousands. Undoubtedly they stayed until lured away by some fresh address from a stump or the tail of a wagon. For the crowds were without form as they collected, listened, shouted "Amen!" and "Hallelujah!" and drifted off to find neighbors or refreshments or more preaching. The din can only be guessed at. The guilty were groaning and sometimes screaming at the top of their lungs, and those who felt that they were saved were clapping their hands, shouting hymns, and generally noising out their exultation. There were always hecklers at the meetings too, and some of them were no doubt shouting irreverent remarks at the faithful. Crying children added their bit, and tethered horses and oxen stamped, bawled, and whinnied to make the dissonance complete. Someone said that the meeting sounded from afar like the roar of Niagara. At night the campfires threw weird shadow-patterns of trees across the scene, and the whole moving, resounding gathering appeared to be tossing on the waves of some invisible storm. As if to etch the experience into men's memories, there were real rainstorms, and the drenched participants were thrown into fresh waves of screaming as thunder and lightning crashed around them.

All in all a memorable enough episode. And yet still stranger things happened to put the brand of the Lord's sponsorship on Cane Ridge's mass excitement. Overwhelmed with their sensations, some men and women lay rigid and stiff on the ground for hours in a kind of catalepsy. One "blasphemer" who had come to scoff at the proceedings tumbled from his saddle unconscious and remained so for a day and a half. There was something incredibly compelling in what was going on. One remembered testimony came from a reasonably hardheaded young man named James Finley. Later in life Finley became a Methodist preacher, but in 1801 he was, except for a better-than-average education, a typical frontiersman. He had a small farm, a new wife, and a vigorous love of hunting. He had come to the Cane Ridge meeting out of curiosity, but as he looked on, he was taken with an uncontrollable trembling and feelings of suffocation. He left the campground, found a log tavern, and put away a glass of brandy to steady his nerves. But they were beyond steadying. All the way home he kept breaking out in irrational fits of laughter or tears. Many a spirit, returning from Cane Ridge, must have been moved in the same near-hysterical way.

A holy frenzy seemed to have taken hold of the West. Throughout the frontier communities, the ecstasy of conversion overflowed into the nervous system. At Cane Ridge, and at a hundred subsequent meetings, the worshipers behaved in ways that would be unbelievable if there were not plenty of good testimony to their truth. Some got the "jerks," a spasmodic twitching of the entire body. They were a fearful thing to behold. Some victims hopped from place to place like bouncing balls. Sometimes heads snapped from side to side so rapidly that faces became a blur, and handkerchiefs whipped off women's heads. One preacher saw women taken with the jerks at table, so that teacups went flying from their hands to splash against log walls. Churchmen disagreed about the meaning of these symptoms. Were they signs of conversion? Or demonstrations of the Lord's power, meant to convince doubters? Peter Cartwright, a famous evangelist of a slightly later era, believed the latter. He told of a skeptic at one of his meetings who was taken with the jerks and in a particularly vicious spasm snapped his neck. He died, a witness to the judgment of Omnipotence but gasping out to the last his "cursing and bitterness." Besides the jerks, there were strange seizures in which those at prayer broke into uncontrollable guffaws or intoned weird and wordless melodies or barked like dogs.

It was wild and shaggy, and very much a part of life in the clearings. Westerners wanted to feel religion in their bones. In their tough and violent lives intellectual exercises had no place, but howls and leaps were something that men who were "half-horse and half-alligator" understood. It was natural for the frontier to get religion with a mighty roar. Any other way would not have seemed homelike to people who, half in fun and half in sheer defensiveness, loved their brag, bluster, and bluff.

Yet there was something deeper than mere excitement underneath it all. Something fundamental was taking place, some kind of genuine religious revolution, bearing a made-in-America stamp. The East was unhappy with it. For one thing, camp-meeting wildness grated on the nerves of the educated clergy. All of this jigging and howling looked more like the work of Satan than of God. There were ugly rumors, too, about unsanctified activities at the meetings. Some candidates for salvation showed up with cigars between their teeth. Despite official condemnation, liquor flowed free and white-hot on the outskirts of the gatherings. It might be that corn did more than its share in justifying God's ways to man. Then there were stories that would not down which told how, in the shadows around the clearing, excited men and women were carried away in the hysteria and, as the catch phrase had it, "begot more souls than were saved" at the meeting. All these tales might have had some partial truth, yet in themselves they did not prove much about frontier religion. As it happened, a part of every camp-meeting audience apparently consisted of loafers and rowdies who came for the show and who were quite capable of any sin that a Presbyterian college graduate was likely to imagine.

Yet it was not the unscrubbed vigor of the meetings that really bothered conservatives in the Presbyterian Church. Their fundamental problem was in adjusting themselves and their faith to a new kind of democratic urge. Enemies of the revivals did not like the success of emotional preaching. What would happen to learning, and all that learning stood for, if a leather-lunged countryman with a gift for lurid word pictures could be a champion salvationist? And what would happen—what *had* happened—to the doctrine of election when the revival preacher shouted "Repent!" at overwrought thousands, seeming to say that any Tom, Dick, or Harry who felt moved by the Spirit might be receiving the promise of eternal bliss? Would mob enthusiasm replace God's careful winnowing of the flock to choose His lambs? The whole orderly scheme of life on earth, symbolized by a powerful church, an educated ministry, and a strait and narrow gate of salvation, stood in peril.

Nor were the conservatives wrong. In truth, when the McGreadys and Stones struck at "deadness" and "mechanical worship" in the older churches, they were going beyond theology. They were hitting out at a view of things that gave a plain and unlettered man little chance for a say in spiritual affairs. A church run by skilled theologians was apt to set rules that puzzled simple minds. A church which held that many were called, but few chosen, was aristocratic in a sense. The congregations of the western evangelists did not care for rules, particularly rules that were not immediately plain to anyone. In their view, the Bible alone was straightforward enough. Neither would they stand for anything resembling aristocracy, whatever form it might take. They wanted cheap land and the vote, and they were getting these things. They wanted salvation as well—or at least free and easy access to it—and they were bound to have that too. If longer-established congregations and their leaders back east did not like that notion, the time for a parting of the ways was at hand. In politics, such a parting is known as a revolution; in religion, it is schism. Neither word frightened the western revivalists very much.

The trouble did not take long to develop. In McGready's territory, a new Cumberland Presbytery, or subgroup, was organized in 1801. Before long it was in a battle with the Kentucky Synod, the next highest administrative body in the hierarchy. The specific issue was the licensing of certain "uneducated" candidates for the ministry. The root question was revivalism. The battle finally went up to the General Assembly, for Presbyterians a sort of combined Congress and Supreme Court. In 1809 the offending revivalistic presbytery was dissolved. Promptly, most of its congregations banded themselves into the separate Cumberland Presbyterian Church. Meanwhile, Barton Stone, Richard McNemar, and other members of the

northern Kentucky wing of camp-meeting Presbyterianism were also in trouble. They founded a splinter group known as the "New Lights," and the Kentucky Synod, as might have been
foreseen, lost little time in putting the New Lights out, via heresy proceedings. Next, they
formed an independent Springfield Presbytery. But like all radicals, they found it easier to
keep going than to apply the brakes. In 1804 the Springfield Presbytery fell apart. Stone and
some of his friends joined with others in a new body, shorn of titles and formality, which carried the magnificently simple name of the Christian Church. Later on, Stone went over to the
followers of Thomas and Alexander Campbell, who called themselves Disciples of Christ. Richard McNemar, after various spiritual adventures, became a Shaker. Thus, ten years after
Cane Ridge, the score was depressing for Presbyterians. Revivalism had brought on innumer-
able arguments, split off whole presbyteries, and sent ministers and congregations flying into
the arms of at least four other church groups. That splintering was a stronger indictment than
any conservative could have invented to bring against Cane Ridge, or against its western
child, the camp meeting.

A dead end appeared to have been reached. But it was only a second-act curtain. In the
first act, religion in the West, given up for lost, had been saved by revivalism. In the second,
grown strong and rambunctious, it had quarreled with its eastern parents. Now the time was
at hand for a third-act resolution of the drama. Both sides would have to back down and compromise. For the lesson of history was already plain. In religious matters, as in all matters, East
and West, metropolis and frontier, were not really warring opposites. Each nourished the other, and each had an impact on the other. Whatever emerged as "American" would carry some
of the imprint of both, or it would perish.

On the part of the West, the retreat consisted of taming the camp meeting. Oddly
enough, it was not the Presbyterians who did that. By 1812 or so, they had drawn back from
it, afraid of its explosive qualities. But the Methodists were in an excellent position to make
use of revivalism and all its trappings. They had, at that time at least, no educated conservative wing. They welcomed zealous backwood preachers, even if they were grammatically defi-
cient. In fact, they worked such men into their organization and sent them, under the name
of "circuit-riders," traveling tirelessly on horseback to every lonely settlement that the wilderness spawned. The result was that the Methodists were soon far in the lead in evangelizing
the frontier. They did not have to worry about the claims of limited election either. Their
formal theology did not recognize it. With a plain-spoken and far-reaching ministry freely
offering salvation to all true believers, Methodism needed only some kind of official harvest
season to count and bind together the converts. The camp meeting was the perfect answer.
By 1811, the Methodists had held four or five hundred of them throughout the country; by
1820, they had held a thousand—by far the majority of all such gatherings in the nation.

But these meetings were not replicas of Cane Ridge. They were combed, washed, and made
respectable. Permanent sites were picked, regular dates chosen, and preachers and flocks given
ample time to prepare. When meeting time came, the arriving worshipers in their wagons were
efficiently taken in charge, told where to park their vehicles and pasture their teams, and given
a spot for their tents. Orderly rows of these tents surrounded a preaching area equipped with
sturdy benches and preaching stands. The effect was something like that of a formal bivouac
just before a general's inspection. Tight scheduling kept the worship moving according to plan—
—dawn prayers, eight o'clock sermons, eleven o'clock sermons, dinner breaks, afternoon prayers
and sermons, meals again, and candlelight services. Years of experience tightened the schedules,
and camp-meeting manuals embodied the fruits of practice. Regular hymns replaced the dis-
cordant bawling of the primitive era. Things took on a generally homelike look. There were
Methodist ladies who did not hesitate to bring their best feather beds to spread in the tents, and

meals tended to be planned and ample affairs. Hams, turkeys, gravies, biscuits, preserves, and melons produced contented worshipers and happy memories.

There were new rules to cope with disorderliness as well. Candles, lamps, and torches fixed to trees kept the area well lit and discouraged young converts from amorous ways. Guards patrolled the circumference of the camp, and heroic if sometimes losing battles were fought to keep whiskey out. In such almost decorous surroundings jerks, barks, dances and trances became infrequent and finally nonexistent.

Not that there was a total lack of enthusiasm. Hymns were still yelled and stamped as much as sung. Nor was it out of bounds for the audience to pepper the sermon with ejaculations of "Amen!" and "Glory!" Outsiders were still shocked by some things they saw. But they did not realize how far improvement had gone.

Eastern churchmen had to back down somewhat, too. Gradually, tentatively, they picked up the revival and made it part of their religious life. In small eastern towns it became regularized into an annual season of "ingathering," like the harvest or the election. Yet it could not be contained within neat, white-painted meeting-houses. Under the "sivilized" clothing, the tattered form of Twain's Pap Finn persisted. Certain things were taken for granted after a time. The doctrine of election was bypassed and, in practice, allowed to wither away.

Moreover, a new kind of religious leader, the popular evangelist, took the stage. Men like Charles G. Finney in the 1830's, Dwight L. Moody in the 1870s, and Billy Sunday in the decade just preceding the First World War flashed into national prominence. Their meetings overflowed church buildings and spilled into convention halls, auditoriums, and specially built "tabernacles." As it happened, these men came from lay ranks into preaching. Finney was a lawyer, Moody a shoe salesman, and Sunday a baseball player. They spoke down-to-earth language to their massed listeners, reduced the Bible to basic axioms, and drew their parables from the courtroom, the market, and the barnyard. They made salvation the only goal of their service, and at the meeting's end they beckoned the penitents forward to acknowledge the receipt of grace. In short, they carried on the camp-meeting tradition. By the closing years of the nineteenth century, however, the old campgrounds for the most part were slowly abandoned. Growing cities swallowed them up, and rapid transportation destroyed the original reason for the prolonged camp-out. But the meetings were not dead. Mass revivalism had moved them indoors and made them a permanent part of American Protestantism.

All of this cost something in religious depth, religious learning, religious dignity. Yet there was not much choice. The American churches lacked the support of an all-powerful state or of age-old traditions. They had to move with the times. That is why their history is so checkered with schismatic movements—symptoms of the struggle to get in step with the parade. Hence, if the West in 1800 could not ignore religion, the rest of the country, in succeeding years, could not ignore the western notion of religion. One student of the camp meeting has said that it flourished "side by side with the militia muster, with the cabin raising and the political barbecue." That was true, and those institutions were already worked deeply into the American grain by 1840. They reflected a spirit of democracy, optimism, and impatience that would sweep us across a continent, sweep us into industrialism, sweep us into a civil war. That spirit demanded some religious expression, some promise of a millennium in which all could share.

The camp meeting was part of that religious expression, part of the whole revival system that channeled American impulses into churchgoing ways. In the home of the brave, piety was organized so that Satan got no breathing spells. Neither, for that matter, did anyone else.

June 1959

XII

The Debts We Never Paid

Robert Wernick

The deficit seems so large, and the spending so overwhelming and uncontrollable. Can the states and the nation ever get out from under the stack of bills and red ink? These seemingly modern questions, were in fact of intense concern in the mid nineteenth century United States. The speculative insanity that helped bring on the Panic of 1837, would likewise leave many states with difficult debts. Robert Wernick gives a lively discussion of the various means by which the crises were met in the country.

William Wordsworth, the most benign of poets laureate and best remembered for his idyllic view of daffodils and country maidens, was capable, when provoked, of flashes of baleful fire. Thus, in a sonnet published in 1845:

> All who revere the memory of Penn
> Grieve for the land on whose wild woods his name
> Was fondly grafted with a virtuous aim,
> Renounced, abandoned by degenerate Men
> For state-dishonour black as ever came
> To upper air from Mammon's loathsome den.

These "degenerate Men" were the citizens of the commonwealth of Pennsylvania, and their reputation was low in the early 1840's. "I never meet a Pennsylvanian at a London dinner," wrote the Reverend Sydney Smith in a letter to a newspaper, "without feeling a disposition to seize and divide him; to allot his beaver to one sufferer and his coat to another—to appropriate his pocket—handkerchief to the orphan, and to comfort the widow with his silver watch, Broadway rings and the London Guide, which he always carries in his pockets. How such a man can set himself down at an English table without feeling that he owes two or three pounds to every man in company I am at a loss to conceive: he has no more right to eat with honest men than a leper has to eat with clean men."

The reason for these outbursts? Pennsylvania, caught in the great depression that began with the Panic of 1837, had stopped paying interest on its bonds, thousands of which had been sold to English middle-class families like the Wordsworths and the Smiths. It is hard to imagine proper Pennsylvania doing anything of this sort. And, it is only fair to mention at once, it did resume payments in full in a couple of years, and received a commendatory footnote in Wordsworth's collected works. The Wordsworth family held on through the dark period. Sydney Smith, on the other hand, sold his holdings at a forty per cent loss and sourly announced that he was switching to Abyssinian securities. But few defaulting states showed as much conscience as Pennsylvania.

Our schoolbooks and our political orators tend to leave us with the impression that the American pioneer went west and opened up the country with nothing but his axe, his Kentucky rifle, and his McGuffey's *Reader*. If he had, he would have been condemned to a semibarbarous life in a log hut, trading surplus swine to an occasional peddler for calico and gunpowder. To open the way to a glorious and profitable future he needed two mechanisms which are now in ill repute among his descendants: Bureaucratic Planning, in the form of state-built canals and railroads that could take his produce to market cheaply; and Foreign Aid, in the form of capital from overseas to pay for these means of transportation.

The huge construction projects necessary were far beyond the means of private enterprise. There was little or no surplus capital in the United States available for investment. New York State found the solution by borrowing seven million dollars, mostly in England, to build the Erie Canal. This was so spectacularly successful—it opened the markets of the world to western grain, it made New York City the business capital of the country, and in addition it made enormous profits—that every other state, from staid old Pennsylvania to savage little Arkansas out in its wilderness, wanted to do likewise. The federal government at this period did not believe in spending money on public improvements, and so it was up to the states to draw up their own projects and raise their own funds.

Unlike the Pakistanis and the Ghanaians of today, the impecunious leaders of nineteenth-century states could not wheedle money out of cold-warring Great Powers. But there was plenty of private money in western Europe. The bourgeoisie there was beginning to cash in on the profits of the Industrial Revolution, and the money markets of London and Amsterdam were awash in funds waiting for lucrative investment opportunities. In Europe there were always wars or the threat of wars, and capital might go up in smoke any minute. But across the Atlantic was the brand new land of America, with no enemies except ragged Native Americans, with unlimited resources, and moreover willing to pay considerably higher interest than European borrowers. The American states needed cash desperately, just to keep a minimum of governmental activity and commerce going, and though most of them could get away with paying six per cent interest, others were forced to go up to ten, fifteen, and even higher. The state of California, starting life from scratch in 1850, with a nonexistent treasury, offered thirty-six per cent on its first bond issue.

Every report from America emphasized the growth, the fantastic growth. And the Americans were generally believed to be thrifty and reliable. Hadn't the government at Washington paid off the entire national debt in 1835 and started passing out its annual surplus in loans to the states? (Those loans, incidentally, are still on the books, no state ever having offered to repay them.) No wonder that all England—bankers, dukes, clergymen, widows, orphans, poets laureate—hurried to invest. And to urge investors on even more, the bond-issuing states sent over special agents, fast-talking Yankees, to pass out prospectuses and spread the good tidings of perpetual profits.

Not all these agents and prospectuses were honest. Some extolled the perfectly valid attractions of the Erie Canal, but others urged investment in some malarial mud flat of the kind so caustically described by Dickens in *Martin Chuzzlewit*. Many an American community might well erect a statue to the Unknown Swindler who euchred the foreigners into getting it started.

In 1839 and 1840, when times were hard, pressure was brought by foreign investors and by certain Whig newspapers to try to get the federal government to assume the states' debts, which, after a decade of borrowing, amounted to more than 150 million dollars. The movement did not get very far, one of the arguments used against it in the press being that if the states defaulted, English investors would be willing to sell the bonds at a fraction of their face value; worthy Americans could buy them up, and when the states were able to resume paying interest, the money would stay in the land of the free instead of going into the coffers of the bloated English.

An attractive theory. But wouldn't it make the bloated English tighten their purse strings the next time they were asked for funds? Well, it did. When the United States government, protesting that it was not responsible for the financial transactions of the individual states, tried to float a loan in Europe in 1842, there were no takers. Americans travelling abroad were subjected to indignities. "An American gentleman of the most unblemished character," reported the London *Times,* "was refused admission to one of the largest clubs in London on the sole grounds that he belonged to a republic that did not fulfil its engagements." But if the English chose to be stuffy, the agents and their prospectuses could move on to fresh territory. The great American railroad boom of the 1850's—cut short by the Panic of 1857—attracted a considerable sum of German money. By the time of the mining boom after the Civil War, the English were back enthusiastically in the market. "The average Britisher," said a journalist of that period, "does not in the least object to being swindled, provided it is done by one of his own countrymen, and if by a body of them with a Duke's name as director, it is positively delightful." A notorious swindle like the case of the Emma Mine Company (an enterprise that had been guaranteed respectable by half a dozen members of Parliament, a U.S. senator, a Yale professor, and the American ambassador to the Court of St. James') probably drew more silver out of the pockets of guileless Englishmen than was ever extracted from the mine itself, out in the wilds of Utah.

Such swindles were of course reprehensible, but not unprecedented in the dog-eat-dog world of finance. What rankled—what rankles still in some quarters—was the way sovereign states, which even at that early date were ever ready to lecture foreign countries on the principles of morality, calmly tore up their obligations.

It is easy to see how the states, even assuming the best will in the world, got themselves into trouble. American prosperity in the 1830's was dazzling. It was "perhaps the most extraordinary financial period the world has ever seen," said the *North American Review* after the crash of 1837. Everything was getting bigger and more efficient. Everybody was making money. Only the vast emptiness of the western sky was the limit. Or so it seemed. The state of Michigan, entering the Union with a population of less than 200,000 citizens, almost all of whom were living on subsistence farms, immediately floated a five-million-dollar loan for public works. Trustingly, it allowed two banks to buy its bonds on the installment plan. The banks had paid about half of the cash value of the bonds when they went bankrupt; not, however, before they had placed the bonds, at full value, as collateral on loans. Although Michigan made several half-hearted attempts to settle up with the bondholders, the result was general dissatisfaction.

In all, eight states defaulted on their obligations in the years 1840-42. Some made heroic efforts to keep up the payments—Maryland scooped up its public school funds, Pennsylvania sold railroads it had built at a cost of thirty million dollars for eleven million dollars. Indiana, where financial difficulties were compounded by wholesale thefts perpetrated by the state officials in charge of the bond sales, entered into long and bitter negotiations with the bondholders and finally agreed to allow them a degree of compensation from the revenues of the canal system that the bonds had built. But within a couple of years, the canals were driven into bankruptcy, partly because of competition from the railroads the state was building alongside them.

Florida was more straightforward and thoroughgoing. It simply wiped out its debt by legislative fiat. This debt was created while Florida was still a territory, and it was backed up by mortgages on property that the territorial legislature had arbitrarily valued at $15 or more an acre, though the market price was between $1.50 and $5. When the day of reckoning came, the legislature voted that it did not possess "nor was it ever invested with the authority to pledge the faith of the Territory." Foreign bondholders were by now learning many things about the peculiarities of the American federal system: this particular lesson cost them 3.9 million dollars.

In 1841 Arkansas defaulted on its bonds; a constitutional amendment (some forty years later) made it illegal ever to pay them. And in Mississippi, the story was even worse. This state had, during the 1830's, chartered two banks, the Planters' and the Union, and issued some eighteen million dollars in bonds to get them going. These banks financed the great cotton plantations which covered most of the fertile land in the state. After the Panic of 1837 a touch of recklessness crept into their mode of operation. They speculated strongly in cotton futures; and the most carefree investor might have been disturbed to learn that the Union Bank was refusing to show its books to the state commissioners because "their minds were biased."

But as long as the price of cotton was going up, nobody cared. The English were delighted to buy the bonds, and the Mississippians were even more delighted to sell them. When news came that five million dollars' worth had been unloaded on the London Exchange in 1838, "the smoke of great guns," says the *Encyclopedia of Mississippi History*, "filled the capital city [Jackson] with a pillar of cloud by day and bonfires and illuminations lighted it with a pillar of fire by night."

Within three years a different sound was coming out of Mississippi. Estates that had cost $30,000 were being sold for $3,200. The banks were broke. The balance in the state treasury in 1842 was thirty-four cents. Governor Alexander McNutt, described in the histories of the time as a man of "slovenly appearance and intemperate habits," had in 1839 proclaimed that "the honor of the state must be preserved unsullied." He discovered in 1841 that there had been certain technical defects in the sale of the bonds: they were not supposed to be sold below par, but some of them had been—perhaps because there were different definitions of the word "par" in America and in England. Consequently he moved to declare all the bonds null and void. The legislature rebuffed him that year, but thought better of it later. In 1852, the state's High Court of Errors and Appeals ruled that the bonds were a legal obligation, despite any irregularities in their sale; the only practical effect of this decision was to deprive the judges of any chance of ever being elected to office in Mississippi. Sacred obligations were all very well in their way, but not if they meant that people were going to have to pay taxes. "The beds on which your wives and children sleep," said a newspaper, "the tables on which you eat your daily bread will be taken by the excise men for the benefit of those who sleep in splendid brick palaces, who sleep in mahogany bedsteads, eat with gold knives and forks, and drink champagne as the ordinary beverage of the day." Are we going to make our children serfs, asked the Governor, to "Baron Rothschild, with the blood of Judas and Shylock in his veins, who has advanced money to the Sublime Porte and taken as security a mortgage upon the holy city of Jerusalem and the sepulchre of our Savior"? That was the kind of talk that appealed to the voters, and a series of electoral triumphs established "the sacred truth that the toiling millions never should be burdened with taxes to support the idle few."

The action of Mississippi received great criticism from the world at large. A learned judge tried to explain to the more civilized British bondholders that it was unfair to judge Mississippians as you would Londoners. They were more like Highland chieftains: "They mean to pay, but they did not expect when they contracted the debt to distress themselves about the payment. If a friend wants a thousand dollars for a loan or a gift, he can have it, though perhaps a creditor wants it also."

Friends before creditors remained the watchword as the years went by. In 1875, an article was added to the Mississippi state constitution forbidding any payment on either the Planters' or the Union Bank bonds. It was added at the suggestion of General Adelbert Ames, then governor, a man detested as a vile carpetbagger by the conservative Democrats of the state. But by 1890, when the Democrats regained control of the state government and rewrote the constitution, they were careful not to leave out the repudiation clause.

By that time, buyers of state bonds had many fresh wounds to weep over. All the states that had joined the Confederacy came out of the Civil War in financial chaos. Their treasuries held nothing but worthless paper. Half of their taxable property had been destroyed by the invading armies or set free by the Emancipation Proclamation. The Reconstruction governments imposed by Northern arms had to borrow money to get a semblance of normal life going again. Bonds were issued more or less haphazardly, and squads of agents were dispatched to Europe to unload them for what they could get. Prudent investors noted that the regimes issuing these bonds were not very stable and that if they were overthrown, their paper would not be worth any more than the Confederacy's. But there were plenty of imprudent investors.

Modern historians have restored some of the reputation of the Reconstruction governments. The older schoolbooks are full of carpetbaggers, illiterate freedmen turned legislators, the forty-cent spittoons in the South Carolina legislature replaced by eight-dollar cuspidors, and so forth. The reconsidered view is that the carpetbag governments passed a good deal of useful legislation, and were not notably more extravagant and corrupt than the North's state governments of that time—it was the scandalous Gilded Age—or the Grant administration in Washington, not to speak of certain state governments of more recent times. But the southerners who wrested control of their states from Reconstructionists did not take this view. They were revolutionists come to power by force or the threat of force, and their attitude toward their predecessors' debts was much like the attitude of, say, Che Guevara toward Batista's.

These new southern regimes were forbidden by the Fourteenth Amendment to pay the debts incurred for fighting the Civil War. It seemed only logical to them to repudiate likewise the debts of the governments that had been imposed by the Northern armies. They were all the happier to do so because great quantities of the carpetbag bonds had been sold in the North. The Yankees, who could no longer be beaten on the battlefield, could at least be squeezed in their tender pocketbooks. That innocent investors abroad would also be squeezed does not appear to have been a consideration.

In courtly Virginia, which until the Civil War had an unblemished financial record, the work of repudiation was known as "readjustment." Once undertaken, it was carried on with vigor. The former Confederate states not only cancelled all the Reconstruction bonds, they pushed right ahead and scaled down by fifty per cent or more the bonds they had issued before the war began. They probably lost more than they gained in the process, for their credit remained low for a couple of generations, and in the great industrial boom of the half century following Appomattox they had to limp along far behind the rest of the country.

Not that a northern state wouldn't resort to the same kind of financial shenanigans, when the occasion required. Minnesota had an unfortunate experience constructing railroads in the 1850's, and did not honor its bonds at all until 1880, when it finally paid fifty per cent of their face value.

But with this action, the great era of financial irresponsibility on the part of state governments may be considered closed. America was by now generating its own surplus capital (though still a debtor nation by some 3.5 billion dollars at the start of the First World War), and was becoming a self-appointed guardian of international financial morality. In the early years of this century, when countries such as Nicaragua and the Dominican Republic had difficulties paying their debts, they were apt to find the United States Marines stationed in their customs- houses making collections. Why, asked many a curious widow and orphan in Europe, couldn't similar measures be taken against Mississippi and Indiana? In the 1840's, hot-blooded creditors of the states had talked of swooping down with an army from Canada. Cooler heads sought recourse in the law, but the law was little comfort. The courts did indeed agree that the federal Constitution forbade the states to tear up their contracts. But to get their money back, the bondholders would have to sue the states, and the Eleventh Amendment to the Constitution says that a state may not be sued by a private citizen without its consent. None of the delinquent states has ever given its consent.

Ingenious lawyers, glimpsing all those millions of dollars in perfectly valid obligations, have tried again and again to figure out a way of getting into that paradise. But the flaming sword of the Eleventh Amendment has always kept them out. Except once. In 1904 the state of South Dakota found itself in possession of some North Carolina bonds which had been left by a citizen for the use of the state university. In the case of *South Dakota vs. North Carolina* (192 U.S., 286-354) the Supreme Court held for the plaintiff, and North Carolina had to fork over $27,400. The shock was so great that North Carolina promptly made a deal with some private holders in England to buy off their bonds—at a low price, but paid in hard cash.

Other aggrieved parties have had no such luck. Some private citizens tried deeding defaulted North Carolina bonds to, say, Massachusetts, since one sovereign state may sue another, but the Supreme Court held that this was only a dodge to get around the Eleventh Amendment and would hear nothing of it. No more did it pay attention to the principality of Monaco, which had inherited some bonds and tried to sue the state of Mississippi in 1930.

That same year, the Great Depression was beginning, and Great Britain was trying to get out of paying its war debt to the United States. American politicians and American newspapers swelled with righteous disapproval. Some of the loudest disapproval came from, yes, Mississippi; its Representative John Rankin led the assault on President Hoover's debt moratorium. "One of the boldest schemes of financial buccaneering ever attempted," he called it; Governor McNutt would surely have used stronger language.

In March, 1930, Lord Redesdale, father of the Mitford girls, rose in the House of Lords to move that the repudiated American state debts, which he estimated to amount, with accrued interest, to seventy-eight million pounds, be applied against the British war debt, thus enabling the United States to rub out "a painful and shameful page" from their history and "raise them from the level of Russia." (Russia, at the time, was the only sovereign nation to have repudiated its debts.) The Earl of Limerick supported Lord Redesdale and pointed out that the interest, if compounded, would bring the sum due to over one billion dollars. Lord Ponsonby, for the government, which was anxious not to disturb the London Naval Conference then in progress, held that the state debts were the result of private transactions and that for the British government to attempt to collect them would be impracticable; and Lord Redesdale grouchily subsided.

And there the matter rests. Still in their owners' strongboxes and solicitors' files they lie, the gaily engraved obligations of the deadbeat states. And there, while we go on lecturing defaulters and admonishing new states to meet their obligations, they will go on lying. The descendants of the widows and orphans of the 1840's still subscribe to the annual bulletins of the Council of Foreign Bondholders, and yearly scan the melancholy news. There may be grounds for hope of some sort of accommodation with various Central American defaulters. But on the Planters' Bank bonds of Mississippi, like the czarist Russian four per cents, the news is always bad.

December 1964

XIII

THE THANKLESS TASK OF NICHOLAS TRIST

Richard M. Ketchum

Nicholas P. Trist adroitly managed to negotiate a favorable end to the Mexican-American War despite difficulties with General Scott, President Polk and Mexican officials. For this great service, he was fired from the State Department, and nearly driven into bankruptcy. Richard M. Ketchum explains the trials and tribulations of this American diplomat during the war with Mexico.

As winter wore on into the spring of 1847, the hope grew in Washington that the year-old war with Mexico might be settled soon. The nation's first major foreign conflict had been an unpopular affair from the beginning; a large number of Americans seem to have thought it would be a short skirmish, followed by a rich land-grab, and were disappointed when the Mexicans showed no immediate signs of collapsing or negotiating. When President James K. Polk learned of General Winfield Scott's victory on March 27 at Veracruz, he concluded that the moment was auspicious for peace talks and, with the agreement of his Cabinet, looked about for a man he might send to Scott's headquarters to be on the scene should the Mexicans decide to sue for peace.

A Democrat who had already decided not to seek re-election in 1848, the President was eager for the war to end, but he had no intention of appointing someone who would make political hay out of an important peace mission. He realized he had to select someone "who would be satisfactory to the country . . . [yet] such is the jealousy of the different factions of the Democratic party in reference to the next Presidential Election toward each other that it is impossible to appoint any prominent man." And so it was that Nicholas Philip Trist was chosen for one of the strangest, most misunderstood, most productive assignments in American diplomatic history.

At the time Polk plucked him out of near-anonymity for greater things, Trist was the chief clerk in the State Department. This meant that he was second-in-command to the Secretary, James Buchanan—a position he had attained largely through his intimate connections with some of the towering figures in United States politics. Trist had been born in 1800 in Charlottesville, Virginia, where his grandmother was a close friend of Thomas Jefferson, and as a result of that relationship Nicholas and his brothers were invited to come to Monticello for an extended visit in 1817. There Nicholas promptly fell in love with Mr. Jefferson's granddaughter Virginia Jefferson Randolph (a tall girl of "not great personal charms," as Trist's outspoken mother described her) and asked permission to marry her. Virginia's mother and Nicholas' found this prospect chilling, since he was only eighteen and she seventeen;

September and young Trist's departure for the Military Academy at West Point came none too soon to suit either of them. At the academy the new cadet showed certain traits that remained with him all his life: he hated restrictions and discipline; he was frequently ill (with his frail constitution—he was 6 feet tall and weighed only 120 pounds—he had difficulty throwing off colds); he worried incessantly; he wrote interminable letters to his family and friends; and he persisted in a belief that Virginians were a very special people, superior to the inhabitants of other parts of the country. At West Point he became a close friend of young Andrew Jackson Donelson, nephew of the hero of New Orleans—an association that was to have an important effect on his later career.

In the summer of 1821 Trist returned to Monticello, determined to quit West Point, marry Virginia Randolph, and take up the law. This time he was granted permission to propose to his inamorata but lost his nerve at the crucial moment and instead wrote her a letter the next day: "The interview of yesterday," he admitted, "was for the purpose of making a declaration of a passion that you must have often read in me." But once again he was rebuffed, this time by the girl herself, who did not want to leave her family just then and suggested that Trist return to Louisiana—where he had grown up—and read law there. He followed her advice, and three years later he was back at Monticello, where they were married at last on September 11, 1824.

Trist continued his study of the law with Thomas Jefferson and became the feeble ex-President's part-time secretary, riding and walking companion, and confidant. In long talks together Jefferson spoke to him about his views on all the events and personalities of the day, and the old man and the young one developed a truly close friendship. When the Trists' first child was born in May, 1826, she was named for Jefferson's wife; the baby was Jefferson's first great-grandchild and the only one he lived to see, for by this time he was confined to bed most of the time. Trist was with him almost constantly, writing his last letters and conversing for hours with the man who had befriended him. The old statesman was determined to live until July 4, the fiftieth anniversary of the Declaration of Independence he had written, and his last weeks were a triumph of will. All through the night of July 3 Trist remained at his side; with an effort Jefferson asked if it were midnight yet, and when Trist replied that it was, the dying man smiled and murmured, "Ah, just as I wished." A few hours later he was dead.

To Trist, as an administrator of Jefferson's estate, fell the chief burden of settling the former President's chaotic financial affairs (less than five thousand dollars remained in his bank account when he died, and the estate was sorely pressed for funds to run Monticello and support the large family that continued to live there). But despite the demands made upon him, Trist completed his law studies and in November, 1826, was admitted to the Virginia bar. Then followed a brief and unsuccessful ownership of a newspaper, until Trist received an offer of a clerkship in the Department of State from the Secretary, Henry Clay. The job paid fourteen hundred dollars a year, and he accepted with pleasure. Luckily, when Andrew Jackson became President in 1829, Trist's friendship with Jefferson, Madison, and Jackson's nephew Donelson was remembered; unlike so many victims of the spoils system, he was allowed to stay on in his job. Soon Trist and his wife became regulars at White House dinners; Jackson was especially interested in hearing from them about Jefferson's political beliefs, his views on emancipation of the slaves, and his ideas concerning religious freedom.

At the Jefferson memorial birthday dinner in 1830 Trist gave what was technically the chief toast—to the memory of the late President—but his remarks were considerably overshadowed by those of Andrew Jackson: this was the famous occasion on which Jackson rose to his feet, fixed would-be secessionist John C. Calhoun with a steely eye, and stated unequivocally, "Our Union: It must be preserved."

At this time Trist's fluent knowledge of Spanish made him one of the principal State Department informants on Latin-American countries; he was also beginning to handle most of the correspondence between the United States and Russia while James Buchanan was minister there. And opportunity knocked, oddly enough, as a result of a grand social brouhaha at the White House. By spring of 1830 the members of Jackson's Cabinet had taken sides over Peggy O'Neale Eaton, a former barmaid who had become the second wife of John Eaton, the Secretary of War, and while the President stubbornly supported her, the Cabinet officers (except Secretary of State Martin Van Buren) and their wives would have nothing to do with her. Mrs. Andrew Jackson Donelson withdrew as the President's hostess rather than call on her, and suddenly Trist was asked to assume Donelson's place as Jackson's private secretary.

Diplomats, congressmen, and Cabinet officers transacted business through him; it was a demanding, time-consuming position of great responsibility and long hours, from which Trist—fortunately for his relations with his family—was relieved in 1831 by Donelson's reconciliation with his uncle. Then, after two more years in the State Department, Trist received a presidential appointment that promised an opportunity to do something on his own. By now a man of polished manners, impeccable connections, keen insight, and with a broad grounding in foreign affairs, he became consul at the Cuban port of Havana.

He had not been in Havana long before he realized that it had been a mistake to come; it was not a good post for anyone with ambition. The tedious tropical hours found Trist writing incredibly long letters and reports to Washington—reports so full of trivia one wonders if the recipients ever finished reading them (one communication to the Senate Committee on Finance contained fifty-two closely written pages). This was, however, one of the few times in his life that Trist made anything like enough money; he seems to have picked up substantial sums outside his job through notary fees and by investing funds that were deposited with him. But in 1839 some ugly charges were made against Trist—accusations of inefficiency, failure to support American interests, and abetting the slave trade—and his conduct was reviewed by a congressional committee. Although the congressmen gave him a clean bill of health, Trist seems to have been negligent, at the very least, and perhaps even guilty of some of the charges made against him. Certainly many U.S. captains who touched at Havana were highly critical of the consul and his activities. In any case, merit—or the lack of it— sometimes counted for less than the spoils system, and in 1841 Trist received word from the new Whig Secretary of State, Daniel Webster, that he was relieved of his consular duties. Four years later the political tides changed once more, James K. Polk became President, Trist's old friend James Buchanan was appointed Secretary of State, and Trist was named chief clerk of the department. The dying Andrew Jackson, ever a man to support a friend, wrote to Polk endorsing Trist for the job, which paid two thousand dollars a year.

And so it came about, early in 1847, that President Polk decided to send Nicholas P. Trist as his emissary to Mexico, there to await the proper moment to enter into negotiations with a shaky Mexican government. Despite his disappointing performance in Cuba, Trist seemed a natural for the post: in addition to his fluency in Spanish he was thoroughly knowledgeable about the workings of the State Department; as a loyal Democrat he was known to Polk and to members of the Cabinet, yet he had never been active in politics and appeared to have no ambitions in that direction. His assignment, quite simply, was to make his way as inconspicuously as possible to General Winfield Scott's headquarters in Mexico and to forward to the enemy government, via the American commanding general, a proposed treaty of peace drafted by the Secretary of State and approved by administration leaders in Washington. If, by the time he arrived there, the Mexicans had already designated a plenipotentiary empowered to conclude a treaty, Trist was to begin negotiations with him on the basis of the American draft. Its terms were quite definite and had been drawn by Polk and Buchanan in the uneasy awareness that the congressional opposition was ready to pounce on the slightest misstep as a means of repudiating the administration on "the Mexican question." This draft treaty had been submitted to the Cabinet on April 13; revised and approved by both President and Cabinet, it was delivered on April 15, 1847, to Nicholas P. Trist, who was designated a "commissioner plenipotentiary" and bidden Godspeed.

Secrecy, of course, was absolutely vital to the mission, and Polk had every confidence in the discretion of his emissary; but Trist had been gone less than a week when reports of his assignment appeared in the *New York Herald,* the *National Intelligencer, Niles' Weekly Register,* and other newspapers. Polk was understandably furious and alternated between blaming Trist and the State Department for the unpardonable leak (finally he settled on the latter as the most likely source and took a dislike to Buchanan that hardened as time wore on). From New Orleans the unsuspecting Trist wrote one of his wearisome letters to his chief; in thirty verbose pages the only real news he gave Buchanan was that he had arrived in Louisiana after travelling overland via Charleston, Augusta, and Mobile, whence he had taken a steamer to New Orleans. Travelling incognito as "Doctor Tarreau," a French merchant, he had stayed at a "French auberge, of the economical order," rather than at one of the better hotels where someone might recognize him and become suspicious.

For all his precautions Trist managed to call a good deal of attention to himself by his painstaking selection of a vessel to carry him quickly toward his destination; from New Orleans he sailed across the Gulf of Mexico in eight days, arriving on May 6 at Veracruz, where he learned that a supply train would leave on the eighth for Scott's headquarters. And here Trist made a monumental error.

He bore with him a letter of appointment from Buchanan, giving him "full diplomatic powers" to sign a treaty in the name of the United States. He also had two copies of the treaty *projet,* or draft—one of them sealed, for the Mexicans—and his instructions were to place the sealed copy in the hands of General Scott for forwarding to the Mexican authorities. But unfortunately, instead of delivering this document to Scott personally and informing him of its contents, Trist chose to remain at Veracruz and to write a letter to the General in which he requested that the sealed dispatch be delivered to the Mexican minister of foreign affairs. With this communication he enclosed one from William L. Marcy, the Secretary of War, which ordered Scott to transmit the sealed letter to the Mexicans and informed him that "Mr. Trist, an officer from our department of foreign affairs, next in rank to its chief," was now at Army headquarters.

Scott exploded. Under the best of circumstances he was a proud man, excruciatingly sensitive of his reputation and quick to detect a slight whether or not one was intended. Temperament aside, there was also the fact that he was a prominent Whig—a political foe of the administration in Washington—and had long since fallen out with President Polk. In fact, at the time Polk gave Scott command of the Army in May, 1846, the tactless General had written the President an offensive letter complaining about Democratic place-seekers and then had confided to Secretary of War Marcy that he had no stomach for placing himself "in the most perilous of all positions:—a fire upon my rear, from Washington, and the fire in the front, from the Mexicans." Polk's furious reaction had been to excuse Scott from field command in Mexico, leaving him to stew in the capital while Zachary Taylor won the victories and the glory. Finally, in November, 1846, Scott was sent to command the movement on Veracruz and Mexico City, but Polk neither forgave nor forgot. He wrote in his diary:

General Scott has acted with so little discretion since he assumed the command that the confidential plans of the Government which were confided only to himself have been made so public that every Mexican may know them . . . . His vanity is such that he could not keep the most important secrets of the Government which were given to him. He is . . . making such a parade before the public in all he does that there is danger that the objects of the campaign may be entirely defeated. . . .

Such a background was not one to make Scott warm to Trist, and what was to have been a co-operative mission between the two was immediately thrown into jeopardy. Still in the dark about the contents of the proposed treaty, Scott wrote an outraged answer to Trist's first letter. It began: "I see that the secretary of War proposes to degrade me, requiring that I, as commander-in-chief of this army, shall defer to you, the chief clerk in the Dep't of State, the question of continuing or discontinuing hostilities." After getting that out of his system, he indicated that since there was no real Mexican government, he could not forward the dispatch anyway.

Here Nicholas Trist, had he had his wits about him, would have recognized his initial error and attempted to patch things up with the General. But no, he sent off one of his endless communications—an eighteen-page letter that Scott termed "sarcastic, burning, and impolite." By now Polk's peace mission was completely off the rails. Scott, assuming Trist to be an ally of Polk and Buchanan (both of whom he mistrusted because they had opposed his appointment as commanding general), now believed that the government in Washington was deliberately trying to prevent him from having a voice in a truce with the Mexicans. Trist, no less suspicious, wrote his wife that Scott was "decidedly the greatest imbecile that I have ever had anything to do with" and soon was exchanging further angry letters with him. By May 29—more than three weeks after Trist arrived to negotiate a peace with the Mexican government—he had still not even met the U.S. Commander in Chief, who wrote him a curt note referring to one of Trist's thirty-page onslaughts as a "farrago of impudence, conceit, and arrogance."

Fortunately for posterity, both men were now being taken to task by their chiefs: Buchanan wrote Trist telling him that this was no time for a personal vendetta—the government, he said, could not indulge its representatives in a quarrel; Marcy told off Scott in similar fashion. Despite their differences and their abraded nerve ends, both men were good Americans, and they soon realized how detrimental to the nation's interests their conduct was. Nicholas Trist took the initial step to heal the rift: on June 25 he sent Scott a note that was for the first time free of rancor, and Scott replied at once, saying that he would be quite willing to forget the recent unpleasantness. Just then Trist fell ill, causing Scott to feel more compassionate toward him; on July 6 a box of guava marmalade was delivered to the diplomat's sickbed from the Commander in Chief, and with this peace offering the feud ended as suddenly as it had begun. A few days later the two met for the first time and established an immediate *entente cordiale;* soon contrite letters were on their way to Washington from both of them to their respective departments, requesting that the earlier, angry letters of complaint be removed from the files.

But by this time, naturally enough, the President of the United States was thoroughly disgusted with both his representatives. In addition to what he knew from other sources of the Trist-Scott feud, he had been receiving confidential dispatches from Scott's second-in-command, General Gideon J. Pillow, Polk's former law partner in Tennessee, who lost no opportunity to put Scott (and, after the *rapprochement,* Trist) in the worst possible light. Pillow was no fool; he wanted the top job himself, and thanks in part to his machinations, Polk gave renewed consideration to removing Scott from command.

Because of the horrendous delays in getting word from the battlefield to Washington—it often took three or four weeks for a message to reach the capital—there was an Alice-in-Wonderland aspect to the whole affair by this time, so that while Polk fumed at the White House over the lack of progress, events in Mexico were actually pushing matters toward a settlement. In August, Trist met for the first time with the Mexican peace commissioners, who balked at parting with Texas south of the Nueces River and a portion of Upper California. Since the Rio Grande boundary was a *sine qua non* of Trist's instructions, he broke off the talks; but he agreed to submit the Mexican proposal to Washington. Meanwhile the course of the war made peace inevitable: on September 14 the Americans captured Mexico City, Santa Anna and the government fled, and Trist observed that "total dissolution" of the country was at hand. In this state of chaos Mexico would neither negotiate nor fight.

But as far as Washington knew, the unpopular war was merely dragging on, and President Polk could take no comfort from the fact that his Democrats were outnumbered in the House 117 to 110. Having heard further from Pillow that Trist was "acting unwisely," he concluded that no good could possibly come of the peace mission and told the Secretary of State to order his "commissioner plenipotentiary" to return home. So on October 6 Buchanan, unaware that Mexico City had fallen, wrote Trist telling him how conditions had changed since the previous April, reminding him of the American lives and treasure that had been squandered since then, and informing him, finally, that he was recalled. If Trist had written a treaty by the time he received these instructions, the Secretary added, he should of course bring it home with him; but if not, he should not delay his departure even though he might be in the midst of negotiations with the Mexicans. The next day, probably out of friendship and to soften the blow of Trist's recall, Buchanan followed up his official letter with a chatty personal note telling his friend how much he looked forward to having him back in the department again.

Two weeks later—on October 21—letters Trist had written on September 28 were received in Washington, making it clear that he had discussed terms with the Mexicans that exceeded his carefully drafted instructions. That was too much for Polk: his commissioner had "embarrassed future negotiations," the President spluttered. His conduct was "much to be regretted," since he had evidently encouraged the Mexicans to hope for better conditions than he had any right to promise them.

In November, when Trist finally received his letter of recall, along with other letters criticizing his actions, he characteristically sat down and wrote a lengthy justification of his conduct during the negotiations. Time and events certainly seemed to support Trist's hopes that a settlement would be reached before long. He was convinced that the Mexican peace party would form a government; Santa Anna, the defeated leader, had resigned the presidency, and the army had not rallied to him when he fled the Mexican capital. He had been succeeded by Manuel de la Peña y Peña, the president of the supreme court, who appointed a peace advocate as his minister of relations. But just at that moment, with the Mexicans on the verge of peace talks, Trist's recall had arrived. To his wife he wrote of his bitter disappointment; he intended to resign from the State Department, he told her, and "bid adieu *forever* to official life." Over and above his personal chagrin he could not understand why his government—if it sincerely desired peace, as he assumed—did not replace him with another peace commissioner. On December 1, when no word of a replacement had reached him, Trist decided to ignore his recall and stay in Mexico to write a treaty. He had concluded that he could not permit the present opportunity to slip by, and on December 6 he wrote to inform Buchanan of his decision. Even if new commissioners were appointed now, he argued, they could not arrive in time to salvage the situation, and if the opportunity were lost now, it might be gone forever. As for the boundaries, he realized that those limits included in his original instructions were the maximum to which the Mexicans could agree. With great sensitivity Trist wrote, "however helpless a nation may feel, there is necessarily a point beyond which she cannot be expected to go under any circumstances, in surrendering her territory as the price of peace."

One hopes that President Polk was spared the full catalogue of Trist's arguments, since his letter ran to sixty-five pages, but in any event Polk reacted predictably. He ordered Trist out of Army headquarters at once and instructed the United States military commander to inform the Mexicans that Nicholas P. Trist was no longer acting for the United States government. Separately, the President had also decided to replace Scott, having heard from Pillow and other subordinate officers that Scott was taking all the credit for victory over the Mexicans. (Robert E. Lee, a young colonel who had participated in that victory, wrote sadly to a friend concerning the dissensions in the Army. "No one can regret them more than I do. They have clouded a bright campaign. . . . The affair I suppose will soon be before the court . . . but I suspect that if one party [Scott] has been guilty of harshness . . . the other [Pillow and other dissident officers] has been guilty of insubordination.")

Trist responded to adversity by writing still more letters, assuring Buchanan that it was not personal vanity but devotion to duty that prompted him to remain in Mexico. Since he had not been replaced, he repeated, he would stay and achieve a peaceful settlement out of regard for both nations. At long last, on December 30, 1847, peace negotiations began in the town of Guadalupe Hidalgo, outside Mexico City. Trist was handicapped by having not even a secretary to assist him, so he was obliged to keep minutes while listening to the Mexican proposals. Each night he retired to write voluminous letters to Buchanan and to his wife.

On January 25 he was able to inform the Secretary of State that the terms of a treaty had been agreed upon. He had obtained the boundaries called for in his original instructions with only a slight variation at the western extremity; but he believed that the new line, which included the fine port of San Diego, fulfilled his orders in principle, and it was acceptable to the Mexicans. The defeated government was to be paid an indemnity of $15,000,000 for the territory taken by the United States, and the victors were to assume claims against Mexico up to $3,250,000. On his own hook, Trist had worked out a solution to the status of Mexicans living in the ceded lands. If they elected to move out of what was now U.S. territory, they could take their belongings with them, without penalty; if they decided to remain, they could retain their Mexican citizenship provided that within a year they announced their intention to do so—otherwise they would become U.S. citizens.

On February 2, 1848, after a rash of delays caused by the Mexican commissioners, Trist wrote proudly to Buchanan informing him that the Treaty of Peace, Friendship, Limits, and Settlement had been signed that day at Guadalupe Hidalgo. Since Trist now had to remain in Mexico to testify at a court of inquiry ordered by President Polk to examine the charges brought by several members of Scott's staff concerning the conduct of the war, he asked James L. Freaner, correspondent for the *New Orleans Delta,* to carry the treaty back to the United States. As Robert Arthur Brent has written, the completed treaty was the most important achievement of Trist's life. If Trist had acted "at times negligently, at others without tact," he had nonetheless never lost sight of his objective, which was the establishing of peace between Mexico and the United States. "His success," Brent adds, "was the glory of the Polk administration; his disgrace was his own to bear."

And the signs all pointed to disgrace now. When Buchanan brought the treaty to Polk at the White House on February 19, the President was still angry over Trist's behavior, although he was forced to admit that the document met all the conditions given to Trist in April, 1847.

After thinking the matter over, Polk informed his Cabinet that he would submit the treaty to the Senate. If he did not do so, he reasoned, Congress might react by refusing to appropriate money to keep the Army in Mexico, and Polk would have to withdraw the troops without a peace treaty. The Whigs who had attacked the war so bitterly would surely make political capital out of his failure to end it, especially when the treaty embodied the very terms laid down by Polk himself. And finally, Polk was keenly aware of the immense value of the lands ceded by this treaty to the United States. So on February 23—against the advice of Buchanan, who wanted to demand even more territory from the defeated Mexicans—Polk sent the treaty to the Senate, including with it a remarkable note recommending that it be debated on its own merits and without reference to the unfortunate actions of Nicholas P. Trist. The Senate responded by requesting from the President all correspondence relating to Trist's mission, and members of the Foreign Relations Committee informed Polk that they would recommend rejection—not because of the terms of the treaty but because Trist had written it after his recall.

Polk fought back at once. The senators were usurping the powers of the Chief Executive, he stated firmly; the Senate might consider the treaty itself, but not how it had been made—that was the prerogative of the President. There was formidable opposition to the treaty: Thomas Hart Benton led a group of Democrats who opposed ratification on moral grounds—the United States, they said, had no right to any territory other than Texas south to the Nueces River; Daniel Webster, leading the Whig forces, opposed it on the basis that the United States would thereby acquire too much territory; and another group of Democrats was against it because the United States did not get *enough* land. But on March 10, with four senators not voting, the treaty was finally approved by a vote of thirty-eight to fourteen.

And what of the treaty's chief advocate? Poor Trist, after wrangling with Army authorities over his right as an American citizen to remain in Mexico, was placed under arrest as the only means of getting him to leave the country where he had toiled for so long. When he rejoined his family in Washington at last, on May 17, 1848, thirteen months had elapsed since his departure, and he found himself dismissed from government service in disgrace. Buchanan, now completely out of favor with the President, could not help him. (Polk had grown increasingly suspicious of his Secretary of State because of his presidential aspirations: "No candidate for the presidency ought ever to remain in the Cabinet," Polk noted in his diary. "He is an unsafe adviser.") And the President, of course, wanted nothing to do with Trist. Although Trist, more than any other man, was responsible for fulfilling Polk's ambition of rounding out the natural boundaries of the United States, the President could not bring himself to forgive his act of disobedience. Indeed, since Trist had been on a secret mission and therefore was paid out of the President's special funds, he was even denied his full pay by the Chief Executive, who cut off his salary as of November 16, when he received his recall.

In a memorial to Congress, Trist pleaded his cause: he had not sought the appointment as peace commissioner; he had been asked to render a great service to his country; in doing so, he had saved thousands of lives and millions of dollars; he had acquired a vast territory for the United States, extending our western boundary to the Pacific and fixing firm boundaries between Mexico and the United States where none had existed. Surely a man who had achieved that deserved recognition? But the Congress was not in a forgiving mood either.

Virtually destitute, Trist and his wife moved to West Chester, Pennsylvania, in July of 1848. Fortunately, a few friends—Winfield Scott among them—offered him help. During his stay there several writers came to him in search of information about the great men he had known: Henry S. Randall, for his biography of Jefferson; James Parton, for his biography of Jackson; Thomas Hart Benton, for assistance on his *Thirty Years' View*. By 1855, with his wife running a school for young ladies, Nicholas Trist was reduced to taking a job as a clerk for the

Wilmington and Baltimore Railroad Company, where he eventually worked up to paymaster at a salary of $112.50 a month. It was a bitter lot for a man who had been so close to the nation's great and had done so much for his country.

As the Civil War approached, Trist was drawn again to politics—for the New York *World* he wrote an article quoting Jefferson's and Madison's views on secession. To General Scott, a Virginian who was now commanding general of the Union Army, he wrote that he was also a southerner by birth and a Yankee by adoption, but that his sympathies and those of his wife lay with the North and with preservation of the Union. Now and again Trist's friends tried to help him obtain a government job. In 1861 Scott wrote to the Secretary of the Treasury, Salmon P. Chase, stating that Trist had been wronged by Polk and neglected by Taylor, Fillmore, Pierce, and Buchanan; the nation owed Nicholas Trist a great debt, the old soldier added. But Chase did nothing. Finally, in 1870, Senator Charles Sumner made an eloquent speech in Trist's behalf, reminding the Senate of his signal contributions, and a year later Trist received the sum of $14,559.90—money that was owed him for his salary and expenses in Mexico twenty-three years earlier. It came none too soon, for he had had to give up his railway job a year earlier, and the Trists were poverty-stricken. In the summer of 1870 President Grant appointed him postmaster in Alexandria, Virginia. He was paid $2,900 a year, which was more money than he had earned at any time since 1841, but he had less than four years to enjoy this munificence. On February 11, 1874, after suffering a stroke, Trist died.

Anyone wishing to contemplate the part chance plays in human destiny might give some thought to the career of Nicholas P. Trist. His act of rare courage and principle for a cause he believed to be right cost him the support of the President and brought him dismissal, disgrace, poverty, and the total disregard of posterity. Most historians have neglected him entirely or dismissed him as a man of no ability, overlooking the fact that Trist was a victim of an unpopular war and an administration that neither understood nor sympathized with his difficulties or his aspirations. Immovable on matters of principle, Trist determined to do what he considered right. And for this, as well as for the tangible effects of his deed, he deserves better of his country.

What the nation obtained as a result of the treaty he executed singlehandedly was the boundary of the Rio Grande and the cession of territory between that river and the Pacific Ocean—which includes the present states of California, Nevada, Utah, New Mexico, Arizona, a corner of Wyoming, and the western slope of Colorado. Because of the efforts of Nicholas P. Trist, James K. Polk is remembered as the President who, except for Jefferson, added more territory to the nation that any other. When Polk left office the United States was half again as large as when he took the oath. As a final irony, while Nicholas P. Trist and the Mexicans were reaching final agreement in Guadalupe Hidalgo, gold was discovered at Sutter's Mill in California, with consequences beyond all imagining.

August 1970

XIV

The Nature of Southern Separatism

David Potter

Why the South became a section has long concerned historians of the Civil War era. David M. Potter, in his last great contribution to American history, gives a penetrating analysis of this complex and difficult topic.

Ten days after the election of Lincoln, the Augusta, Georgia, *Daily Constitutionalist* published an editorial reflecting on what had happened to American nationalism:

The most inveterate and sanguine Unionist in Georgia, if he is an observant man, must read, in the signs of the times, the hopelessness of the Union cause, and the feebleness of the Union sentiment in this State. The differences between North and South have been growing more marked for years, and the mutual repulsion more radical, until not a single sympathy is left between the dominant influences in each section. Not even the banner of the stars and stripes excites the same thrill of patriotic emotion, alike in the heart of the northern Republican and the southern Secessionist. The former looks upon that flag as blurred by the stain of African slavery, for which he feels responsible as long as that flag waves over it, and that it is his duty to humanity and religion to obliterate the stigma. The latter looks upon it as the emblem of a gigantic power, soon to pass into the hands of that sworn enemy, and knows that African slavery, though panoplied by the Federal Constitution, is doomed to a war of extermination. All the powers of a Government which has so long sheltered it will be turned to its destruction. The only hope for its preservation, therefore, is out of the Union. A few more years of unquiet peace may be spared to it, because Black Republicans cannot yet get full possession of every department of the Government. But this affords to the South no reason for a moment's delay in seeking new guards for its future safety.[1]

When the *Constitutionalist* declared that not a single sympathy was left between the two sections, it exaggerated the degree to which Unionism had been eroded. The tenacity with which Maryland, Virginia, North Carolina, Kentucky, Tennessee, Missouri, and Arkansas clung to the Union during the next five months proved that Unionism retained much vigor. The great body of Americans, in both the North and the South, still cherished their images of a republic to which they could respond with patriotic devotion, and in this sense American nationalism remained very much alive—so much alive, in fact, that it was able to revitalize itself speedily after four years of devastating war. But though they cherished the image, the sectional conflict had neutralized their many affinities, causing antislavery men to depreciate the value of a Union which was flawed by slavery, and causing men in the slaveholding states to give the defense of the slave system such a high priority that they could no longer offer loyalty to a Union which seemed to threaten that system. As these forces of repulsion between North and South came into play, the southern states were, at the same time, drawn closer together by their common commitment to the slave system and their sense of need for mutual defense against a hostile antislavery majority. Southern separatism had been developing for several decades, and how it was about to end in the formation of the Confederate States of America. Historians have spoken of this separatism as "southern nationalism," and of the Confederacy as a "nation." Yet it is clear that much of the old devotion to the Union still survived among many citizens throughout the South and even dominated the action of some southern states until they found themselves forced to fight on one side or the other. Therefore, one must ask: What was the nature of southern separatism? What was the degree of cohesion within the South on the eve of the Civil War? Had the cultural homogeneity of the southern people, their awareness of shared values, and their regional loyalty reached the point of resembling the characteristics of nationalism? Were they drawn together by a sense of separate destiny which required separate nationhood, or were they rather impelled to united action by their common fears of forces that seemed to threaten the foundations of their society?[2]

The understanding of any so-called nationalism—indeed of any development involving sustained cohesive behavior on the part of a large group of people—is complicated by two kinds of dualism. One of these is the dualism of objective and subjective factors, or, one might say, of cultural realities and states of mind. Cohesion can scarcely exist among an aggregate of people unless they share some objective characteristics. Classic criteria are common descent (or ethnic affinities), common language, common religion, and most important and most intangible of all, common customs and beliefs. But these features alone will not produce cohesion unless those who share them also share a self-consciousness of what they have in common, unless they attach distinctive value to what it shared, and unless they feel identified with one another by the sharing. A second dualism lies in the interplay between forces of attraction and forces of repulsion. Wherever and whenever nationalism has developed in notably vigorous form, it has been in circumstances of conflict between the nationalizing group and some other group. In such a situation, the rejection of the out-group not only strengthens the cohesion of the in-group, but imparts to the members of the in-group a greater awareness of what they share. Indeed, it gives them new things to share—common danger, common efforts against the adversary, common sacrifice, and perhaps a common triumph. Sometimes it even impels them to invent fictitious affinities. Thus, conflict and war have been the great catalysts of nationalism, and forces of repulsion between antagonistic groups have probably done more than the forces of affinity within compatible groups to forge the kind of unity that translates into nationalism.

The problem of the South in 1860 was not a simple one of southern nationalism versus American nationalism, but rather one of two loyalties coexisting at the same time—loyalty to the South and loyalty to the Union. Because these loyalties were soon to be brought into conflict, they have often been categorized as "conflicting loyalties," with the implication that if a person has two political loyalties they are bound to conflict, that one of the two must be illegitimate, and that a right-minded person would no more maintain two loyalties then he would commit bigamy. But in fact, strong regional loyalties exist within many nations, and they existed in the United States in other areas besides the South. There was nothing inherently incompatible between regional loyalties and national loyalties as long as they could both be aligned in a pattern in which they remained congruent with one another instead of being at cross-purposes with one another. Any region which had enough power in the federal government could always prevent federal policy and regional policy from coming into any sort of major collision. But the South, by 1860, no longer had such power, or at least no longer had confidence of maintaining such power. Thus the loyalties of southerners became "conflicting loyalties," not necessarily because they loved the Union less but because they had lost the crucial power to keep them from conflicting.[3]

But what were the factors of affinity making for cohesion within the South in 1860, and what were the factors of repulsion between the South and the rest of the Union which gave negative reinforcement to southern unity?

The vast and varied region extended from the Mason-Dixon line to the Rio Grande and from the Ozarks to the Florida Keys certainly did not constitute a unity, either physiographic or cultural. But the whole area lay within what may be called the gravitational field of an agricultural economy specializing in staple crops for which plantations had proved to be effective units of production and for which Negro slaves had become the most important source of labor. This, of course, did not mean that all white southerners engaged in plantation agriculture and owned slaves—indeed only a small but very influential minority did so. It did not even mean that all of the states were heavy producers of staple crops, for the cotton states were only in the lower South. But it did mean that the economy of all of these states was tied, sometimes in secondary or tertiary ways, to a system of plantation agriculture.

Agricultural societies tend to be conservative and orthodox, with strong emphasis on kinship ties and on the observance of established customs. If land is held in great estates, such societies tend to be hierarchical and deferential. Thus, even without slavery, the southern states would have shared certain attributes to a high degree. But the presence of slavery had dictated conditions of its own, and these too were shared very widely throughout the South. Indeed they became the criteria for determining what constituted the South.

A slave system, since it means the involuntary subordination of a significant part of the population, requires a social apparatus distinctively adapted in all its parts to imposing and to maintaining such subordination. In the South, this subordination was also racial, involving not only the control of slaves by their masters but also the control of a population of 4 million blacks by 8 million whites. Such a system cannot be maintained simply by putting laws on the statute books and making formal records that one individual has acquired legal ownership of another. It is axiomatic that the enslaved will tend to resist their servitude and that the slaveowners must devise effective, practical means of control. The first requisite is that the system shall be able to deal with the contingency of insurrection. This alters the priorities, for though the system of subordination may have originated as a means to an end—to assure a permanent labor supply for the cultivation of the staple crops—the immediacy of the hazard of insurrection soon makes the subordination of the slaves an end in itself. This was what Thomas Jefferson meant when he said, "We have a wolf by the ears."

The question of the extent to which the South stood in real danger of slave insurrection is a most difficult one, complicated by the fact that the white South could never for a moment rid itself of the fear of insurrection, yet at the same time could never admit even to itself, much less to others, that its "civilized," "contented," and "loyal" slaves might some day massacre their masters.[4] The fear was probably out of proportion to the actual danger. But the point is that white southerners shared, subjectively, a fear of what the slaves might do, and, objectively, a social system designed to prevent them from doing it.

From the time of Spartacus, all slaveholding societies had lived with the danger of slave revolt. But for the South, no reminders from antiquity were needed. On the island of Santo Domingo, between 1791 and 1804, black insurrectionists under a series of leaders including Toussaint L'Ouverture and Jean Jacques Dessalines had risen in revolt, virtually exterminating the entire white population of the island and committing frightful atrocities, such as burying people alive and sawing them in two. Survivors had fled to New Orleans, Norfolk, and other places in the United States, and southerners could hear from their own lips the stories of their ordeal. Santo Domingo lived as a nightmare in the mind of the South.[5] Within the South itself, of course, there were also revolts or attempted revolts.[6] Gabriel Prosser led one at Richmond in 1800. Some sort of conspiracy under the leadership of Denmark Vesey apparently came near to hatching at Charleston in 1822. Nat Turner led his famous insurrection in Southampton County, Virginia, in 1831. All of these were negligible compared with Santo Domingo or even with revolts in Brazil,[7] but, each one hit an exposed nerve in the southern psyche. Also there were local disturbances. Altogether, one historian has collected more than two hundred instances of "revolts," and while there is reason to believe that some of these were wholly imaginary and that many others did not amount to much, still every one is a proof of the reality of southern apprehensions if not of the actual prevalence of the danger.[8] On isolated plantations, and in districts where blacks heavily outnumbered whites, the peril seemed a constant one. Every sign of restlessness in the slave quarters, every stranger seen along a lonely road, every withdrawn or cryptic look on a slave face, even the omission of some customary gesture of deference, might be the forewarning of nameless horrors lurking just beneath the placid surface of life.

This pervasive apprehension explains much, of course, about southern reaction to the antislavery movement. The southerners were not deeply concerned with what the abolitionists might persuade Congress or the northern public to do—indeed the whole elaborate territorial controversy had many of the aspects of a charade—but with what they might persuade the slaves to do. Southerners were acutely sensitized to direct abolitionist efforts at incitation, such as Henry H. Harnett's speech at a national Negro convention in 1843 in which he urged slaves to kill any master who refused to set them free.[9] It was seldom difficult to make an equation between abolitionist exhortation and slave violence. Thus southerners tried to link Nat Turner's revolt in August 1831 with the first appearance of the *Liberator* eight months previously, but in truth it appears likely that Turner was more influenced by an eclipse of the sun in February than by William Lloyd Garrison in January. Twenty-eight years later, however, John Brown made the equation explicit: a white abolitionist was caught trying to rouse the slaves to revolt. Brown's tying of the bond between abolition and slave revolt gave electrifying importance to what might otherwise have been dismissed as an act of suicidal folly.

This concern about antislavery propaganda as a potential cause of slave unrest also explains in part why white southerners seemed so oblivious to the great difference between the moderate attitude of an "ultimate extinctionist" like Lincoln and the flaming abolitionism of an "immediatist" like Garrison. When southerners thought of extinction it was in terms of Santo Domingo and not in terms of a gradualist reform to be completed, maybe, in the twentieth century. From their standpoint, the election to the presidency of a man who stated flatly that slavery was morally wrong might have a more inciting effect upon the slaves than denunciatory rhetoric from the editor of an abolitionist weekly in Boston.[10]

Since the determination to keep blacks in subordination took priority over other goals of southern society, the entire socioeconomic system had to be conducted in a way that would maximize the effectiveness of racial control. This went far beyond the adoption of slave codes and the establishment of night patrols in times of alarm.[11] It meant also that the entire structure of society must be congruent with the objective, and no institutional arrangements should be countenanced which would weaken control. The blacks should live on plantations not only because plantations were efficient units for cotton production, but because in an era prior to electronic and bureaucratic surveillance, the plantation was a notably effective unit of supervision and control. Also, it provided maximum isolation from potentially subversive strangers. Slaves should be illiterate, unskilled, rural workers not only because the cotton economy needed unskilled rural workers for tasks in which literacy would not increase their usefulness, but also because unskilled rural workers were limited in their access to unsupervised contacts with strangers, and because the illiterate could neither read seditious literature nor exchange surreptitious written communication. In fact, the conditions of employment in the cotton culture seemed to fit the needs of a slave system as neatly as the conditions of slavery fitted the needs of employment in the cotton culture, and if cotton fastened slavery upon the South, it is also true that slavery fastened cotton upon the South.

Even beyond these broad relationships, the system of subordination reached out still further to require a certain kind of society, one in which certain questions were not publicly discussed. It must give blacks no hope of cultivating dissension among the whites. It must commit the nonslaveholders to the unquestioning support of racial subordination, even though they might suffer certain disadvantages from a slave system in which they had no economic stake. This meant that books like *The Impending Crisis* must not circulate, and, indeed, universal education, extending literacy indiscriminately to all lowerclass whites, need not be encouraged. In a mobile society it would be harder to keep slaves firmly fixed in their prescribed positions; therefore, the society must be relatively static, without the economic flexibility and dynamism of a money economy and a wage system. The more speculative a society became in its social thought, the more readily it might challenge the tenets of the established order. Therefore the South tended toward a religion which laid major emphasis on personal salvation and on a Bible-based orthodoxy; toward an educational system which stressed classical learning; and toward reforms of a pragmatic kind, such as better care for the blind, rather than reforms associated with ideology.[12] In short, the South became increasingly a closed society, distrustful of isms from outside and unsympathetic toward dissenters. Such were the pervasive consequences giving top priority to the maintenance of a system of racial subordination.[13]

By 1860, southern society had arrived at the full development of a plantation-oriented, slaveholding system with conservative values, hierarchical relationships, and authoritarian controls. No society is complete, of course, without an ethos appropriate to its social arrangements, and the South had developed one, beginning with a conviction of the superior virtues of rural life. At one level, this conviction embodied a Jeffersonian agrarianism which regarded landowning cultivators of the soil as the best kind of citizens, because their landownership and their production for use gave them self-sufficiency and independence, uncorrupted by commercial avarice—and also because their labor had dignity and diversity suitable to well-rounded men. But at another level, the commitment to rural values had led to a glorification of plantation life, in which even slavery was idealized by the argument that the dependence of the slave developed in the master a sense of responsibility for the welfare of the slaves and in the slaves a sense of loyalty and attachment to the master. This relationship, southerners argued, was far better than the impersonal, dehumanized irresponsibility of "wage slavery, which treated labor as a commodity."

From an idyllic image of slavery and plantation conditions, it was but a short step to the creation of a similar image of the planter as a man of distinctive qualities. Thus, the plantation virtues of magnanimity, hospitality, personal courage, and loyalty to men rather than to ideas held a social premium, and even the plantation vices of arrogance, quick temper, and self-indulgence were regarded with tolerance. From materials such as these, in an era of uninhibited romanticism and sentimentality, the southern upper class built a fully elaborated cult of chivalry, inspired by the novels of Sir Walter Scott and including tournaments, castellated architecture, a code of honor, and the enshrinement of women. Thus, with a mixture of self-deception and idealism, the South adopted an image of itself which some men used as a fiction to avoid confronting sordid reality, while others used it as a standard toward which to strive in order to develop, as far as they were able, the better aspects of human behavior that were latent even in a slaveholding society.[14]

One other belief shared by the men of the South in 1860 was especially important because they felt just uncertain and insecure enough about it to be almost obsessively insistent and aggressive in asserting it. This was the doctrine of the inherent superiority of whites over Negroes. The idea was not distinctively southern, but it did have a distinctive significance in the South, for it served to rationalize slavery and also to unite slaveholders and nonslaveholders in defense of the institution as a system, primarily, of racial subordination, in which all members of the dominant race had the same stake.

This racial prejudice against Negroes cannot, of course, be dismissed as nothing but a rationalization to justify their subordination of the blacks, for in fact it was in part just such prejudice which had originally made blacks and Indians subject to enslavement, while servants of other races were not. Initially, the prejudice may have stemmed from the superiority which technologically advanced societies feel over less advanced societies; it may have reflected something of the attitude of Christians toward the "heathen"; it may have reflected the universal antagonism of in-groups and out-groups or the universal distrust of the unfamiliar. In these aspects, prejudice may even be regarded as a relatively innocent form of ethnocentrism, uncorrupted by consideration of self-interest. But once it became firmly tied to slavery, prejudice began to have certain functional uses which added immeasurably both to the strength of slavery and also to its brutalizing quality. Racial prejudice and slavery together created a vicious circle in which the assumed inferiority of the blacks was used as justification for their enslavement, and then their subordination as slaves was used to justify the belief that they were inferior. The stigma of race increased the degradation of slavery, and servile status, in turn, reinforced the stigma of race.[15]

Doctrines of race not only served to minimize the potentially serious economic divisions between slaveholders and nonslaveholders, but also furnished southerners with a way to avoid confronting an intolerable paradox: that they were committed to human equality in principle but to human servitude in practice. The paradox was a genuine one, not a case of hypocrisy, for though southerners were more prone to accept social hierarchy than men of other regions, still they responded very positively to the ideal of equality as exemplified by Jefferson of Virginia and Jackson of Tennessee. In their politics, they had moved steadily toward democratic practices for whites, and in fact it was argued, with a certain plausibility, that the system of slavery made for a greater degree of democracy within that part of the society which was free, just as it had made for democracy among the freemen of ancient, slaveholding Athens.[16] Still, this only made the paradox more glaringly evident, and no doubt it was partly because of the psychological stress arising from their awareness of the paradox that southern leaders of the late eighteenth and early nineteenth centuries had played with the idea of some day eliminating slavery. That was, in part, why the South had acceded to the exclusion of slavery from the Northwest Territory in 1787 and to the abolition of the African slave trade in 1808. It was why a limited number of southerners had emancipated their slaves, especially during the half-century after the Declaration of Independence, and why a greater number had indulged themselves in a rhetoric which deplored slavery without exactly condemning it. Some had even joined antislavery societies, and southerners had taken the lead in emancipating slaves and colonizing them in Liberia. Thus, for a generation, the great paradox had been masked by the vague and pious notion that at some remote future, in the fullness of time and God's infinite wisdom, slavery would pass away.[17]

By the 1830s, however, this notion had begun to lose its plausibility, for even the most self-deceiving of wishful thinkers could not completely ignore the changes under way. In the lower South the great cotton boom was extending slavery westward across Georgia, Alabama, Mississippi, and Louisiana, and into Arkansas and Missouri. Texas had set up as an independent slaveholding republic. The traffic in slaves between these new states and the older centers of slavery was probably greater in magnitude than the traffic from Africa to the thirteen colonies had ever been.[18] Compared to the birth rate of new slaves, the rate of emancipation was as nothing. Meanwhile, the New England states, New York, Pennsylvania, and New Jersey had abolished slavery.[19] Concurrently, northern anti-slavery men had begun to abandon their tone of gentle, persuasive reproachfulness in discussing slavery and had fallen not only to denouncing slavery as a monstrous sin, but also to castigating slaveholders, as hideous sinners.[20] One should not accept the apologia that the South would itself have got rid of slavery if this indiscriminate onslaught had not compromised the position of the southern emancipationists,[21] but it does seem valid to say that, in the face of such bitter condemnation, white southerners lost their willingness to concede that slavery was an evil—even an inherited one, for which Yankee slave sellers and the southern slave buyers of the eighteenth century shared responsibility. Instead they responded by defending slavery as a positive good.[22] But this made all the more stark the contradiction between equality in theory and servitude in practice, and their only escape was to deny that the blacks were qualified for equality on the same basis as other men. Some theoreticians of race even denied that blacks were the descendants of Adam, which was a long step toward their exclusion not only from equality but also from the brotherhood of man.[23]

With the theory of race thus firmly linked to the theory of slavery, the belief in Negro inferiority was as functional and advantageous psychologically as slavery itself was economically. The belief could be used to justify a certain amount of ill treatment of the blacks and even hostility toward them, since, lacking full humanity, they did not deserve fully human treatment and might justifiably be despised for their inherent deficiencies. By maintaining slavery, the South had violated its own ideal of equality, but by adopting racist doctrine it had both perverted and rejected the ideal, as the only way, other than emancipation, to escape from their dilemma.

All these shared institutions, practices, attitudes, values, and beliefs gave to southern society a degree of homogeneity and to southerners a sense of kinship.[24] But a sense of kinship is one thing, and an impulse toward political unity is another. If one searches for explicit evidence of efforts to unify the South politically because of cultural homogeneity, common values, and other positive influences, rather than as a common negative response to the North, one finds relatively little of it.

Yet any separatist movement in the middle of the nineteenth century could scarcely fail to absorb some of the romantic nationalism that pervaded the Western world. At the Nashville convention in 1850, Langdon Cheves of South Carolina had appealed to all the slaveholding states, "Unite, and you shall form one of the most splendid empires in which the sun ever shone, one of the most homogeneous populations, all of the same blood and lineage [note that to Cheves the black population was invisible], a soil the most fruitful and a climate the most lovely."[25] At about the same time, another South Carolinian had declared that as long as the South was in the Union, it occupied a false and dangerous position as "a nation within a nation."[26]

During the fifties, the spirit of southernism continued to grow. For example, in 1852, the governor of South Carolina spoke of "our place as a Southern Confederacy amongst the nations of the earth."[27] Near the end of the decade a Virginia Unionist complained that Alabamians denounced "anyone who professes the smallest love of the Union as a traitor to his country, namely the South."[28] When secession came, many southerners who favored it held back from separate state action because they wanted the South to act as a unit. Thus the principal opponent of immediate secession in Alabama wrote to a friend in Tennessee, "I resisted the secession of Alabama to the last moment, not because I doubted that it must come sooner or later, but because I preferred to wait until you in Tennessee were ready to go with us."[29] Even more, some southerners who chose to remain with the Union at the same time prepared to defend other southerners who might choose to go out of it. A Missouri newspaper declared that the border states, "while they are devoted to the Union, . . . will not stand idly by and see their sister States—bone of their bone and flesh of their flesh-trampled in the dust. They will not do it."[30]

Even when men in the southern states saw their political destiny as being outside the American union, they did not necessarily visualize a southern republic as the alternative. In 1832, John Pendleton Kennedy declared, "Virginia has the sentiments and opinions of an independent nation," but he meant independence of the Gulf Coast states as well as the Yankees.[31] Twenty-eight years later, Kennedy denounced South Carolina's secession as "a great act of supreme folly and injustice passed by a set of men who have inflamed the passions of the people."[32]

State loyalty no doubt gave ground to regional loyalty between the 1830s and the 1860s, but localism by no means ceased to compete with southernism. It is significant that Robert E. Lee, who was opposed to secession, had no thought of resigning his commission in the United States army until Virginia seceded, but then he "went with his state." It is perhaps also significant that the vice-president of the Confederacy, who had repeatedly hampered its power by his localistic objections, when imprisoned at Fort Warren after the war wrote, "My native land, my country, the only one that is country to me, is Georgia."[33]

The "set of men" whom Kennedy denounced as inflaming the passions of the people might have included at least four well-known southern figures. Two of these, Edmund Ruffin of Virginia and William Lowndes Yancey, might well be labeled southern nationalists, for they both had the vision of a South united by shared distinctive qualities, and both seemed to care more for the South as a whole than for their own states. The other two, Robert Barnwell Rhett of South Carolina and James D. B. De Bow of Louisiana, were also major actors in the secession movement, but for them a united South was primarily an alliance against the North. If nationalism means something more than bitterness against another country, it would be difficult to show that Rhett and De Bow were southern nationalists.

Ruffin, as early as 1845, had declared, "We shall have to defend our rights by the strong hand against Northern abolitionists and perhaps against the tariffites," and he had formed an intense aversion to all Yankees. He later boasted that he was "the first and for some years the only man in Virginia who was both bold and disinterested enough to advocate the dissolution of the Union." After working steadily for more than a decade to publicize the cause of southern rights, Ruffin came forward early in 1858 with a proposal for a League of United Southerners, of which he besought Yancey to assume the leadership. The League was to consist of citizens who would pledge themselves to defend and secure the constitutional rights and interests of the southern states. Members might form local clubs or chapters, which could sent delegates to a general council. "By discussion, publication, and public speeches," the League would have its impact upon the public mind of the South and would offset the excessive individualism with which many southerners approached public questions. In 1860, after Lincoln's election, Ruffin wrote, "If Virginia remains in the Union under the domination of this infamous, low, vulgar tyranny of Black Republicanism, and there is one other state in the Union that has bravely thrown off the yoke, I will seek my domicile in that state and abandon Virginia forever." True to his word, Ruffin went to South Carolina to encourage secession there in December, and to Georgia and to Florida during the weeks that followed, for the same purpose. In April, this sixty-seven-year-old champion of secession was given the distinction of firing one of the first shells in the bombardment of Fort Sumter. In the spring of 1865, utterly broken and unwilling to survive the Confederacy, he took his own life by shooting himself.[34]

Ruffin's friend and associate Yancey was another southerner who had proven extremely jealous in the assertion of southern rights, both in Congress in 1845—1847 and in his refusal to support the Democratic party in 1848 because it would not affirm the rights of slavery in the territories. But his public advocacy of southern separatism came much later and was somewhat inhibited until 1861 by the general stigma attached to the idea of disunion. By 1858, however, he seems to have become fully committed to the idea of a southern republic. In that year, he followed up Ruffin's proposal by organizing at Montgomery the first chapter of the League of United Southerners. In the same year, at a meeting in Montgomery of one of the annual commercial conventions, he sought to stress the southern rather than the purely states' rights theme by addressing his auditors as "My Countrymen of the South," and by suggesting that their gathering was "a foreshadow of a far more important body" which must "ere long assemble upon Southern soil" if injustice and wrong should "continue to rule the hour and the councils of the dominant section of this country." It was at this time also that Yancey put the rhetorical question: "Are you ready, countrymen? Is your courage up to the highest point? Have you prepared to enter upon the great field of self-denial as your fathers did, and undergo, if necessary, another seven years of war in order that you and your posterity may enjoy the blessings of liberty?" But perhaps his most straightforward statement was in a letter to a fellow Alabamian, also in 1858: "No national party can save us; no sectional party can do it. But if we could do as our fathers did, organize Committees of Safety all over the cotton states, (and it is only in them that we can hope for any effective movement), we shall fire the Southern heart—instruct the Southern mind—give courage to each other, and at the proper moment, by one, organized, concerted action, we can precipitate the cotton states into a Revolution."[35]

James D. B. De Bow made his contribution to the southern cause primarily by serving as editor, from 1846, of *De Bow's Review*, the most vigorous and effective of antebellum southern periodicals. With an enlightened feeling for breadth of coverage, he made the *Review* a vehicle for distributing information about the South as a whole and, especially, the southern economy. In the late fifties, he became one of the foremost advocates of secession. No southern nationalist exceeded him in zeal, but under analysis, his southernism seems to be about one part concern for the unity and cultural integrity of the South and nine parts hostility toward abolition and the economic hegemony of the North. If there had been no abolitionists, it appears that De Bow might have remained, as he began, an exultant spokesman of expansionist American nationalism.[36]

Robert Barnwell Rhett, affiliated with the Charleston *Mercury* since 1830, had been demanding separation from the North intermittently for a generation. His speech at Grahamville, South Carolina, on July 4, 1859, was a prelude to the final push by the fire-eaters, for Rhett declared that the South should either prevent the election of a Republican president in 1860 or secede. In his peroration he began with the incredible statement that he had spent twenty years trying to preserve the Union, and then, he said, "I turned at last to the salvation

of my native land—the South—and in my latter years did all I could to dissolve her connection with the North, and to establish for her a Southern Confederacy." A toast was drunk that
day to "The election of a Black Republican President—the signal for the dissolution of the
Federal Union and the establishment of a Southern Confederacy."[37]

For all the electrifying rhetoric on this and other occasions there were no committees of
correspondence, and the League of United Southerners apparently never expanded beyond
three towns in Alabama. There was, however, one widespread southern organization, though
it never did anything effective for the cause of southern nationalism. In 1859, at Louisville,
Kentucky, a somewhat itinerant promoter and self-styled general, George F. Bickley, launched
a fraternal enterprise which he called the Knights of the Golden Circle. Whether Bickley really had gorgeous dreams of a tropical empire or was merely selling such dreams to earn a living
is not clear, but during 1860 he spent much of his time perambulating the South recruiting
knights. The KGC, taking shrewd advantage of the spirit of filibusterism both in the South
and in other parts of the country, and also of the rising tide of southernism, proposed that
Mexico be acquired for the United States through negotiation with Benito Juárez. This annex-
ation would solve the difficulties of the South as a minority section by bringing twenty-five
new slave states into the Union. But if the North should spurn this glorious opportunity, or if
sectional antagonisms should lead to disruption of the Union, the South could make the an-
nexation alone and create a great tropical empire extending in a golden circle from the tip of
Florida, around the shores of the Gulf of Mexico, to the Yucatán Peninsula. The southern
press lavished an astonishing amount of favorable attention upon this hare-brained scheme,
and General Bickley, a man not given to understatement, claimed a membership of 65,000
Knights in September 1860, and 115,000 in November. Probably one figure was as reliable as
the other. In any case, the Knights played no significant part in 1861 in either forming or up-
holding the southern Confederacy.[38]

The southern commercial conventions provided perhaps the best opportunities to coordinate the impulses of southern nationalism. At first, they had carefully disavowed any spirit of
sectional antagonism, even toasting the North and proclaiming a purpose to emulate the enterprise of their northern brothers. But at Charleston in 1854, Albert Pike of Arkansas advo-
cated a program of southern joint action in the form of a corporation, chartered and financed
by the fifteen slave states collectively, to build a Pacific railroad by the southern route. Pike
also introduced overtly, perhaps for the first time at any of these conventions, the theme of
disunion. The South, he said, should seek equality with the North within the Union, but if
the South "were forced into an inferior status, she would be better out of the Union than in
it." The following year at New Orleans, one delegate proposed the reopening of the African
slave trade, another complained that the monopoly of northern textbooks in southern schools
made for an education that was "unsouthern," and the St. Louis *Democrat* denounced the
conventions as disunionist. At Richmond in 1856, a toast was offered which for the first time
defined the boundaries of a prospective southern republic: "on the North by the Mason-Dixon line, and on the South by the Isthmus of Tehuantepec, including Cuba and all other lands
on our Southern shore which threaten Africanization."

In the last four conventions, held at Savannah, Knoxville, Montgomery, and Vicksburg
from 1856 to 1859, politicians and fire-eaters had largely replaced businessmen as the dominant delegates, and the meetings had become to a great extent rallies in support of disunion
and a southern nation. At Savannah, the chairman spoke of "the beloved Southern section"
and addressed his auditors as "free citizens of the South." The *New York Times* concluded that
the primary object of the conventions was "to separate in the public mind of the South,
Southern interests from national interests," while the Louisville *Journal* denounced most of

the members of the convention as "brazen-faced disunionists . . . as thoroughly treasonable as the vilest conclave that ever polluted the soil of South Carolina."[39]

The convention at Montgomery in 1858 marked a high tide of militant southernism. With Ruffin, Yancey, and Rhett all in attendance, disunion had a field day, but the discussions also revealed the lack of a united South and the dilemma which secessionists would face: if they forced the issue, they might destroy the southern unity they were seeking to create; if they waited for such unity to become complete, they might never act. Yancey spoke eloquently of "a unity of climate, a unity of soil, a unity of production, and a unity of social relations." The business committee harmoniously endorsed the League of United Southerners. But when Yancey called for reopening the African slave trade, Roger Pryor of Virginia charged that his real purpose was dissolution of the Union. He, Pryor, would not dissolve it on this ground. Questioned as to the ground on which he would be willing to dissolve it, he replied, "Give me a case of oppression and tyranny sufficient to justify a dissolution of the Union, and give me a united South, and then I am willing to go out of the Union." A delegate retorted that if Pryor had to wait for an undivided South, he would never secede, but Pryor, not at all abashed, told him to remember that, in case of war, "the first onset would have to be met by Virginia, and one must not expect of her the same inordinate enthusiasm felt by others not as vulnerably situated as she." The impasse was partially broken by a more conservative Alabamian, Henry Hilliard, who suggested that the election of a Black Republican to the presidency would result in the subversion of the government and the dissolution of the Union—with the implication that the former would justify the latter. Pryor agreed that the election of a Republican president would probably be sufficient grounds for secession, adding that in such an event Virginia would be as ready to act as Alabama.[40]

Since nationalism is frequently as much a negative phenomenon as a positive one, it does not disprove the reality of southern nationalism to say that the southern movement arose primarily from antagonism to the North. Yet one is left with a feeling that the South did not want a separate destiny so much as it wanted recognition of the merits of southern society and security for the slave system, and that all the cultural ingredients of southern nationalism would have had very little weight if that recognition and that security had been forthcoming. Southern nationalism was born of resentment and not of a sense of separate cultural identity. But the cultural dissimilarities of North and South were significant enough to turn a campaign for the protection of southern interests into a movement with a strong color of nationalism. This does not mean that there was *never* a deeply felt southern nationalism. There was. But it resulted from the shared sacrifices, the shared efforts, and the shared defeat (which is often more unifying than victory) of the Civil War. The Civil War did far more to produce a southern nationalism which flourished in the cult of the Lost Cause than southern nationalism did to produce the war.

Even the manifestoes of the self-appointed custodians of southernism do not reflect the impulse to fulfill the unique potentialities of a unique society. Their complaint was not that the Union inhibited a robust but repressed culture struggling to be born, but rather that their cultural dependence upon the Yankees was humiliating. Why must southern children study textbooks written and published in the North, and incompatible with southern values? Why must southern readers subscribe to northern magazines instead of supporting southern journals which published southern authors? The frequency and the plaintiveness of this question is evidence of the rather self-conscious literary irredentism of a very small number of southern writers, but it also affords striking proof of the lack of cultural self-consciousness on the part of a large number of southern readers who ignored these pleas and continued to get their reading matter from the North. What the South's struggling authors wanted was not separation from the North but recognition by the North. Why must northern critics insist, they wanted to know, on lauding the doggerel of John Greenleaf Whittier while ignoring the genius of William Gilmore Simms? It was intolerable to have the *Atlantic Monthly* characterizing the South as a coarse and sordid oligarchy unhallowed by antiquity and unadorned by culture. But instead of separation, what they wanted was to escape the condescension of the metropolis toward the provinces, to attain some literary triumph which would force the North to acknowledge southern merit. Meanwhile, they retorted in kind, disparaging northern society as mercenary, materialistic, hypocritical, Godless, ill-mannered, and lacking in any class of gentlemen.[41] In 1858 a prominent Tennessee historian declared, "The high-toned New England spirit has degenerated into a clannish feeling of profound Yankeeism. . . . The masses of the North are venal, corrupt, covetous, mean, and selfish." But "the proud Cavalier spirit of the South," he added, not only remained but had become "intensified."[42] Early in 1860, Robert Toombs remarked in the Senate, "The feeling of a common interest and a common destiny, upon which foundations alone society can securely and permanently rest, is . . . rapidly passing away."[43] Later in the same year, conditions reminded Francis Lieber of what Thucydides had said of Greece at the time of the Peloponnesian War: "The Greeks did not understand each other any longer, though they spoke the same language."[44] As the secession movement got under way, the antitheses were drawn sharper and the stereotypes became caricatures. The "Yankee-Union" was "vile, rotten, infidelic, puritanic, and negro-worshipping."[45] The people of the South were descended from Cavaliers, the people of the North from Roundheads; the people of the South from the conquering Normans of 1066; the people of the North from the subjugated race of Saxons.[46] With such dualisms as these, it was an easy step to the view that the day for brotherhood was "past, irrevocably past," or that the North and the South must separate, not because of Lincoln's election, but because of "the incompatibility growing out of two systems of labor, crystallizing about them two forms of civilization."[47]

In December 1860, when South Carolina seceded, she gave formal affirmation to all these ideas in an Address of the People of South Carolina. "The Constitution of the United States," it declared, "was an experiment. The experiment consisted, in uniting under one Government, peoples living in different climates, and having different pursuits and institutions." In short, the experiment failed. Instead of growing closer together, the sections grew farther apart. By 1860, "their institutions and industrial pursuits, have made them, totally different peoples. . . . All fraternity of feeling between the North and the South is lost, or had been converted into hate; and we, of the South, are at last, driven together, by the stern destiny which controls the existence of nations."[48]

During the secession winter, the South produced a ceaseless flow of statements such as these—all affirmed with such intensity that they suggest the rise of southern nationalism to a fully matured, triumphant, and unchallenged fulfillment.[49] If antipathy toward the Yankees and antipathy toward the American Union could be equated, this inference might be valid. But feelings of anger and fear which part of a society may feel toward another part are not the same as the cultural differences between two distinct civilizations. Nor did hostility toward other elements in the Union necessarily imply hostility toward the Union itself. There was still a vigorous Union nationalism remaining in the South, and in spite of all the emotional fury, there was probably more cultural homogeneity in American society on the eve of secession than there had been when the Union was formed, or than there would be a century later. Most northerners and most southerners were farmer folk who cultivated their own land and cherished a fierce devotion to the principles of personal independence and social equalitarianism. They shared a great pride in the Revolutionary heritage, the Constitution and "republican institutions," and an ignorance about Europe, which they regarded as decadent and infinitely inferior to the United States. They also shared a somewhat intolerant, orthodox Protestantism, a faith in rural virtues, and a commitment to the gospel of hard work, acquisition, and success. Southern aristocrats might disdain these latter attributes, but the cotton economy was itself prime evidence of southern possession of them. The development of steamboats and railroads and the telegraph had generated an internal trade which bound the sections increasingly closer economically and had generated a nationwide faith in American progress and in the greatness of America's destiny. The South participated in all of these experiences, and the crisis of 1860 resulted from a transfer of power, far more than from what some writers have called the divergence of two civilizations.[50]

The degree to which southern nationalism still fell short of a culmination was evident from the continued devotion to the Union of a large part of the population of the South. In the election of 1860, southern voters had had a choice between two stout defenders of the Union—Douglas and Bell—and one candidate who denied that he favored disunion. The Unionist candidates carried 49 percent of the vote in the seven states of the original Confederacy.[51] Even after Lincoln's election, Unionism survived in those state and maintained dominance in the upper South. A high proportion of former Whigs, who had supported Bell in the election, boldly reaffirmed their Unionism. The Vicksburg *Whig* declared, "It is treason to secede." It also predicted the consequences of secession: "strife, discord, bloodshed, war, if not anarchy." Disunion would be a "blind and suicidal course."[52] The Unionists also castigated the secessionists for their irresponsibility. The governor of Louisiana said regretfully that the dissolution of the Union was spoken of, "if not with absolute levity, yet with positive indifference"; and Alexander H. Stephens complained that the secessionists really did not want redress for their grievances; they were "for breaking up" merely because they were "tired of the govnt."[53] In the upper South, the Unionists reminded one another of the importance of their material ties with the North. Senator Crittenden of Kentucky had pointed out in 1858 that "the very diversity of . . . resources" of the two sections led to interdependence and was "a cause of natural union between us." In 1860 a Tennessee newspaper declared: "We can't do without their [the North's] productions, and they can't do without our Rice, Sugar, and Cotton."[54]

Besides, the Union itself remained a priceless asset, an "empire of freemen," in the words of one southern president, with "the most stable and permanent Government on earth."[55] "As a nation," said a North Carolina newspaper, "We possess all the elements of greatness and power. Peace smiles upon us from all quarters of the globe; a material prosperity, unparalleled in the annals of the world, surrounds us; our territory embraces almost the entire continent; we enjoy widespread intelligence and universal plenty; we are happy; WE ARE FREE."[56]

Southern nationalism had arrived, but Union nationalism had by no means departed. Sometimes, indeed, a man might declare his allegiance to both, in the same breath. Thus, Alexander H. Stephens as early as 1845 had said, "I have a patriotism that embraces, I trust, all parts of the Union, . . . yet I must confess that my feelings of attachment are most ardent towards that with which all my interests and associations are identified. . . . The South is my home—my fatherland."[57]

To one who thinks of nationalism as a unique and exclusive form of loyalty, the divisions of the South between Union nationalism and southern nationalism, and the movement of individuals from one camp to the other, will look like some sort of political schizophrenia. But if one thinks of nationalism instead as but one form of group loyalty, it becomes easier to see that the choice between Union nationalism and southern nationalism was basically a question of means—a question of whether the slaveholding society would be safer in the Union or in a southern Confederacy. The South had fared extremely well in the Union of

1787, with its bisectional balance, its lack of centralized power, and most of all, its indulgent attitude toward slavery. As these advantages dwindled, men began to speak of the Union of 1787 as the "Old Union," and the South cherished its memory with nostalgia and reverence, as "the Union of our Fathers." In 1861 the New Orleans *Picayune* opposed secession and called instead for "the reconstruction of the old Union."[58]

Not only did southerners think fondly of a nation within which the southern social system had been secure. They also said quite directly that the security of their system was the criterion by which they should choose between the existing nation and the incipient one. Many recognized that even if a southern confederacy were successfully formed, its existence would not prevent slaves from fleeing north to freedom, would not silence abolitionist attacks on slavery, and would probably mean an abandonment of the rights which slavery, under the Dred Scott decision, enjoyed in the territories. The South would have to resist antislavery in any case, and so perhaps it could fight more effectively inside the Union than outside. Abolitionists might be more dangerous as foreign neighbors than as fellow citizens. The Union, said Benjamin F. Perry of South Carolina, "should be saved as a bulwark against abolition."[59] Secession would endanger slavery more than Lincoln would. Alexander H. Stephens warned that nothing was more dangerous for the South than "unnecessary changes and revolutions in government." He considered "slavery much more secure in the Union than out of it" and thought that Lincoln would make "as good a President as Fillmore did."[60] Hershel V. Johnson, a secessionist in 1850 but converted to Unionism by 1860, offered a simple and pragmatic explanation for his change: "I had become satisfied that Slavery was safer in than out of the Union."[61] The *North Carolina State Journal* denied that the essential problem was a conflict of loyalties. "The question," it said, "is not union or disunion, but what shall she [North Carolina] do to protect herself."[62]

As long as the North and the South had remained fairly equal in economic and political power, and as long as slavery had been immune to serious attack, the two sections had coexisted in a reasonably harmonious way. They could differ and even quarrel fiercely over various political questions without placing the Union in great danger. But as time passed, the sections ceased to be evenly balanced, and slavery lost its immunity. These simultaneous developments had an overpowering effect in the South. They generated a feeling of being on the defensive, the psychology of a garrison under siege.[63]

At the beginning of the century, the population of the slave states had been equal to that of the North, and the South had had 40 percent of the total white population. But by 1860, northerners outnumbered southerners in a ratio of 6:4 in total population and 7:3 in white population. At the beginning of the century, Virginia and Kentucky might talk about the power of individual states to prevent enforcement of the Alien and Sedition Acts, but they really did not need to resort to such minority devices, for they still had enough political muscle to put a Virginian into the White House in 1801 and to keep the presidency in the hands of southerners for forty-two of the next fifty years. But by 1860, a man might win the presidency without even being on the ticket in most of the southern states. The increasing discrepancies in wealth, productive capacity, and technological advancement were equally apparent. William L. Yancey told a New York audience in 1860, "You have power in all the branches of the government to pass such laws as you like. If you are actuated by power, or prejudice, or by the desire of self-aggrandizement, it is within your power . . . to outnumber us and commit aggression upon us." The South was not only in a minority but, more ominously, in a permanent and dwindling minority.[64]

Its power was dwindling, moreover, at the very time when the South found itself exposed to increasingly sharp attack by antislavery spokesmen. During the first forty years of the republic, slavery had certainly been criticized, but it had virtually never been threatened. Antislavery men had been gradualists, who proposed no sudden action; emancipationists, who relied on reasoned appeals to the slaveholders to practice voluntary manumission; colonizationists, whose program looked to the removal of the blacks along with the removal of slavery. Slavery had been respectable, and eight of the first twelve men who reached the presidency were slaveholders. Until 1856, no major political party had ever, at the national level, made a public pronouncement against slavery, and in northern cities, mobs that included "gentlemen of property and standing" had hounded and harassed the abolitionists.[65] But in the 1830s, the abolitionist had captured the antislavery movement, demanding immediate, involuntary emancipation enforced by law, denouncing all slaveholders with unmeasured invective, and even sometimes proclaiming the equality of the blacks.[66] Antislavery parties had appeared for the first time in the 1840s, and a major antislavery party in the mid-fifties. In 1856 the Republicans had branded slavery as a relic of barbarism, and in 1860 they had elected to the presidency a man who said that slavery must be put on a course toward ultimate extinction. In 1859 many northerners had mourned the hanging of a would-be leader of slave insurrection. Meanwhile, slavery had been disappearing from the Western world and remained significant only in Brazil, Cuba, and the southern United States.

If the government of the United States should pass into the control of opponents of slavery, as it seemed about to do in 1860, the South had realistic reason to fear the consequences, not so much because of legislation which the dominant party might adopt, but because the monolithic, closed system of social and intellectual arrangements upon which the South relied for the perpetuation of slavery might be disrupted. Once Lincoln was in office, he could appoint Republican judges, marshals, customs collectors, and postmasters in the South. This would strike a heavy blow at the mystique of planter control which had been vital to the maintenance of the southern system. With their political domination challenged, the planter class might lose some of their social ascendancy also. More explicitly, Lincoln might appoint abolitionists or even free Negroes to public office in the South. And even if he did not do this, the new Republican postmasters would refuse to censor the mails or to burn abolitionist papers.[67] The temptation of postmasterships might attract some nonslaveholding southerners and make them the nucleus of an antislavery force in the South. For a slave system vitally dependent upon the solidarity of the whites, this loomed as a frightful menace. It was irrelevant to say that the Republicans did not constitute a threat because they still lacked the majorities which would enable them to enact legislation in Congress. They did not need to enact legislation.[68]

By 1860, southerners were acutely conscious of their minority status and their vulnerability to abolitionist agitation. After Harpers Ferry, a wave of fear swept through the South, subsiding somewhat in the spring and then rising again during the presidential campaign. There were reports and more reports of dark conspiracies for slave revolts, engineered by abolitionist incendiaries infiltrating the South in guises such as peddlers and itinerant piano tuners. Though seldom verified, the rumors were usually rich in details of plots uncovered; murder, rape, and arson prevented; and malefactors punished. For a time, the atmosphere was such that any fire of unknown origin or any white southerner's death of obscure causes might set off a report of arson or poisoning. And editors, no more immune than their readers, transformed into "news items" the fantasies of a society obsessed with fears of slave insurrection and with apocalyptic visions of terrible retaliation.[69]

When Lincoln's election came at last, the people of the slaveholding states were not united in any commitment to southern nationalism, nor to a southern republic, nor even to political separatism. But they *were* united by a sense of terrible danger. They were unit-ed, also, in a determination to defend slavery, to resist abolitionism, and to force the Yan-kees to recognize not only their rights but also their status as perfectly decent, respectable human beings. "I am a Southern man," a Missouri delegate had asserted in the Baltimore convention, "born and raised beneath the sunny sky of the South. Not a drop of blood in my veins ever flowed in veins north of Mason's and Dixon's line. My ancestors for 300 years sleep beneath the turf that shelters the bones of Washington, and I thank God that they rest in the graves of honest slaveholders."[70]

Motivated by this deeply defensive feeling, the people of the South also tended to accept an interpretation of the Constitution maximizing the autonomy of the separate states. Ac-cording to this view, each state, when ratifying the Constitution, had retained its full sover-eignty. The states had authorized the federal government, as their agent, to administer for them collectively certain of the functions which derive from sovereignty, but they had never transferred the sovereignty itself, and they could resume the exercise of all sovereign functions at any time by an act of secession, adopted in the same kind of state convention that had rati-fied the Constitution. However arid, and antiquarian it may now seem, the acceptance of this doctrine by a majority of the citizens of the Old South gave to it a historical importance inde-pendent of its validity as a constitutional theory. It is impossible to understand the rift be-tween North and South without recognizing that one factor in this rift was a fundamental disagreement between the sections as to whether the American republic was a unitary nation in which the states had fused their sovereign identities or a pluralistic league of sovereign po-litical units, federated for certain joint but limited purposes. Perhaps the United States is the only nation in history which for seven decades acted politically and culturally as a nation, and grew steadily stronger in its nationhood, before decisively answering the question of whether it was a nation at all. The framers of the Constitution had purposely left this question in a state of benign ambiguity. They did so for the best possible reason, namely that the states in 1787 were in hopeless disagreement about it, and some would have refused to ratify an explic-itly national Constitution. Thus, the phrase "*E pluribus unum*" was a riddle as well as a motto. The utmost which the nationalists of 1787 could accomplish was to create the framework within which a nation might grow, and to hope it would grow there. But the legal question of the nature of the Union had been left in doubt and became a subject of controversy. The lead-ing spokesmen on both sides were lawyers who confined themselves largely to drawing refined inferences from the exact wording of the Constitution and following every clue as to the in-tentions of the framers. In this kind of deductive reasoning, as it turned out, the defenders of state sovereignty had quite a strong case, made up essentially of five arguments:

First, at the time of the Articles of Confederation, proposed in 1777 and ratified in 1781, the states had explicitly included a statement that "each state retains its sovereignty, freedom and independence," and the treaty by which Britain recognized independence in 1783 named each of the thirteen states individually and acknowledged them to be "free, sovereign and in-dependent states."[71]

Second, when the Constitution was framed in 1787, it was ratified by each state, acting separately and for itself only, so that the ratification of the requisite number of states (nine) would not have made any other state a member of the "more perfect union" under the Consti-tution unless that other state ratified.[72] It was true that the preamble said, "We the people of the United States . . . do ordain and establish this Constitution," and Daniel Webster, the Great Expounder of the Constitution and the great oracle of nationalism, had rung the changes on "We the people" as a proof that the citizens of all the states were merged into a consolidated Union.[73] But the term "people" was not used to indicate that one people instead of thirteen peoples were ratifying, but rather to distinguish between action by state govern-ments and action by citizens exercising their ultimate power. Under the Articles, the central government had derived its power from the state governments *and* they in turn had derived their power from the people. Hence the central government could act only upon the state governments and not upon any citizens directly. But under the state constitutions and the Constitution of 1787, the people of each state (or the peoples of the thirteen states), by two separate acts, established for themselves two separate governments—a state government, oper-ating locally for that state only, and a central government, operating collectively for the states together. Neither government had created the other; neither was subordinate to the other; they were coordinate governments, both sanctioned directly by the action of citizens, both operating directly on citizens without having to mediate through the machinery of the other government, and both subject to the ultimate authority, not of one or the other,[74] but of the constituencies which had established them. It was a truly dualistic system. This was the real implication of the term "We the people," and in the Convention the framers had originally planned a phrasing which would have avoided the confusion that later arose. They had agreed to list by name, one after another, "the people" of each of the thirteens states, severally, as the ordained and establishing parties. But recognizing the awkwardness that would result if the Constitution should name as a member of the Union a state whose people later refused to rat-ify, they substituted the term "We the people of the United States," using it as a plural and not as a singular term.[75]

Third, the proceedings of the Convention showed clearly that its members had deliber-ately taken up the question of whether the federal government could coerce a state govern-ment, and had positively refused to confer any such power.[76]

Fourth, at the time of ratification, three states had specifically reserved their right to re-sume the powers which they were granting by their acts of ratification.[77]

Fifth, the continued integrity of the states was reflected in the structural features of the new government which provided that the states should be represented equally in the Senate, that the states alone could cast electoral votes for president, that the states alone could ratify amendments to the Constitution, and that, under the Tenth Amendment in the Bill of Rights, "The powers not delegated to the United States by the Constitution nor prohibited by it to the States are reserved to the states respectively, or to the people."[78]

From these arguments, the political theorists of the South had developed the doctrine of state sovereignty and, from it, of the right of secession. The Virginia and Kentucky Res-olutions of 1798, written by Jefferson and Madison, had asserted state sovereignty and had declared each state to be "the judge . . . of the mode and measure of redress" in cases in which the federal government might violate the Constitution. In 1803, St. George Tucker of Virginia, in a treatise on the Constitution, had asserted that each state, "still sovereign, still independent . . . is capable . . . to resume the exercise of its functions to the most un-limited extent." Later, Spencer Roane and John Taylor of Virginia and Robert Y. Hayne of South Carolina, in his famous debates with Webster, all added cogent affirmations of state sovereignty. In 1832, Calhoun's state papers on Nullification gave classic formulation to the same doctrine. Calhoun did not want to secede, and did not emphasize a doctrine of secession, but he made explicit his view that a state's ultimate recourse was to withdraw from the Union. In 1840, Abel P. Upshur of Virginia published a treatise which a modern critic has called "perhaps the strongest historical analysis for the support of state sovereignty . . . ever . . . written." Three years later, Henry St. George Tucker, a law profes-sor like his father, compiled the existing arguments and added some of his own. Before his death in 1850, Calhoun again discussed the nature of the Union in his *Discourse on the*

Constitution. By this time, the doctrine of secession had become, for a majority of political-ly minded southerners, a fundamental tenet of southern orthodoxy.[79]

There were, to be sure, a good many southerners who preferred to claim instead a right of revolution, as asserted in the Declaration of Independence. But the southern majority had committed itself to the right of secession during the crisis of 1846—-1850, and James M. Mason, in 1860, was able to say, "Fortunately for the occasion and its consequences, this is not an open question in Virginia. Our honored state has ever maintained that our Federal sys-tem was a confederation of sovereign powers, not a consolidation of states into one people. . . . Whenever a state considered the compact broken, and in a manner to endanger her safety, such state stood remitted, as in sovereign right, to determine for herself . . . both the mode and measure of redress."[80]

Against the defenders of this doctrine, the defenders of nationalism did not come off as well as they might have, partly because they accepted the assumption that the nature of the Union should be determined by legal means, somewhat as if it were a case in the law of con-tracts. Yet in fact, the nature of the Union had been changing constantly, as the states in-creased in number until those which had created the Union were outnumbered by those which the Union had created. Between 1804 and 1865, the Constitution was not once amended, the longest such interval in American history. But while the text of the charter re-mained the same, the republic itself was transformed.

A thousand forms of economic and cultural interdependence had developed. Such chang-es do not occur without corresponding changes in the attitude of the people, and in a century of rampant nationalism throughout the Western world, there were probably no people who carried national patriotism and self-congratulation to greater lengths than the Americans, and this included the South. Regardless of arrangements made in 1787, nationalism changed the nature of the Union and began to answer the riddle of *pluribus* or *unum*. But nationalism grew at different rates and in different ways in North and South, and by 1860, the sections found themselves separated by a common nationalism. Each was devoted to its own image of the Union, and each section was indistinctly aware that its image was not shared by the other. The South had no idea how ruthlessly its northern Democratic allies were prepared to deal with anyone who tried to tamper with the Union. The North had no idea how fiercely south-ern Unionists who valued the Union for themselves would defend the right of other southern-ers to reject it for *them*selves and to break it up without being molested.

The dual focus of southern loyalties, even as late as 1860, has led one author to say very aptly that the South by then had become a kingdom, but that it did not become a nation until thrust into the crucible of the Civil War.[81] Within this kingdom there was sharp disagreement between the advocates of a southern Confederacy and those who favored remaining in the Union. Yet underneath the disagreement was consensus on two important points. Most southern Unionists shared with secessionists the conviction that no state should be forced to remain in the Union, and most of them also believed in secession as a theoretical right. Whether it was justified or opportune could still be debated. But for southerners generally, the *right* of a state to secede, if it chose to do so, had become an article of faith.

Endnotes

1. Dwight Lowell Dumond (ed.), *Southern Editorials on Secession* (New York, 1931), p. 242.

2. "The only question is . . . can the Union and slavery exist together." William Henry Trescot to William Porcher Miles, Feb. 8, 1859, quoted in Steven A. Channing, *Crisis of Fear: Secession in South Carolina* (New York, 1970), p. 69.

3. David M. Potter, "The Historian's Use of Nationalism and Vice Versa," in his *The South and the Sectional Crisis* (Ba-ton Rouge, 1968), pp. 34–83.

4. On southern fears of slave insurrection, see especially Clement Eaton, *Freedom of Thought in the Old South* (Durham, N.C., 1940), pp. 89–117; Eaton, *The Growth of Southern Civilization, 1790–1860* (New York, 1961), pp. 72–97; John S. Kendall, "Shadow over the City" [New Orleans], *LHQ*, XXII (1939), 142–165; Harvey Wish, "The Slave Insurrection Panic of 1856," *JSH*, V (1939), 206–222; Ollinger Crenshaw, *The Slave States in the Presidential Election of 1860* (Baltimore, 1945), pp. 89–111; Channing, *Crisis of Fear*, pp. 17–62, 92–93, 264–273; Kenneth M. Stampp, *The Peculiar Institution: Slavery in the Ante-Bellum South* (New York, 1956), pp. 132–140; also, citations in note 6, below.

5. Winthrop D. Jordan, *White Over Black: American Attitudes toward the Negro, 1550–1812* (Chapel Hill, 1968), pp. 375–386.

6. Joseph Cephas Carroll, *Slave Insurrections in the United States, 1800–1865* (Boston, 1938); Herbert Aptheker, *American Negro Slave Revolts* (New York, 1943); Marion D. deB. Kilson, "Towards Freedom: An Analysis of Slave Revolts in the United States," *Phylon*, XXV (1964), 175–187; Harvey Wish, "American Slave Insurrections before 1861," *JNH*, XXII (1937), 299–320; Nicholas Halasz, *The Rattling Chains: Slave Unrest and Revolt in the Antebellum South* (New York, 1966); R. H. Taylor, "Slave Conspiracies in North Carolina," *NCHR*, V (1928), 20–34; Davidson Burns McKibben, "Negro Slave Insurrections in Mississippi, 1800–1865," *JNH*, XXXIV (1949), 73–90; William W. White, "The Texas Slave Insurrection of 1860," *SWHQ* LII (1949), 259–285; Wendell G. Addington, "Slave Insurrections in Texas," *JNH*, XXXV (1950), 408–434; Edwin A. Miles, "The Mississippi Slave Insurrection Scare of 1835," *JNH*, XLII (1957), 48–60.

7. For these insurrections see Aptheker and Carroll, cited in note 6. Also, John M. Lofton, *Insurrection in South Carolina: The Turbulent World of Denmark Vesey* (Yellow Springs, Ohio, 1964); Richard C. Wade, "The Vesey Plot: A Reconsideration," *JSH*, XXX (1964), 143–161; Carl N. Degler, *Neither White nor Black: Slavery and Race Relations in Brazil and the United States* (New York, 1971), pp. 47–51; John W. Cromwell, "The Aftermath of Nat Turner's Insurrection," *JNH*, V (1920), 208–234; F. Roy Johnson, *The Nat Turner Slave Insurrection* (Murfreesboro, N.C., 1966); Herbert Aptheker, *Nat Turner's Slave Rebellion* (New York, 1966); Kenneth Wiggins Porter, "Florida Slaves and Free Negroes in the Seminole War, 1836–1842," JNH, XXVIII (1943), 390–421; Porter, "Negroes and the Seminole War, 1817–1818," *JNH*, XXXVI (1951), 249–280.

8. Aptheker, *American Negro Slave Revolts*.

9. Benjamin Quarles, *Black Abolitionists* (New York, 1969), pp. 225–235; Howard H. Bell, "National Negro Conventions of the Middle 1840's: Moral Suasion versus Political Action," *JNH*, XLII (1957), 247–260; Bell, "Expressions of Negro Militancy in the North, 1840–1860," *JNH*, XLV (1960), 11–20.

10. When John Slidell made a farewell address before leaving the Senate after Louisiana's secession, he declared that Lincoln's inauguration would have been regarded by the slaves as "the day of their emancipation." *Congressional Globe*, 36 Cong, 2 sess., pp. 720–721. Also, on Dec. 12, 1860, John Bell wrote a public letter in which he said the "simple announcement to the public that a great party at the North, opposed to slavery, has succeeded in electing its candidate to the Presidency, disguise it as we may, is well calculated to raise expectations among slaves, and might lead to servile insurrection in the Southern States." Quoted in Mary Emily Robertson Campbell, *The Attitude of Tennesseans toward the Union 1847–1861* (New York, 1961), pp. 147–148.

11. H. M. Henry, *The Police Control of the State in South Carolina* (Emory, Va., 1914); Ulrich Bonnell Phillips, *American Negro Slavery* (New York, 1918), pp. 489–502, on slave codes and the policing of slaves.

12. Clement Eaton, "The Resistance of the South to Northern Radicalism," *NEQ* VIII (1935), 215–231.

13. "The whole social institutions of the people in the slave-holding states rested as they then supposed upon the stability of the right, which was involved with the ownership of slaves. It was reputed to be the cornerstone of that society, which for ages had rested upon it, and which it was supposed would be overthrown at its removal. All of the transactions of life were based upon it; all of the arrangements for the progress of society were made with reference to it; . . . It was thus that the remarkable unanimity was produced in all of these states. No other cause would have produced it." A. G. Magrath, Nov. 20, 1865, quoted in Charles Edward Cauthen, *South Carolina Goes to War* (Chapel Hill, 1950), p. 72. See also Eaton, *Freedom of Thought*, pp. 280–332.

14. Ulrich Bonnell Phillips, *Life and Labor in the Old South* (Boston, 1929); William E. Dodd, *The Cotton Kingdom* (New Haven, 1919); Avery O. Craven, *The Coming of the Civil War* (New York, 1942), pp. 17–38; J. G. Randall and David Donald, *The Civil War and Reconstruction* (2nd ed.; Boston, 1969), pp. 29–49; Eaton, *Growth of Southern Civilization*, pp. 295–324; Eugene Genovese, "Marxian Interpretations of the Slave South," in Barton J. Bernstein (ed.), *Toward a New Past: Dissenting Essays in American History* (New York, 1968), pp. 90–125; Genovese, "The Slave South: An Interpretation," in his *The Political Economy of Slavery* (New York, 1965), pp. 13–39; William H. Dodd, "The Social Philosophy of the Old South," *American Journal of Sociology*, XXIII (1918), 735–746; Wilbur J. Cash, *The Mind of the South* (New York, 1941), Book 1 Rollin G. Osterweis, *Romanticism and Nationalism in the Old South* (New Haven, 1949) Louis Hartz, *The Liberal Tradition in America* (New York, 1955), part IV, "The Feudal Dream of the South"; John Hope Franklin, *The Militant South, 1800–1861* (Cambridge, Mass., 1956); William R. Taylor, *Cavalier and Yankee: The Old South and the American National Character* (New York, 1961); Clement Eaton, *The Mind of the Old South* (Baton Rouge, 1964); David Donald, "The Proslavery Argument Reconsidered," *JSH*, XXXVII (1971), 3–18; Jay B. Hubbell, "Cavalier and Indentured Servant in Virginia Fiction," *SAQ*, XXVI (1927), 23–39; Esther J. Crooks and Ruth W. Crooks, *The Ring Tournament in the United States* (Richmond, 1936); William O. Stevens, *Pistols*

at Ten Paces: The Story of the Code of Honor in America (Boston, 1940); Guy A. Cardwell, "The Duel in the Old South: Crux of a Concept," *SAQ*, LXVI (1967), 50–69; David Donald, "The Southerner as Fighting Man," in Charles G. Sellers (ed.), *The Southerner as American* (New York, 1966), pp. 72–88; Grace Warren Landrum, "Sir Walter Scott and His Literary Rivals in the South," *American Literature*, II (1930), 256–276; George Harrison Orians, *The Influence of Walter Scott upon America and American Literature before 1860* (Urbana, Ill., 1929); Orians, "Walter Scott, Mark Twain and the Civil War," *SAQ*, XL (1941), 342–359.

15. Two major studies, neither of which is wholly responsible for the interpretation above, but which dominate the extensive literature dealing with the origins and nature of racial prejudice and racial subordination in the Negro-white context, are Jordan, *White Over Black,* and David Brion Davis, *The Problem of Slavery in Western Culture* (Ithaca, N.Y., 1966).

16. Eaton, *Growth of Southern Civilization*, pp. 152, 158, 307–309; Fletcher M. Green, "Democracy in the Old South," *JSH*, XII (1946), 3–23; Frank L. and Harriet C. Owsley, "The Economic Basis of Society in the Late Ante-Bellum South," *JSH*, VI (1940), 24–45; Blanche H. Clarke, *The Tennessee Yeoman, 1840–1860* (Nashville, 1942); Herbert Weaver, *Mississippi Farmers, 1850–1860* (Nashville, 1945); Frank L. Owsley, *Plain Folk of the Old South* (Baton Rouge, 1949); Fabian Linden, "Economic Democracy in the Slave South: An Appraisal of Some Recent Views," *JNH*, XXXI (1946), 140–189; James C. Bonner, "Profile of a Late Ante-Bellum Community," *AHR*, XLIX (1944), 663–680.

17. On antislavery in the early South, see citations in chap. 2, note 26. Also, John Spencer Bassett, *Anti-Slavery Leaders of North Carolina* (Baltimore, 1898); Ruth Scarborough, *The Opposition to Slavery in Georgia Prior to 1860* (Nashville, 1933); H. M. Wagstaff (ed.), *North Carolina Manumission Society, 1816–1834* (Chapel Hill, 1934); Early Lee Fox, *The American Colonization Society, 1817–1840* (Baltimore, 1919); P. J. Staudenraus, *The African Colonization Movement, 1816–1865* (New York, 1961); Beverley B. Munford, *Virginia's Attitude toward Slavery and Secession* (New York, 1909); Asa Earl Martin, *The Anti-Slavery Movement in Kentucky Prior to 1850* (Louisville, 1918); Merton L. Dillon, *Benjamin Lundy and the Struggle for Negro Freedom* (Urbana, Ill., 1966); Matthew T. Mellon, *Early American Views on Negro Slavery* (Boston, 1934); Richard Beale Davis, *Intellectual Life of Jefferson's Virginia, 1790–1830* (Chapel Hill, 1964).

18. Frederic Bancroft, *Slave-Trading in the Old South* (Baltimore, 1931), pp. 269–364, 382–406.

19. Arthur Zilversmit, *The First Emancipation: The Abolition of Slavery in the North* (Chicago, 1967).

20. For changes in the tone of abolitionist literature, see note 66, below.

21. Hilary A. Herbert, *The Abolition Crusade and Its Consequences* (New York, 1912).

22. William Sumner Jenkins, *Pro-Slavery Thought in the Old South* (Chapel Hill, 1935); William B. Hesseltine, "Some New Aspects of the Proslavery Argument," *JNH*, XXI (1936), 1–14; Eric L. McKitrick (ed.), *Slavery Defended: The Views of the Old South* (Englewood Cliffs, N.J., 1963); Harvey Wish, *George Fitzhugh, Propagandist of the Old South* (Baton Rouge, 1943); Eugene D. Genovese, *The World the Slaveholders Made* (New York, 1969), part II: "The Logical Outcome of the Slaveholders' Philosophy," pp. 115–244; Wilfred Carsel, "The Slaveholders' Indictment of Northern Wage Slavery," *JSH*, VI (1940), 504–520; Robert Gardner, "A Tenth Hour Apology for Slavery," *JSH*, XXVI (1960), 352–367; Ralph E. Morrow, "The Proslavery Argument Revisited," *MVHR*, XLVIII (1961), 79–94; Alan Dowty, "Urban Slavery in Pro-Southern Fiction of the 1850s," *JSH*, XXXII (1966), 25–41; Lewis M. Purifoy, "The Southern Methodist Church and the Pro-Slavery Argument," *JSH*, XXXII (1966), 325–341; Jeannette Reid Tandy, "Pro-Slavery Propaganda in American Fiction of the Fifties," *SAQ*, XXI (1922), 41–50, 170–178.

23. William R. Stanton, *The Leopard's Spots: Scientific Attitudes toward Race in America, 1815–1859* (Chicago, 1960), pp. 110–112, 155–160.

24. "There is a community of interest and feeling between the fifteen Southern States, fully as great, perhaps greater, than existed between the original thirteen," Augusta, Georgia, *Daily Chronicle and Sentinel,* Nov. 13, 1860, quoted in Dumond, *Southern Editorials*, p. 232.

25. Quoted in Nathaniel W. Stephenson, "Southern Nationalism in South Carolina in 1851," *AHR*, XXXVI (1931), 314–335.

26. William H. Trescot, *The Position and Course of the South* (Charleston, 1850), pp. 6–18.

27. Message of Governor John H. Means in 1852, quoted in Cauthen, *South Carolina Goes to War*, p. 6.

28. Eugene Blackford to Mary L. Minor, Nov. 9, 1860 quoted in Crenshaw, *Slave States in the Election of 1860*, p. 251.

29. Jeremiah Clemens to Solon Borland, quoted in Durward Long, "Unanimity and Disloyalty in Secessionist Alabama," *CWH*, XI (1965), 259.

30. St. Louis Missouri Republican, Nov. 21, 1860, in Dumond, *Southern Editorials*, p. 259.

31. Jay B. Hubbell, "Literary Nationalism in the Old South," in David Kelley Jackson (ed.), *American Studies in Honor of William Kenneth Boyd* (Durham, N.C., 1940), p. 177.

32. Hubbell, *The South in American Literature* (Durham, N.C., 1954), p. 487; also, William P. Trent, *English Culture in Virginia* (Baltimore, 1889).

33. Myrta Lockett Avary (ed.), *Recollections of Alexander H. Stephens* (New York, 1910), p. 253.

34. Avery Craven, *Edmund Ruffin, Southerner: A Study in Secession* (New York, 1932), quotations from pp. 107, 162, 198. The text of the constitution of the League of United Southerners is in John Witherspoon Du Bose, *The Life and Times of William Lowndes Yancey* (2 vols.; Birmingham, Ala., 1892), I, 377–378.

35. Du Bose, *Life of Yancey*, I, 358–360, 376; Joseph Hodgson, *The Cradle of the Confederacy, or the Times of Troup, Quitman, and Yancey* (Mobile, 1876); Austin L. Venable, "William L. Yancey's Transition from Unionism to State Rights," *JSH*, X (1944), 331–342; Venable, "The Public Career of William Lowndes Yancey," *AR*, XVI (1963), 200–212; Eaton, *The Mind of the Old South*, pp. 202–221; Alto L. Garner and Nathan Stott, "William Lowndes Yancey: Statesman of Secession," *AR*, XV (1962), 190–202; Malcolm C. McMillan, "William L. Yancey and the Historians: One Hundred Years," *AR*, XX (1967), 163–186, *De Bow's Review*, XXIV (1858), 578–588.

36. Ottis Clark Skipper, "J. D. B. De Bow, the Man," JSH, X (1944), 404 423; Skipper, *J. D. B. De Bow, Magazinist of the Old South* (Athens, Ga. 1958); Robert F. Durden, "J. D. B. De Bow: Convolutions of a Slavery Expansionist," JSH, XVII (1951), 441–461.

37. Laura A. White, *Robert Barnwell Rhett, Father of Secession* (New York, 1931), is standard and excellent. A more recent study is H. Hardy Perritt, "Robert Barnwell Rhett, South Carolina Secession Spokesman" (Ph.D. dissertation, University of Florida, 1954). Perritt, "Robert Barnwell Rhett's Speech, July 4, 1859," in J. Jeffery Auer (ed.), *Anti-Slavery and Disunion, 1858–1861: Studies in the Rhetoric of Compromise and Conflict* (New York, 1963), pp. 98–107, is especially pertinent to the paragraph above.

38. Ollinger Crenshaw, "The Knights of the Golden Circle: The Career of George Bickley," *AHR*, XLVII (1941), 23–50; C. A. Bridges, "The Knights of the Golden Circle: A Filibustering Fantasy," *SWHQ*, XLIV (1941), 287–302; Jimmie Hicks, "Some Letters Concerning the Knights of the Golden Circle in Texas, 1860–1861," *SWHQ*, LXV (1961), 80–86; Roy Sylvan Dunn, "The KCC in Texas, 1860–1861," SWHQ, LXX (1967), 543–573.

39. Herbert Wender, *Southern Commercial Conventions, 1837–1859* (Baltimore, 1930), pp. 123–129, 155–156, 162–228.

40. *Ibid.*, pp. 208–209, 214–217, 220–222. Robert R. Russel, *Economic Aspects of Southern Sectionalism, 1840–1861* (Urbana, Ill., 1924), pp. 123–150; John G. Van Deusen, *The Ante-Bellum Southern Commercial Conventions* (Durham, N.C., 1926); Weymouth T. Jordan, *Rebels in the Making: Planters' Conventions and Southern Propaganda* (Tuscaloosa, Ala., 1958).

41. On literary and cultural nationalism in the South, see titles by Hubbell, above in notes 31, 32; by Osterweis and Eaton, cited in note 14; and also: Merle Curti, *The Growth of American Thought* (New York, 1943), pp. 427–453; John S. Ezell, "A Southern Education for Southrons," *JSH* XVII (1951), 303–327; Howard R. Floan, *The South in Northern Eyes, 1831–1861* (Austin, 1958).

42. J. G. Ramsey to L. W. Spratt, quoted in James Welch Patton, *Unionism and Reconstruction in Tennessee* (Chapel Hill, 1934), p. 3.

43. *Congressional Globe*, 36 Cong. I sess., appendix, pp. 88–93.

44. Thomas Sergeant Perry (ed.), *The Life and Letters of Francis Lieber* (Boston, 1882), p. 314.

45. Joseph Carlyle Sitterson, *The Secession Movement in North Carolina* (Chapel Hill, 1939), p. 238. See also William Howard Russell, *Pictures of Southern Life* (New York, 1861), pp. 5–8.

46. Osterweis, *Romanticism and Nationalism*, pp. 110, 148.

47. Clarence Phillips Denman, *The Secession Movement in Alabama* (Montgomery, Ala., 1933), p. 89; Cauthen, *South Carolina Goes to War*, p. 40. See also Henry T. Shanks, *The Secession Movement in Virginia, 1847–1861* (Richmond, 1934), p. 166.

48. Edward McPherson (ed.), *Political History of the United States during the Great Rebellion* (Washington, 1876), pp. 12–15.

49. "We separated because of incompatibility of temper; we are divorced, North from South, because we have hated each other so." Mary Boykin Chesnut, *A Diary from Dixie* (Boston, 1949), p. 20.

50. For a classic statement of the homogeneity of American culture in all parts of the country in the generation before the Civil War, see Allan Nevins, *Ordeal of the Union* (2 vols.; New York, 1947), I, 34–112. Also, J. G. Randall and David Donald, *The Civil War and Reconstruction* (2nd ed.; Lexington, Mass., 1969), pp. 1–28 and esp. p. 29; Randall, *Lincoln: The Liberal Statesman* (New York, 1947), pp. 41–43, 49–54; Carl Bode, *The Anatomy of American Popular Culture, 1840–1861* (Berkeley, 1959).

51. Thomas B. Alexander, "Persistent Whiggery in the Confederate South, 1860–1877," *JSH*, XXVII (1961), 307.

52. Quoted in Percy Lee Rainwater, *Mississippi: Storm Center of Secession, 1856–1861* (Baton Rouge, 1938), p. 164.

53. Jefferson Davis Bragg, *Louisiana in the Confederacy* (Baton Rouge, 1941), p. 2; Ulrich Bonnell Philips (ed.), *The Correspondence of Robert Toombs, Alexander H. Stephens, and Howell Cobb*, AHA Annual Report, 1911, II, 526.

54. *Congressional Globe*, 35 Cong., I sess., pp. 1153–1159; Campbell, *Attitude of Tennesseans*, p. 140.

55. Zachary Taylor's first annual message, Dec. 4, 1849, James D. Richardson (ed.), *A Compilation of the Messages and Papers of the Presidents* (11 vols.; New York, 1907), V, 9.

56. Dumond, *Southern Editorials*, p. 227. James L. Orr of South Carolina said, "When this government is destroyed, neither you, nor I, your children nor my children will ever live to see so good a government reconstructed." Quoted in Laura A. White, "The National Democrats in South Carolina, 1850 to 1860," *SAQ*, XXVIII (1929), 381.

57. *Congressional Globe*, 28 Cong., 2 sess., appendix, p. 314.

58. Howell Cobb to Absalom H. Chappell, Feb. 7, 1851, in Phillips (ed.), *Toombs, Stephens, Cobb Correspondence*, p. 221; New Orleans *Picayune*, quoted in Willie Malvin Caskey, *Secession and Restoration of Louisiana* (University, La., 1938), p. 36. See also Campbell, *Attitude of Tennesseans*, p. 171; Richard Harrison Shryock, *Georgia and the Union in 1850* (Durham, N.C., 1926), pp. 293–294.

59. Benjamin Franklin Perry, *Biographical Sketches of Eminent American Statesmen* (Philadelphia, 1887), pp. 171–180.

60. Stephens to J. Henly Smith, July 10, 1860, in Phillips (ed.), *Toombs, Stephens, Cobb Correspondence*, pp. 486–487.

61. Percy Scott Flippin, *Herschel V. Johnson of Georgia: State-Rights Unionist* (Richmond, 1931), p. 93.

62. Sitterson, *Secession Movement in North Carolina*, p. 213.

63. Rich in relevant data and quotations in Jesse T. Carpenter, *The South as a Conscious Minority, 1789–1861* (New York, 1930).

64. Emerson David Fite, *The Presidential Campaign of 1860* (New York, 1911), pp. 301–329.

65. Leonard L. Richards, *Gentlemen of Property and Standing: Anti-Abolition Mobs in Jacksonian America* (New York, 1970).

66. For the mild tone of earlier abolitionist literature, see Locke and Adams, as cited in chap. 2, note 26. For the increasingly militant tone after 1831, see titles in chap. 2, note 28; also, Herbert Aptheker, "Militant Abolitionism," *JNH*, XXVI (1941), 438–484; Bell, "Expressions of Negro Militancy," pp. 11–22; Bell, "National Negro Conventions," pp. 247–260; Quarles, *Black Abolitionists*, John Demos, "The Antislavery Movement and the Problem of Violent Means," *NEQ*, XXXVII (1964), 501–526; Martin Duberman (ed.), *The Antislavery Vanguard: New Essays on the Abolitionists* (Princeton, 1965), pp. 71–101, 270–298, 417–451; James B. Stewart, *Joshua R. Giddings and the Tactics of Radical Politics* (Cleveland, 1970); Stewart, "The Aims and Impact of Garrisonian Abolitionism, 1840–1860," *CWH*, XV (1969), 197–209; Lewis Curtis Perry, "Antislavery and Anarchy: A Study of the Ideas of Abolitionism before the Civil War" (Ph.D. dissertation, Cornell University, 1967). For the impact of this militancy on the South, Arthur Y. Lloyd, *The Slavery Controversy, 1831–1860* (Chapel Hill, 1931); Henry H. Simms, "A Critical Analysis of Abolitionist Literature," *JSH*, VI (1940), 368–382; Simms, *A Decade of Sectional Controversy, 1851–1861* (Chapel Hill, 1942), pp. 146–168; Simms, *Emotion at High Tide: Abolition as a Controversial Factor* (n.p., 1960).

67. For the importance of postal censorship to the South see Clement Eaton, "Censorship of the Southern Mails," *AHR*, XLVIII (1943), 266–280; William Sherman Savage, *The Controversy over the Distribution of Abolition Literature, 1830–1860* (Washington, 1938).

68. Roy F. Nichols, *The Disruption of American Democracy* (New York, 1948), pp. 352–353. For southern anxiety about the nonslaveholding whites, see Hesseltine, "Some New Aspects of the Proslavery Argument"; *Channing Crisis of Fear*, pp. 254–256.

69. Crenshaw, *Slave States in the Election of 1860*, pp. 89–111; Nichols, *Disruption*, pp. 351, 367.

70. N.C. Claiborne, June 22, 1860, in Murat Halstead, *Caucuses of 1860* (Columbus, 1860), p. 239.

71. Henry Steele Commager (ed.), *Documents of American History* (7th ed., 2 vols.; New York, 1963), I, 111, 117.

72. North Carolina did not ratify the Constitution until Nov. 21, 1789, nor Rhode Island until May 29, 1790, and neither was a member of the Union when Washington became president.

73. E.g., speech of Webster in Senate, Jan. 27, 1830, in *Register of Debates in Congress*, 21 Cong., 1 sess., cols. 74, 77. Webster argued that the powers conferred on the new government were perfectly well understood to be conferred, (1) not by any state, or (2) the people of any state, but (3) by the people of the United States. Since the only thing that made the Constitution applicable in any state was ratification by a convention of that state, it is very difficult to see any rational basis for Webster's rejection of (2).

74. It has been argued, of course, that this coordinate status is eliminated and federal ascendancy is established by Article VI of the Constitution, which declares that the Constitution and "the Laws of the United States which shall be made in pursuance thereof ... shall be the Supreme Law of the Land." But under the theory of a dualistic system federal supremacy would not follow. Instead the argument would run that each state, having made two constitutions—one by itself, for local matters controlling only the state government, and the other jointly with other states, for general matters, controlling both state governments and the federal government—does not diminish its autonomy by providing that in cases of conflict between the two, the latter shall take priority. The "supreme law" clause gives a federal statute force only if it is "in pursuance of" the Constitution. Since both constitutions emanated from the same authority, the people of the states, acting severally in one case and jointly in another, the ultimate question was not which constitution should control in cases of conflict, but which government—federal or state—should act as arbiter for the people of the state in construing the constitution in question. Should each state act as its own arbiter, as Jefferson and Madison had argued in the Virginia and Kentucky resolutions of 1798; or should the federal

judiciary act as arbiter, as in the cases of Fletcher v. Peck (1810) and Cohens v. Virginia (1821), when the Supreme Court asserted the power to declare the act of a state legislature void if contrary to the federal Constitution, and to reverse the decision of the highest court of a state?

75. Clinton Rossiter, *1787: The Grand Convention* (New York, 1966), p. 229; for the preamble as reported by the committee on detail, Aug. 6, 1787, and as reported back by the committee on style, see Charles C. Tansill (ed.), *Documents Illustrative of the Formation of the Union of the American States* (Washington, 1927), pp. 471, 989.

76. On May 29, 1787, Edmund Randolph introduced resolutions in the constitutional convention, including a provision that "the National Legislature ought to be empowered . . . to call forth the force of the Union against any member of the Union failing to fulfill its duty under the articles thereof." This was taken up on May 31. Madison was apparently the only speaker. He opposed it on the ground that "the use of force against a state would look more like a declaration of war than an infliction of punishment, and would probably be considered by the party attacked as a dissolution of all previous compacts by which it might be bound." He moved to postpone, and the motion was adopted unanimously. Tansill, *Documents*, pp. 117, 131. Andrew C. McLaughlin, *A Constitutional History of the United States* (New York, 1935), p. 598, offers an argument that the action on this resolution did not mean what it appears to mean.

77. Virginia's ratification, June 27, 1788, specified that "the powers granted under the Constitution being derived from the people of the United States may be resumed by them whensoever the same shall be perverted to their injury or oppression." New York's ratification, July 26, specified, "We the Delegates declare and make known that the Powers of Government may be resumed by the People, whensoever it shall become necessary to their happiness"; Rhode Island, May 29, 1790, adopted the same provision as New York. Tansill, *Documents*, pp. 1027, 1034, 1052.

78. It became a truism that the government under the Constitution was neither wholly federal nor wholly national, but mixed. The best analysis of the nature of this mixture is by Madison in *The Federalist*, number 39. William Paterson declared that "as in some respects, the States all to be considered in their political capacity, and in others as districts of individual citizens the two ideas—instead of being opposed to each other, ought to be combined; that in *one* branch the people ought to be represented; in the other, the states." Tansill, *Documents*, p. 297.

79. The historical literature on the development of the doctrine of secession is scanty. A brief but very able account is Carpenter, *The South as a Conscious Minority*, pp. 171–220. Also see Ulrich Bonnell Phillips, "The Literary Movement for Secession," in *Studies in Southern History and Politics Inscribed to William Archibald Dunning* (New York, 1914), pp. 33–60; William E. Dodd, "John Taylor: Prophet of Secession," in *John P. Branch Historical Papers*, 1908 (Ashland, Va., 1908), pp. 214–252; articles and correspondence of Spencer Roane, *ibid.*, 1905, pp. 51–142, and 1906, pp. 78–183.

80. Carpenter, *South as a Conscious Minority*, pp. 194–200, discusses the preference of some southerners for claiming a right of revolution rather than a right of secession. The quotation from Mason, taken from Richmond *Enquirer*, Nov. 23, 1860, is at p. 200.

81. Henry Savage, Jr., *Seeds of Time: The Background of Southern Thinking* (New York, 1959), pp. 49–136.

$\times \vee$

HOW WE GOT LINCOLN

Peter Andrews

The epic proportions of the Lincoln legend has made a factual analysis of his emergence in the 1860 election especially tenuous. This great man had long been a political leader in Illinois, and once he decided to join the new Republican Party, he became one of Illinois most likely candidates. However, his successful quest for the presidential nomination in 1860 was achieved only with considerable maneuvering. Peter Andrews brings to light the activities of Lincoln's men and how they got him the candidacy of his Party.

In the crowded months between the beginning of the 1860 presidential campaign and the attack on Fort Sumter, it is easy now to see the emergence of Abraham Lincoln as something preordained, as though the issues had manufactured a figure commensurate with their importance. Or at the least, one might imagine a dramatic, hard-fought campaign with Northern and Southern states rallying around their respective candidates. But that's not quite how it happened.

There is drama enough in the 1860 campaign, but most of it does not spring from the election itself. The moment Lincoln was nominated, the issue was settled: He would become the President; he would be faced with the dissolution of the federal Union. The crucial steps on Lincoln's road to the White House came earlier, during the most important party convention in our history—a convention that seemed, at the time, certain to nominate William Henry Seward as Republican party candidate for President of the United States.

The senator from New York cut an odd, slight figure. Spare and angular, Seward looked, one newspaper said, like "a jay bird with a sparrow hawk's bill." His unprepossessing appearance aside, Seward seemed like a man very much in control of his political life as he marched down the Republican side of the Senate chamber on May 7, 1860. Taking his seat, Seward produced a large quantity of snuff and a yellow handkerchief that he waved expansively as he amused his fellow Republicans with a joke or two. There were few things in life Seward enjoyed more than being the focus of attention. The senators who watched him perform understood that they were looking at the next President of the United States. And no one in the chamber was more certain of this than Seward himself.

Four days earlier the Democratic party convention in Charleston had done an extraordinary thing. Deliberately, the delegates had thrown away the forthcoming presidential election. They had met to confirm Senator Stephen A. Douglas of Illinois, the only Democrat who could have reached out beyond the slave-holding South and gathered up enough electoral votes from the border states to win. But insurrection had been in the air at Charleston. The smooth-talking Democrat from Alabama, William Yancey, who took pride in being known as "the Prince of the Fire-Eaters," had his mind not on success within the political system but on secession from the Union. With Yancey calling the shots, the convention turned away from Douglas and refused to nominate anybody. The party would eventually put up two candidates, Douglas and Vice-President John Breckinridge, while a hastily formed splinter group calling itself the Constitutional Union party nominated John Bell of Tennessee.

Yancey had what he wanted. The fragmented Democrats would most likely lose to a Republican committed to abolition. The South would have no choice but to secede.

So the way was left open for the Republicans. A political organization that had been stitched together five years earlier by grafting snippets of Free-Soilers, Know-Nothings, Abolitionists, and runaway Democrats onto the carcass of the old, moribund Whig party had the Presidency within its grasp for the first time. In 1856, with no reasonable chance of victory, the Republicans had nominated the romantic adventurer John Frémont, and lost. Now it was time for a seasoned man of politics. That man was Seward.

The senator had every right to be confident. He was a traditional politician of the day and had played the political game in the traditional manner. He had spoken out on the questions Republicans wanted addressed. He had led them where they wanted to go. Seward had paid his dues, and now it was time to collect.

He had the credentials. An early organizer of the party, Seward led the anti-slavery forces in Congress despite his uninspiring public-speaking style. Indeed, he frequently gave the impression of talking to himself. The great orators such as Daniel Webster and John C. Calhoun had ignored his speeches. But Seward had a keen mind and once, in a moment of inspiration, he described the issue between slave and free as an "irrepressible conflict." The phrase went into the political language of the day, and Seward's followers liked to call themselves "the Irrepressibles."

He had the following. No American politician of the time could claim more devoted supporters. To a party based on opposition to slavery, Seward was more than simply a leader. He was, as the contemporary journalist Isaac Bromley put it, "the central figure of the whole movement, its prophet, priest, and oracle." A presidential election without Seward, Bromley concluded, "would be the play without Hamlet."

He had the money. With a war chest full of dollars culled from New York State political organizations, Seward's campaign manager, Thurlow Weed, had been able to collar Republican leaders by promising "oceans of money" to underwrite not only Seward's campaign but theirs as well.

He had the votes. To secure the nomination, Seward would need 233 delegates. He had 170 in his pocket as he sat in the Senate. If there had been a national primary at the time, Seward would certainly have won it. The Republicans held a number of straw votes before the convention showing him an easy winner. One from Michigan gave him 210 votes and all other candidates 30, while another from the Northwest showed him with 127 and 44 for the rest.

Always meticulous in such matters, Seward started working on a draft of the resignation speech he would give the Senate upon receiving the nomination. But the smooth senator from New York found himself heading into some very rough territory.

In a neat piece of symbolism for the emerging importance of the party's Western reach, the Republican convention was set for Chicago. It was not much of a city. Writing in the mid-1850s, the historian James Parton said that of all American prairie towns, Chicago "was the most repulsive to every human sense." Cattle still crowded the sidewalks, and stables were routinely emptied into Lake Michigan, which provided the city's drinking water. Consumption, cholera, and smallpox were commonplace; Chicago had the highest death rate in the nation. But it was an energetic place. When engineers decided the city streets had to be raised twelve feet to bring them safely above river level, every building in town was jacked up and twelve hundred acres were filled in.

By 1860 Chicago had made itself into a convention city of fifty-seven hotels, eight of them considered deluxe by the town's relaxed standards. And just for the Republicans the city had erected the first building in America specifically constructed to hold a political convention: an immense two-story wooden structure called the Wigwam and billed as "the largest audience room in the United States." Completed only four days before the convention opened, the eighteen thousand square-foot Wigwam could accommodate somewhere between six and fifteen thousand people. With more than twenty thousand Republicans coming to town, it was going to be a tight fit.

Chicago was a good town in which to practice a little political bushwhacking, and Seward, although he carried the cachet that goes with being the front-runner, made an appealing target. He was so confident of the righteousness of his causes that he seemed indifferent to the intensity of the resentment he aroused.

Once when Senator Douglas, exasperated during an all-night Senate session, used the word *nigger*, Seward snapped, "Douglas, no man who spells Negro with two *g*s will ever be elected President of the United States." The line played well back home, but it made Seward enemies. Although there was no evidence to support the charge, many suspected Seward, among other Northern Republicans, of complicity in John Brown's raid on Harpers Ferry the year before. One Richmond newspaper carried an advertisement offering fifty thousand dollars for the head of the "traitor" William Seward.

Several highly placed Republicans disliked the senator as well, and all of them were coming to Chicago. If Seward was to be stopped, the Wigwam was the place where it could be done.

The Republicans began streaming into Chicago in crowds that made the railroad depots "beat like great hearts with their living tide," according to one correspondent. They came in such numbers that some 130 of them had to sleep on pool tables in hotel billiard rooms. They were a rough, contentious group who smelled victory and started their celebrating early. The New York Republicans in particular, said one witness, "can drink as much whiskey, swear as loud and long, sing as bad songs, and 'get up and howl' as ferociously as any crowd of Democrats. . . . "

The imperious Thurlow Weed, nicknamed "Lord Thurlow," led the pack. He set up headquarters at the Richmond House with an abundant supply of good cigars and champagne, and a willingness to promise anything required to secure the remaining 60 votes Seward needed. To back him up with muscle and yelling power for marching in parades and shouting in floor demonstrations, Weed had brought in a gang of roughnecks, among them the former American heavyweight champion Tom Hyer (who in fact was considered by many to be the best-mannered man at the convention).

There were other candidates in the contest besides Seward, but Weed discounted them. Salmon Chase of Ohio yearned to be President, but he seemed too proud to campaign actively for it. Judge Edward Bates of St. Louis, backed by powerful forces within the party, had been tainted by his association with the Know-Nothings and their chauvinistic policies against the foreign-born and Roman Catholics, two important voting blocs with long memories. Simon Cameron, the party boss of Pennsylvania, had presidential ambitions, but Cameron was essentially a deal-maker who could be made content as long as he got something for himself out of the convention. The field was filled out with favorite-son candidates such as William Dayton of New Jersey and Abraham Lincoln of Illinois.

Surveying it all, Weed calculated that although Lincoln was a marginal candidate, he would require scrutiny. In an attempt to give some regional balance to the campaign, Weed offered him second place on the ticket. The offer was tempting, but Lincoln and his advisers refused. They were after bigger game.

Fifty-one years old, Abraham Lincoln was a made-over Whig with considerable local experience and some small national distinction. Born in Kentucky, and raised in Indiana and Illinois, he had worked as a land surveyor and won election as a captain of militia during the Black Hawk War before turning to law. He served for eight years in the Illinois legislature as a Clay Whig and generally could be relied upon to vote down the line with his party. Elected to Congress in 1846, he was turned out after one term, largely because of his opposition to the Mexican War, and afterward returned to Springfield to practice law.

Lincoln attained national recognition ten years later when he ran for the Senate against Douglas. His opening speech declared, famously, that "a house divided against itself cannot stand." It became part of the national conscience, but it cost Lincoln the election. Douglas used the phrase to paint Lincoln as an abolitionist, and Leonard Swett, one of Lincoln's closest advisers, later commented that Lincoln had defeated himself in the first sentence of his first speech. During his famous series of debates with Douglas, Lincoln attempted to backpedal. "I am not . . . in favor of making voters or jurors of Negroes," he said in Charleston, Illinois, "nor of qualifying them to hold office. . . . " But the political damage had been done.

Nevertheless, Lincoln made his national mark. He carried the antislavery issue about as far as most Republicans wished it taken and he had emerged as the leading Republican in Illinois.

Lincoln was woven of genuine homespun—he said "jist" for "just" and "sich" for "such"—but he was no political naif. He had toiled hard for the party and done the scut work of driving Frémont's campaign wagons in 1856. He knew the names of hundreds of precinct and county workers and was careful to keep in contact with them. Lincoln was fiercely ambitious for political advancement. His long-time legal associate, Henry C. Whitney, said Lincoln picked his companions for what they could do for him. Noting that Lincoln used to play billiards with a somewhat disreputable Illinois attorney from time to time, Whitney remarked that "it was the only non-utilitarian thing" he ever saw Lincoln do.

Lincoln and Seward never confronted each other. The struggle was fought out by their supporters in Chicago. Lincoln awaited word of the results in Springfield, while the senator remained in his hometown of Auburn, New York. In a letter to Lincoln marked "Profoundly private," Dr. Charles Ray, editor of the *Chicago Tribune*, laid it out simply enough: "You need a few trusty friends here to say words for you that may be necessary to be said. . . . A pledge or two may be necessary when the pinch comes."

The trusty friends behind Lincoln were solid, practical men of good sense and considerable diligence. Judge David Davis, who had known the candidate since they had both been circuit-riding lawyers in Illinois, served as Lincoln's campaign manager. Weighing close to three hundred pounds, Davis gave the appearance of a sleepy mountain, but he was quick-witted and possessed of a nice political judgment. Charles Ray and his fellow editor Joseph Medill were ready to put the *Tribune* at Lincoln's disposal. The state auditor Jesse Dubois was in Lincoln's camp, as were Judge Stephen Logan, who had once been Lincoln's law partner, and Norman Judd, a prominent railroad attorney who had been instrumental in setting up the Douglas debates.

They compared their man with Seward and were not unhappy. On the principal issue, Lincoln's record was as good. And for a national campaign he was considered less radical.

Seward's ringing "irrepressible conflict" had become something of an embarrassment to someone who hoped to win a national election without goading the South into insurrection.

Seward admitted to a Washington hostess that if the Lord forgave him this time, he would never again put together two such high-sounding words. Lincoln had said almost as much in his "House Divided" speech, but coming from a minor Illinois politician its implications did not fall as stridently upon the ear as they did from a powerful New York senator.

If Lincoln did not have the public record of Seward, that meant also that he did not have as much to defend. There is nothing like being a political front-runner to find out who really doesn't like you, and the more Judge Davis poked around Seward's record, the more possible roadblocks to Seward's nomination he found. Former Democrats, new to the Republican party, were unhappy with Seward's contention that black people should have the vote. Then there were the Know-Nothings, whom Seward had consistently mocked. They were particularly powerful in states such as New Jersey, where the Republicans had no real organization of their own. Indiana and Pennsylvania were also strong Know-Nothing country. The big Northern businessmen, usually a source of strength for Seward, were getting shy about his prominence as a lightning rod for Southern hatred ever since Harpers Ferry and were beginning to worry about their commercial trade with the South. And, oddly for such a moral man, Seward had a hint of corruption about him. Weed had not always been scrupulous about how he raised money for Seward, sometimes resorting to little more than shakedowns from Republican officeholders and the promoters of New York City street railways who relied on Weed to guide their franchises through the legislature. Horace Greeley's *New York Tribune* said that when Seward was governor, the New York legislature was "not merely corrupt but shameless."

Greeley's animosity was difficult to understand. By rights, the two New Yorkers should have been political allies, but they had fallen out somewhere along the line over a matter of political patronage, and now Greeley remained implacable in his opposition to Seward's candidacy.

And then there was the image question. In many ways, Seward, a wealthy corporation lawyer, was in the classic old Whig mold of a well-born moralist telling the people what was good for them whether they wanted to hear it or not. These Whigs had a poor record in winning the White House. The only two Presidents they had been able to elect were dusted-off generals, Harrison and Taylor, who had run on their war records while the Whig leadership made fools of themselves wearing coonskin caps and drinking hard cider, trying to look like men of the people.

But with Lincoln, the Republicans could have a man who really was from humble origins and looked comfortable in the part. Lincoln carefully cultivated his populist appeal. During the Douglas debates, when Douglas and his party arrived in a line of carriages, Lincoln trailed behind in a wagon hauled by oxen. His rail-splitter image was an inspired piece of political flackery conjured up by his supporters. When Lincoln secured the presidential pledge from the state convention on May 9, a group of men dressed as farmers carried in a pair of rails supposedly split by the candidate in 1830. Lincoln went along with the gag—up to a point. "I cannot say whether I made those rails or not, but I am quite sure I have made a great many as good," he said amid applause so great that part of the canvas roof covering the meeting hall collapsed.

Lincoln would do nicely if they could put him over. And that was a question of mathematics. Could Seward be stopped short of 230 delegates and could Lincoln then pick them up before the convention rallied to someone else?

Lincoln had already demonstrated one quality vital to a presidential candidate: he was lucky. Chicago had been chosen as a compromise site before Lincoln was considered a serious candidate. If he had been seen as a contender, the city would have been unacceptable to Seward's people; and if any other place had been chosen, it is unlikely Lincoln's Illinois team could have swung the nomination.

Months before, Lincoln had astutely indicated the basic strategy to be taken. Writing to a delegate from Ohio to thank him for his support, Lincoln said, "If I have any chance, it consists mainly in the fact that the whole opposition would vote for me, if nominated. (I don't mean to include the pro-slavery opposition of the South, of course.) My name is new in the field, and I suppose I am not the first choice of a very great many. Our policy, then, is to give no offense to others—leave them in a mood to come to us if they shall be compelled to give up their first love. . . . "

Davis, having established Lincoln's campaign headquarters in a two-room suite at the Tremont House, had three immediate jobs to do:

First, Seward had to be stopped from winning on the first ballot. Everything depended on that. As far as Davis was concerned, anyone who wouldn't vote for Seward was a Lincoln man. At least for one round.

Second, Lincoln had to be built into something more than a favorite son candidate. Favorite sons would be blown away by the second ballot. Lincoln needed votes from outside Illinois to demonstrate his depth. Davis had hoped for a solid second-place finish from Lincoln on the first ballot—no easy task, because Chase, Cameron, and Bates were all coming to Chicago with more delegates than Lincoln.

Finally, Davis had to play a waiting game and secure as many second-ballot pledges for Lincoln as possible. Once Seward was stalled, it was imperative that Lincoln forge ahead before the convention could gather around someone else.

Davis dispatched his men to meet the various conventioneers as they arrived. Samuel Parks, who was born in Vermont, went to that delegation and Swett went to see his old friends from Maine. Every delegation Davis could get to was visited by Lincoln's men. They carried with them a pair of powerful messages from Davis.

Although they were careful not to disparage Seward, they drove home the point that he was not as solid as he looked. With only New England firmly in the Republican column, the national election would be won or lost in New Jersey, Indiana, Illinois, and Pennsylvania, where Know-Nothing sentiment remained high. The Republicans had to win three of those four doubtful states or lose it all. And these were precisely the four marginal states where Seward was weakest.

Something Seward had said in 1852 now returned to haunt him. When the Whigs of his state wanted to give the venerable Henry Clay a third chance for the Presidency, Seward had written a New York congressman saying, "it is not a question of who we should prefer but whom can we elect." Now the same hard political judgment was to be used against Seward. Even if he was the best man, his party could not elect him.

The second message was the Davis counter to Weed's "oceans of money." Davis had hardly any money at all. He later calculated the total expense of nominating Lincoln, including everything from band music to railroad tickets for delegates, at less than seven hundred dollars. With no cash, Davis did the next best thing he could think of. In effect he established a futures market in Lincoln's cabinet and sold it off chair by chair.

He had to start by securing his own Illinois delegation. Not all of the 22 delegates were solid for Lincoln. Men from the northern part of the state, about a third of the state delegates, were for Seward. Davis handled that by binding the state to vote as a unit.

Lincoln swiftly won Indiana's 26 delegates. Dr. Ray checked in with Medill at the Tremont House to tell him the news that Indiana was committed to Lincoln down the line. Asked how this was done, Ray replied, "By the Lord, we promised them everything they asked." After the election Indiana's Caleb Smith was appointed Secretary of the Interior and William

Dole was given the post of Commissioner of Indian Affairs, where the hours were good and the money excellent.

As Chicago filled up with Republicans, and with the balloting only two days away, Lincoln still trailed Seward by as many as 90 votes, but Davis was happy. Lincoln's cause was moving forward, and he would likely have the solid second-place finish Davis wanted for his man.

The convention took over the city. Seward's men, led by a brass band with bright white and scarlet feathers in their hats, trooped up and down the streets playing the Seward campaign song, "Oh Isn't He a Darling?," as if the election was already over. Inside the hotels the delegates talked politics. As Murat Halstead of the *Cincinnati Commercial* described the scene, "Men gather in little groups, and with their arms about each other, and chatter and whisper as if the fate of the country depended upon their immediate delivery of the mighty political secrets with which their imaginations are big. . . . There are now at least a thousand men packed together in the halls of the Tremont House, crushing each other's ribs, tramping each other's toes, and titillating each other with the gossip of the day; and the probability is, not one is possessed of a single political fact not known to the whole, which is of the slightest consequence to any human being." It was an insistent crowd that surged up to the Wigwam on Wednesday, May 16, for the opening of the convention. One man, a Mr. Johns, delegate-at-large from Iowa, described as "a plain, homespun western farmer, but sound to the core," had walked 150 miles to get to the railroad that would bring him to Chicago. The doors opened and the flood of delegates, newsmen, and spectators poured in. The press tables had the latest in telegraphic equipment but only sixty seats for nine hundred applicants. The standing-room-only delegate floor for forty-five hundred was filled within five minutes. The galleries, which would accommodate gentlemen only in the company of ladies, caused considerable problems for the all-male convention. Schoolgirls were offered a quarter for their company, and one woman, who was offered a half-dollar, refused because she had already accompanied six gentlemen inside and was afraid the police would object if she came in a seventh time. One enterprising Republican attempted to bring in a Native American who was selling moccasins on the street but was rebuffed by the guards, who held that a Native American could not be a woman.

The first day of the convention was given over to forming committees and listening to prayers and speeches blessing various Republican endeavors. David Wilmot gave a stem-winder of an antislavery speech and there was a small flap over the seating of Horace Greeley. Shut out from the New York delegation by Seward, Greeley had managed to get himself seated as a delegate from Oregon. No one seemed to mind very much. There would always be room for Horace Greeley at a Republican convention, although some wag played a joke on the editor by pinning a Seward campaign badge on the back of his coat. George Ashmun of Massachusetts was named president of the convention and presented with a gavel made of wood from Com. Oliver Hazard Perry's flagship *Lawrence*. Knowing a cue when he saw one, Ashmun told the convention, "I have only to say today that all the auguries are that we shall meet the enemy and they shall be ours."

The most spirited debate was whether or not to accept the Chicago Board of Trade's invitation to take a boat ride on Lake Michigan later in the day. After some discussion it was agreed to go, and the convention adjourned until the next day, when the platform was to be adopted and the candidates voted upon.

Davis did not go on the boat ride. Nor did Weed. Both men worked furiously on the Kansas delegation. First the Kansans went over to see Weed for a smoke and a glass of champagne and a spot of politics. Weed surprised and delighted them by knowing most of their names and pouring the wine with a generous hand. As he told them how Seward was unbeatable, one Kansan said the expansive host reminded him of Byron's Corsair—"The mildest mannered man that ever scuttled a ship or cut a throat."

Arriving back at their hotel, the Kansans were greeted by a beatific Horace Greeley all pink and sleek, "looking like a well-to-do farmer fresh from his clover field." Greeley came quickly to the point: " . . . you couldn't elect Seward if you could nominate him . . . to name Seward, is to invite defeat. He cannot carry New Jersey, Pennsylvania, Indiana, or Iowa, and I will bring to you representative men from each of these states who will confirm what I say."

If Greeley had been fronting for Lincoln's men, which he was not (he still had hopes for Bates), he would have been hard put to define their position more clearly. Davis manipulated him masterfully. "We let Greeley run his Bates machine," Swett wrote later, "but got most of them for a second choice."

And for harder cases, Davis had stronger methods.

Gideon Welles, with a Santa Claus beard and an ill-fitting wig, came to Chicago heading up a badly split Connecticut delegation. He was not particularly well disposed toward Seward but was undecided about which way to jump until Lincoln's people talked to him about a cabinet position. Welles went to work and was later named Secretary of the Navy.

At some point Davis got to the influential Blair family of Maryland, which had been politically prominent since the days of Andrew Jackson. With the promise of Maryland's votes on the second ballot, Montgomery Blair was ticketed to be Postmaster General.

Thursday the seventeenth was largely given over to adopting the party platform, and had it not been for the excitement in the air of selecting the next President of the United States, a dreary day's work it would have been. The platform promised something for everyone except, perhaps, the slave-holding Southerners. There was a protective tariff to keep Greeley and Pennsylvania happy. There was a homestead law for the farmers and a Pacific railroad for the West. But there was little fire in the document. The 1856 platform had been given over almost entirely to the question of slavery. The 1860 platform included the issue as one of many before the voters, and not necessarily the most important one. The homestead and tariff planks received more cheers than the plank calling for the limiting of slavery.

So timid were the framers on the question of slavery that they turned down a proposed amendment by Joshua Giddings, an old campaigner in the abolitionist struggle, to reaffirm the line from the Declaration of Independence that "all men are created equal." Giddings, feeling "everything lost, even honor," stormed off the floor. His departure, however, was an empty gesture, for he was back a few minutes later when the New York delegation had the phrase inserted into the platform. As Giddings came back to his seat, William Evarts, Seward's floor manager from New York, commented, "Well, at least we saved the Declaration of Independence."

Unaware of the extent of the headway Davis was making off the convention floor, Seward's people were riding high. The delegates called to start the balloting, and if it had proceeded, Seward, still the leading candidate, would probably have been the party's nominee. But fate and Judge Davis intervened. The convention clerks said the tally sheets were prepared but, for some reason, were not at hand. After some desultory debate, the convention agreed to go to supper and reconvene in the morning.

Davis, "nearly dead from fatigue," would have one more night.

There was a great deal to do, and Davis was the sort of man who had a good eye for the detail as well as the big picture. To ensure that Lincoln was well represented on the floor with demonstrators, a large number of counterfeit tickets were printed and several Lincoln men stayed up all night forging signatures on them. And if Seward was going to have some shouters on the floor, so would Lincoln. Davis rounded up a group of strong-lunged men, including one Dr. Ames, reportedly possessed of lungs so hearty he could be heard across Lake Michigan, and even a stray democrat who apparently had nothing better to do the next day.

Nobody slept very much that night. Seward's band serenaded the streets as politicians crisscrossed the city. Weed reportedly uncorked three hundred bottles of champagne, and Halstead saw Henry Lane of Indiana, "pale and haggard, with cane under his arm, walking as if for a wager," going from one caucus to another trying to bring it home for Lincoln.

Greeley was making the rounds as well. His Bates boom had fizzled and at 11:40 P.M. Greeley telegraphed the *New York Tribune*, saying, "My conclusion, from all that I can gather to-night is, that, the opposition to Gov. Seward cannot concentrate on any candidate, and that he will be nominated."

Davis, however, was far from finished. After Greeley left, he met with members of the New Jersey and Pennsylvania delegations and produced a tabulation showing Lincoln a solid second with many more votes than any other candidate except Seward. Both states said they would caucus and get back to Davis. New Jersey agreed to go along that night, but Pennsylvania would let him know in the morning.

A few hours before the convention was to reconvene on Friday, Judge Joseph Casey from Harrisburg arrived with the deal. Simon Cameron would deliver Pennsylvania on the second ballot if he could be named Secretary of the Treasury. A wire went off to Lincoln saying things looked good if Cameron could be accommodated. Lincoln sent back a startling telegram: "I authorize no bargains and will be bound by none." The wording was simple enough, but what did Lincoln mean by it? He knew Davis was in Chicago making deals for him. That's why Davis was there in the first place. Besides, Lincoln also had said earlier that he wanted that "big Pennsylvania foot" to come down on the scale for him. Surely he did not mean to back off just because the going was getting a little rough. The most likely explanation is that Lincoln expected Davis to continue dealing in his name while he covered himself for the record. The "Rail Splitter" was developing the long view.

As his agents discussed the telegram, Davis cut in sharply, "Lincoln ain't here." The candidate, he went on, "don't know what we have to meet, so we will go ahead, as if we hadn't heard from him, and he must ratify it." Dr. Ray agreed. "We are after a bigger thing than that; we want the Presidency and the Treasury is not a great stake to pay for it."

The extent of just how much Davis actually committed in Lincoln's name has been the subject of debate ever since. When Davis and his team later presented Lincoln with the due bill for political services rendered in Chicago, he responded, "Well, gentlemen, where do I come in? You seem to have given everything away."

The results, however, are certain. Pennsylvania dutifully swung over to Lincoln on the second ballot, and its leader was awarded a seat in Lincoln's cabinet. The sticky-fingered Cameron didn't get the Treasury, however. That went to Salmon Chase of Ohio. Cameron was named Secretary of War and after one inept and corrupt year in office was shipped off to Moscow as the U.S. ambassador to Russia.

On Friday morning the Seward people received their first setback at the door. When Seward's brass band arrived with a thousand supporters, they found they couldn't get in. Their places had been taken by Lincoln men with forged tickets.

The nomination of the candidates was swiftly done with, and it was obvious that only Seward and Lincoln had any clear vocal support. When Seward's name was seconded, his depleted backers gave a good account of themselves. Trying to describe it stretched Halstead to the journalistic limit. He wrote: "The effect was startling. Hundreds of persons stopped their ears in pain. The shouting was absolutely frantic, shrill and wild. No Camanches, no panthers ever struck a higher note, or gave screams with more infernal intensity."

Then it was Lincoln's turn. "Imagine all the hogs ever slaughtered in Cincinnati giving their death squeals together, a score of big steam whistles going," Halstead wrote, "and you conceive something of the same nature. I thought the Seward yell could not be surpassed; but the Lincoln boys were clearly ahead. . . . "

When the shouting finally petered out, it was time to begin the balloting, and things began to unravel quickly for Seward. Maine, voting first, gave Seward 10 and Lincoln 6. Abolitionist New England, which was supposed to be solid for Seward, was starting to crack. New Hampshire cast one wistful vote for Fremont, one for Chase, one for Seward, and 7 for Lincoln. As Evarts tallied up the New England bloc, it showed 32 for Seward, 19 for Lincoln, and the remaining 30 spread out among the field. A lead, but not the kind to start parades for.

When New York was called, its 70 votes gave Seward a tally of 102 to only 19 for Lincoln. But then the senator ran into trouble. New Jersey held its 14 votes for Dayton and Pennsylvania gave Seward 1 1/2 and Lincoln 4, and kept 47 1/2 for Cameron. Virginia, which Seward had counted on, gave him only 8 and Lincoln 14. Henry Lane's eyes glittered when Indiana threw all 26 for Lincoln. By the end of the first ballot Seward led with 173 1/2, some 60 votes shy of the 233 needed to win; Lincoln held a surprisingly strong 102. It was now the two-man fight Davis had wanted, and the victory would go to the one who gained more on the second ballot.

Again it began badly for Seward. Lincoln picked up 2 more votes from New Hampshire, and Vermont abandoned its favorite son and cast all 10 for Lincoln. "This was a blighting blow upon the Seward interest," Halstead wrote. "The New Yorkers started as if an Orsini bomb had exploded." Welles never did deliver Connecticut entirely to Lincoln, but the state stayed out of the Seward column, giving 4 to Lincoln and spreading its other 8 among Bates, Chase, and Cassius Clay, the old war-horse from Kentucky. But when Pennsylvania weighed in with 48 for Lincoln, the rout was on. The results of the second ballot showed Seward hanging on with 184 1/2 and Lincoln with 181.

The third ballot was carried out "amid excitement that tested the nerves." Lincoln crept forward. Massachusetts took 4 of its Seward votes and gave them to Lincoln. Lincoln picked up a 3-vote lead from New Jersey and 4 more from Pennsylvania. Ohio came in with 29 for Lincoln, a gain of 15. He picked up 4 more when Oregon deserted Bates. Up and down the line it was almost all Lincoln. But would it be enough to put him over on this ballot? As the people in the hall tallied up the results, one newspaperman wrote, "a profound stillness suddenly fell upon the Wigwam; the men ceased to talk and the ladies to flutter their fans; one could distinctly hear the scratching of pencils and the ticking of telegraph instruments on the reporters' tables."

The tally showed Seward sagging to 181 and Lincoln at 231 1/2. Another vote and a half would do it.

It was time for one last squeeze. Sometime during the first ballot Medill had wormed his way into the Ohio delegation and sat next to its floor leader, D. K. Cartter. Medill whispered to Cartter that Salmon Chase had only to come to Lincoln and he "can have anything he wants." When the suspicious Cartter asked how he could be certain, Medill assured him by saying, "I know and you know I wouldn't promise if I didn't know."

Cartter, pockmarked and stammering, stood up on a chair and called for attention. "I-I a-a-rise, Mr. Chairman, to a-a-nounce the ch-change of f-four votes, from Mr. Chase to Abraham Lincoln."

It was done.

There was a moment's silence," Halstead noted. "The nerves of the thousands, which through the hours of suspense had been subjected to terrible tension, relaxed, and as deep breaths of relief were taken, there was a noise in the Wigwam like the rush of a great wind, in the van of a storm—and in another breath, the storm was there. There were thousands cheering with the energy of insanity."

One of the secretaries with a tally sheet in his hand shouted over the crowd what they already knew, "Fire the Salute—Abe Lincoln is nominated!" With tears on his cheeks, Evarts, as Seward's floor manager, moved to have the nomination made unanimous. A huge charcoal portrait of Lincoln was brought in for the convention to admire, and one exulting group of his supporters tried to seize the New York banner as a trophy but was fought off.

The Seward crusade was over. It was left to Austin Blair of Michigan to make, in elegiac tones, the speech of the day: 'Michigan, from first to last, has cast her vote for the great Statesman of New York. She has nothing to take back. She has not sent me forward to worship the rising sun, but she has put me forward to say that, at your behests here to-day, she lays down her first, best loved candidate to take up yours . . . she does not fear that the fame of Seward will suffer, for she knows that his fame is a portion of the history of the American Union; it will be written, and read, and beloved long after the temporary excitement of this day has passed away, and when Presidents themselves are forgotten in the oblivion which comes over all temporal things. We stand by him still. . . . " Other Seward supporters wanted to eulogize their man, but the convention was in a mood to celebrate and cut them off.

Back home, each candidate received the word by telegram. Always the pessimist, Lincoln had assumed he would lose and that the convention, after failing to nominate Seward on the first ballot, would turn to either Bates or Chase. When the wire arrived telling him of his victory, Lincoln accepted congratulations from his friends and said, "There is a lady over yonder on Eighth Street who is deeply interested in this news; I will carry it to her."

In Auburn, Seward read the telegram: "Lincoln nominated third ballot." There was no change of expression on his face. "Well," he said, "Mr. Lincoln will be elected and has some of the qualities to make a good President."

Earlier that evening Seward's friends had dragged a cannon up near his house to be used when the good news arrived. Quietly the six-pounder was wheeled away, and a few hours later, still primed with Seward shot and powder, it fired a salute to Abraham Lincoln, the next President of the United States.

November 1988

XVI

PRISON CAMPS OF THE CIVIL WAR

Bruce Catton

The horrors of the Civil War are manifold. Perhaps none so poignant as the fate of captured soldiers. With the breakdown of the exchange system, both North and South turned to the prison camp. No one involved on either side can escape blame for its deficiencies. Bruce Catton sheds light on this horrid system and the South's most "notorious" figure.

On the tenth day of November, 1865, a pale, black-whiskered little man named Henry Wirz, a used-up captain in the used-up army of the late Confederate States of America, walked through a door in the Old Capitol Prison at Washington, climbed thirteen wooden steps, and stood under the heavy crossbeam of a scaffold, a greased noose about his neck. On the platform with him—with him, but separated from him by the immense gap which sets apart those who are going to live from those who are about to die—there was a starchy major in the Federal Army. To this major Captain Wirz turned, extended his hand, and offered his pardon for the thing which the Federal major, detailed to take charge of a hanging squad, was about to do.

"I know what orders are, Major," said Captain Wirz. "I am being hung for obeying them."

The two men shook hands and drew apart. The drop was sprung, Captain Wirz dangled briefly at the end of a rope, died, and the thing was over. And across the northern part of the recently reunited United States many people took note and rejoiced that a villain who richly deserved hanging had finally got what was coming to him.

If the people of the North in the fall of 1865 had used the language of the late 1940s they would have said that Captain Wirz was a war criminal who had been properly convicted and then had been hanged for atrocious war crimes. Today, with the more sober perspective of nearly a century of peace, the business looks a little different. The language of the Old Testament would have been better; Wirz was a scapegoat, dying for the sins of many people, of whom some lived south of the Potomac River, while others lived north of it.

Indeed, the sins were not really sins at all, but simply wrongs—grievous wrongs against humanity, done by people who had meant to do no wrongs at all; wrongs done because of hasty action taken under immense pressure, growing out of human blundering and incompetence and the tangles of administrative red tape, with final responsibility traceable to the blinding passions born of a bewildering war. They took place in the South and they took place in the North, and some 50,000 Northern and Southern boys died because of them. In the fall of 1865 Captain Wirz died because of them too, and this did not help anybody very much except that it did provide a scapegoat.

Wirz had been commandant of Andersonville Prison, the hideous prison pen set up in February of 1864 by the dying Confederacy as a proper place to keep Union prisoners of war. First and last, more than 30,000 Union prisoners were kept there, and about 12,000 of them died, and the ones who did not die had a miserable time of it, so when the war ended there was a great clamor to punish someone. Henry Wirz stood in the path of that clamor, and he swung from a scaffold for it, leather straps about his arms and legs, a black mask over his contorted face; and somehow that was not quite the end of it.

The end of it could not come until enough years had passed to enable people to take a more detached view. The view that can be had now shows, quite simply, nothing much more than the fact that dreadful things happen in time of war, that these dreadful things are the fault of war itself rather than of individual people; and that when the business is all over, there is apt to be enough accumulated ill will lying around to create an explosion.

Wirz was born in Switzerland and by profession was a doctor. He came to America in 1849 after the death of his first wife, lived in Kentucky and then in Louisiana, remarried, and enlisted in a Louisiana volunteer regiment in 1861 after the fall of Fort Sumter. He was wounded in the right arm and shoulder in a battle early in the war, and the wound never healed properly. Wirz went back to duty for a time, but in 1863 he got leave and went to Europe for what he hoped would be better medical treatment. An operation was performed on his arm but it was not successful; the arm remained weak and painful, and Wirz—who was brusque and something of a martinet to begin with—grew irritable and snappish. Returning to the Confederacy, eventually, he was assigned early in 1864 to duty at the newly established prison camp at Andersonville, in the heart of Georgia.

Andersonville was destined to become the horrible example of the Civil War prison camp system, but the system itself was basically monstrous. At a time when all prison camps, in the North and South alike, were extremely bad, Andersonville became the worst of the lot, but it differed from the others in degree rather than in kind. Wirz obviously lacked the administrative capacity that a man in his job ought to have had, but given the circumstances under which Andersonville was set up and operated, it would have taken a complete administrative genius to keep the place from becoming anything but a horror.

Originally, the method of handling prisoners during the Civil War was based on a system of exchange. Early in the war the two governments, following long established military precedent, signed a cartel, which was in effect a sort of gentlemen's agreement providing that at frequent intervals the governments would exchange prisoners on a man-for-man basis. There was an intricate table of values: a lieutenant was worth a certain number of privates, a colonel was worth a larger number, and so on, and the bookkeeping occasionally became rather difficult. Many prisoners had to wait a long time for exchange, and now and then the warring governments found it hard to go along with a system which depended finally on mutual cooperation and trust, but in the main the thing worked tolerably well. At the very least it kept the prisoner-of-war population on both sides fairly stable and held the whole problem down to manageable size.

But in 1863 the business began to collapse, for a number of reasons which add up to the fact that the infinite pressures of wartime provided a load too heavy for any gentlemen's agreement to carry.

To begin with, the North had organized a number of black regiments, most of whose members were fugitive slaves, and the South refused to agree that these soldiers, when captured, were subject to ordinary exchange procedure; in retaliation, the North balked at making any exchanges at all. In addition, in the border states each side arrested a number of civilians, and there was endless argument as to whether these people came under the cartel.

When Vicksburg and Port Hudson surrendered in July, 1863, some 35,000 Confederate prisoners were released on parole, and the Federals charged that the Confederate authorities restored these men to duty in violation of the cartel.

Finally, Lieutenant General U. S. Grant became general in chief of the Union armies, and he surveyed the collapsing cartel with a coldly realistic eye. By this time there were more Confederate prisoners in the North than there were Union prisoners in the South, and the Confederacy was much more badly pinched for manpower than was the North. Grant concluded that the cessation of exchange hurt the South and, indirectly but effectively, helped the North. This, he admitted, was rough on the prisoners, but it brought Union victory nearer—and so the Northern government made very little effort to restore the exchange system to its former activity.

Because of all of this the population of Northern and Southern prison camps began to grow and kept on growing, and as it did so the camps became places of great hardship, suffering, and death. The size of the problem is shown by figures which the War Department in Washington compiled in July, 1866. These figures showed that from first to last the North held a total of 220,000 Confederates as prisoners, while the South held 126,000 Unionists. Of these, 26,436 Southerners died in the Northern camps, while 22,576 Northerners died in the Southern camps. The official who drew up the figures hastened to point out that this made the death rate in the Southern camps substantially higher than in the Northern camps, and he added that his estimate of Federal deaths was probably too low anyway.

As it happened, these figures are subject to a great deal of revision. The Northern historian, James Ford Rhodes, studied the whole business forty years later and concluded that the Confederacy had imprisoned some 194,000 Union soldiers and that the North had imprisoned about 215,000 Confederates. The War Department tabulation of deaths was fairly accurate. These figures indicate that by and large neither side had much reason to point any accusing fingers at the other side. Whether they were situated in the North or in the South, prison camps in the Civil War were almost incredibly lethal, and no refinement of figuring leaves one side looking much better than the other.

To understand how appallingly deadly the prison camps really were, one need do no more than reflect on this simple fact: about two and one-half times as many soldiers were exposed to the dangers of the prison camps as were exposed to the dangers of the great Battle of Gettysburg—and the camps killed nearly ten times as many as were killed at Gettysburg.

At the time, good people on both sides felt that their enemies were willfully and maliciously mistreating prisoners in order to kill them, but it is clear by now that nothing much more than sheer human clumsiness was involved. Looking back with the added knowledge of Civil War affairs which is available today, it is easy to understand why the prison camps became so terrible.

Each government, the one at Washington and the one at Richmond, was straining itself and its country's economy to conduct the war. Each government had many things to think of—raising and supporting armies, providing food and munitions and equipment, maintaining its finances and its industries and its transportation system, trying in short to handle an all-out war for which there had been no preparation of any consequence. In all of this, on each side, the conduct of the prison camps usually came last. Whatever time, money, energy, and administrative competence were left over, after the business of fighting the war was taken care of, could be applied to the care of prisoners. As the record proves, this was not nearly enough.

Under any circumstances, indeed, prison camps in that generation were certain to be bad. Even in his own army, when he was far removed from the battlefield and situated where he could get the best care his government could give him, the Civil War soldier existed under conditions that were just barely endurable. His food was bad, his housing was usually atrocious, his medical care was cruelly imperfect; disease and malnutrition killed far more soldiers (leaving those who died in prison entirely out of consideration) than ever died in combat. Just to be in the army at all was a serious danger to life and limb in the 1860s. To be a prisoner of war inevitably intensified that danger, not because anyone planned it that way bur simply because it was bound to happen so.

The Army of the Potomac, for instance, spent the winter of 1863 in camp near Fredericksburg, Virginia, fifty miles from Washington, with plenty of steamers plying an open waterway to bring supplies. In that winter, a number of the soldiers in that army died of scurvy, a malady that comes from nothing on earth but dietary deficiency: in this case, it was the result of a continued diet of salt pork and crackers. (The number of men in that army who died that winter of pneumonia, or of intestinal maladies stemming from bad food and bad sanitation, was ever so much greater than the number that died of scurvy.) These things happened to men who were in winter quarters, within easy traveling distance of their own capital, under a government which was doing its best to provide them with every necessity. This being the case, it is not hard to see why men in prison camps had it really rough.

Andersonville Prison came into existence in February, 1864, under conditions which made it inevitable that it would become the worst of the lot.

The site had been selected a few months earlier, when the Confederate authorities concluded that they needed a prison camp far enough from the fighting fronts to provide security and large enough to accommodate prisoners who would have to be removed from places dangerously near the advancing Federal armies. A sixteen and one-half acre enclosure was set up in a rolling meadow crossed by a little stream, and a stockade was built around it; the first prisoners arrived before the stockade was finished, and before the prison bake-house had been built, and there were no barracks or huts of any kind; and before the authorities could get hold of the situation and get the place into proper order, they began to be swamped by an unceasing influx of prisoners whose rate of arrival constantly outpaced the authorities' efforts to prepare for their reception. The stockade was indeed finished, and the cook-house was completed, but 400 prisoners were arriving every day; by March there were 7,500 of them in the stockade, and by May the enclosure which had been designed to accommodate 10,000 men had 15,000 prisoners, with new ones coming in every week.

Wirz got to Andersonville early in April, and he did his best to cope with the situation, but things were simply out of hand. Many things needed to be done. The prisoners had no housing, except for such foxholes as they might grub out or such makeshift tents as they could put together out of blankets, branches of trees, and odds and ends of planks. The authorities possessed no axes, spades, shovels, picks, or other tools, and found it almost impossible to get any. At about the time Wirz got there, a worried Confederate colonel was reporting that although many prisoners were dying every day, he lacked even implements to dig graves. Wirz said that it was well along in May before he got the tools he had to have, and although he did his best to dig drainage ditches and keep the little stream unpolluted, the problem of sanitation was forever beyond solution. By midsummer he had managed to enlarge the stockade by ten acres, but by now there were 30,000 prisoners and the prison pen was little better than a slimy quagmire. A Confederate officer who inspected the place in August reported that there was just enough room to provide about six square feet of ground for each prisoner, and men were dying at the rate of 100 a day.

It was never possible to do much about it, although Wirz tried. His real problem was beyond him: the Confederate economy, ground down by four years of war, was collapsing, and the task of maintaining a decent prison for 30,000 men was impossible. The ruinous inability even to get tools to build the place was symptomatic. Near the prison there were enough trees to provide lumber for all the barracks, hospitals, and other buildings anyone could have wanted, but the manpower, money, and equipment to turn these trees into lumber and then into prison buildings just were not there. Georgia had a big surplus of food—when Sherman's boys marched through in the fall of 1864 they found more than they could eat, and wasted tons of good food—but the railroads were breaking down, government machinery was doing the same, and Confederate armies were going hungry. When the Confederacy could not even feed its own soldiers, it was not going to be able to give much food to its war prisoners. So the boys at Andersonville got, mostly, corn meal made out of corn with the cobs ground in with it, unsifted, and a good many of them died because of it; they blamed Wirz, as they blamed him because the prison hospital was terrible, and because the whole camp was terrible, and because he was a short-tempered man trying to do an impossible job with next to no help at all; but it was not Wirz's fault. He did his best, his best was not good enough, but nobody's best would have been adequate.

Andersonville, in short, was about as bad as a place could conceivably be. Its horrors were publicized then and have been described in detail at intervals ever since, and there is no point in repeating the catalogue of horrors. But all of the other prison camps were bad, too, and the Northern camps killed their full quota of Southerners.

There was, for instance, a Northern camp at Elmira, New York; another camp in the middle of a prosperous state, this one situated in a country whose economy was booming, maintained by a government which was strong and rich and which was going to live for a long time. In the fall of 1864 the hospital surgeon at Elmira complained to the War Department. In three months, he said, with some 8,347 prisoners in camp, 2,011 had been admitted to the prison hospital, and 775—over a third of those admitted—had died. On the average, he pointed out, there were 451 men in hospital every day and 601 more sick in their quarters, which meant that about one eighth of the number in prison was on the sick list. He added: "At this rate the entire command will be admitted to hospital in less than a year and 36 per cent die." He reported that the entire prison enclosure stank to the high heavens, that a river which flowed through the ground had formed a gummy pond, "green with putrescence, filling the air with its messengers of disease and death," that his applications for medicines were ignored, and that because he had been unable to get straw a good many of his patients had to lie on the hospital floor.

Elmira was a fair sample. There was a Federal prison camp on an island in the Mississippi at Rock Island, Illinois, where more than 1,800 Confederates died; a medical inspector reported that this was partly because smallpox struck the camp and partly because, when the place was laid out, no one had bothered to put up any hospital facilities. Certain barracks were set apart for the purpose, but smallpox patients had to lie in wards with men suffering from lesser ailments, and a Federal doctor complained that there was "a striking want of some means for the preservation of human life which medical and sanitary science has indicated as proper."

At Fort Delaware, on Pea Patch Island near the mouth of the Delaware River, barracks were built on marshy ground which was so soggy that the buildings settled and were in danger of toppling over; cooking facilities were inadequate, sanitary conditions were so bad that typhoid fever was prevalent, and long after the war a marker was erected in memory of the 2,436 Confederate prisoners who died in the place. During 1864 the big prison camp at Point Lookout, Maryland, put over 1,200 Confederate soldiers into their graves. Filth, poor drainage, and overcrowding created a horror at Camp Douglas, on the edge of Chicago, and the president of the United States Sanitary Commission after inspecting the place asserted that the conditions were "enough to drive a sanitarian mad." In the fall of 1864 the colonel who commanded this camp reported that 984 of his 7,402 prisoners were sick, said that there had been "a lack of efficiency in the management of the medical affairs of the post," and complained that many prisoners had scurvy because no vegetables or other antiscorbutics were available.

The climate often added to the prisoners' woes. Southern boys were not used to cold northern winters, and they usually lacked adequate clothing and blankets; the camp for Confederate officers on Johnson's Island, in Lake Erie, seems to have been an especially chilly place, although it must be added that the death rate at this prison was never high. Northern boys, similarly, found the hot summers of the Deep South hard to endure, especially in some of the stockaded camps where they could not get shelter from the sun. The notorious Libby Prison in Richmond, a ponderous building that used to be a tobacco warehouse, was verminous and, like most prisons, served terrible food, but had the advantage of being less than escapeproof; in February, 1864, prisoners dug a tunnel, and 109 of them got out, 48 being recaptured before they could reach the Union lines.

High bounty laws in the North caused special problems in certain Southern prisons, most notably in Andersonville. When a man who enlisted could get more than $1,000 in cash—which was the case in many northern states in 1864—many out-and-out thugs took this route to easy riches, signing up as volunteers with every intention of deserting promptly and re-enlisting under another name somewhere else. Most of them got away with it, but some got into action and were captured by the Confederates before they could desert, and in the prison camps they were dangerous nuisances, forming gangs to rob their fellow prisoners of anything worth taking, from rations to blankets to cash. Since the Confederacy had just barely enough soldiers to guard its prison camps, they were rarely able to police the activities of the prisoners. At Belle Isle, a pen on an island in the James River at Richmond, the commandant confessed that he could do nothing to suppress the gangsters' activities; it was all he could do to keep the whole set of prisoners from escaping en masse. At Andersonville the prisoners themselves formed a vigilance committee and tried and hanged six of the worst gangsters, with Wirz's approval. Eighteen other gangsters who escaped hanging were beaten so badly that three of them died.

Early in the fall of 1864, the warring governments did work out a deal for the exchange of prisoners who were obviously too sick to be put back in combat assignments. The prison authorities at Elmira culled out 1,200 such men and put them on a train for Baltimore, where they would take ship for some Southern port. Federal doctors who met the train protested that many of the men shipped off were in no condition to travel; five had died on the train, sixty more had to be sent off to hospital as soon as they got to Baltimore, and the steamer that was waiting for them had neither doctors, orderlies, nor nurses. The medical officers who had chosen the men to be transferred, these surgeons complained, had been guilty of "criminal neglect and inhumanity," and the commander of the Elmira camp wrote that even though he had sent away 1,200 of his worst cases, his hospital soon was as crowded as ever, with a fearful death rate.

If an indictment can be drawn up against Andersonville, then, indictments can also be brought against the other camps. Andersonville, to be sure, was by all odds the worst place of the lot, and, quite naturally—because it was the worst, and also because it was the biggest—it got the most attention. And when the war ended, Andersonville became, in the eyes of the people of the North, the great symbol of all of the needless suffering the war had caused, the prime example of man's inhumanity to man, which, because it had caused so much misery for so many people, must somehow be punished.

So Wirz was arrested, lodged in prison, and on August 21, 1865, he went on trial before a military commission in Washington. He was charged with conspiring with other Confederate officers to weaken or kill Union prisoners, and with murder "in violation of the laws and customs of war." If Andersonville was the accepted symbol of the barbarities of war, Wirz had become the symbol of Andersonville. The press characterized him as "the Andersonville savage," "the inhuman wretch," and "the infamous captain," and his leading attorney remarked, with some reason, that Wirz was doomed before he even got a hearing.

To the Union soldiers who had been at Andersonville Wirz seemed a villain. They knew that they had suffered infamous treatment; Wirz was the man, as far as they could see, through whom this treatment had come. He had tried to run a decent prison, but no living mortal could have accomplished that at Andersonville, considering all of the handicaps, and anyway the men who had been imprisoned there knew nothing of his efforts or of his problems; they know only that the place had been a hellhole, that he apparently had been in charge of it, and that he was stiff, arrogant, and peevish in his demeanor. The military court clearly shared their feeling. It heard a vast amount of evidence about horrible conditions in the prison, passed lightly over the evidence that went to show that Wirz had tried without success to get these conditions bettered, and refused to hear any testimony which might indicate that Northern prison camps were not very much better than Andersonville. In the end, as might have been expected, Wirz was convicted and was sentenced to be hanged. President Andrew Johnson refused to intervene, and the sentence was carried out.

So on November 10, 1865, Wirz was led into the courtyard at Old Capitol Prison. En route he stopped at the door of a fellow prisoner and asked the man to take care of Mrs. Wirz and the Wirz children, and to do what he could to clear Wirz's name of the stigma which had been put upon it. Then he went on, to meet his death with a cool composure which moved *Leslie's Illustrated* (which had denounced him bitterly during his trial) to remark that there was "something in his face and step which, in a better man, might have passed for heroism."

If there had been a conspiracy to kill Union prisoners, nobody ever heard any more about it. All of the men who had been accused with Wirz were released without trial. The War Department theory that Jefferson Davis, president of the Southern Confederacy, had himself motivated this "conspiracy" evaporated, and Davis too was finally released from his confinement.

Andersonville remained a reproach for years to come, a favorite topic during the 1880s and 1890s for Northern political candidates who sought election by the process of "waving the bloody shirt." But the passage of the years has at last brought a new perspective. Andersonville is now seen as a creation of its time and place, the worst of a large number of war prisons, all of which were almost unbelievably bad. And the real culprit is seen now not as Wirz, the luckless scapegoat, but as war itself.

August 1959

THE NEW VIEW OF RECONSTRUCTION

Eric Foner

For many decades the assessment of the South's reunion with the North has been told in lu-rid terms. Unscrupulous northerners, conscienceless southern trash and illiterate freedmen conspired to destroy decent white victims of the war. These gross distortions have been put into a more balanced perspective by contemporary historians. Eric Foner presents a brief overview of these current perspectives and findings.

In the past twenty years, no period of American history has been the subject of a more thoroughgoing reevaluation than Reconstruction—the violent, dramatic, and still controversial era following the Civil War. Race relations, politics, social life, and economic change during Reconstruction have all been reinterpreted in the light of changed attitudes toward the place of blacks within American society. If historians have not yet forged a fully satisfying portrait of Reconstruction as a whole, the traditional interpretation that dominated historical writing for much of this century has irrevocably been laid to rest.

Anyone who attended high school before 1960 learned that Reconstruction was an era of unrelieved sordidness in American political and social life. The martyred Lincoln, according to this view, had planned a quick and painless re-admission of the Southern states as equal members of the national family. President Andrew Johnson, his successor, attempted to carry out Lincoln's policies but was foiled by the Radical Republicans (also known as Vindictives or Jacobins). Motivated by an irrational hatred of Rebels or by ties with Northern capitalists out to plunder the South, the Radicals swept aside Johnson's lenient program and fastened black supremacy upon the defeated Confederacy. An orgy of corruption followed, presided over by unscrupulous carpetbaggers (Northerners who ventured south to reap the spoils of office), traitorous scalawags (Southern whites who cooperated with the new governments for personal gain), and the ignorant and childlike freedmen, who were incapable of properly exercising the political power that had been thrust upon them. After much needless suffering, the white community of the South banded together to overthrow these "black" governments and restore home rule (their euphemism for white supremacy). All told, Reconstruction was just about the darkest page in the American saga.

Originating in anti-Reconstruction propaganda of Southern Democrats during the 1870s, this traditional interpretation achieved scholarly legitimacy around the turn of the century through the work of William Dunning and his students at Columbia University. It reached the larger public through films like *Birth of a Nation* and *Gone With the Wind* and that best-selling work of myth-making masquerading as history, *The Tragic Era* by Claude

G. Bowers. In language as exaggerated as it was colorful, Bowers told how Andrew Johnson "fought the bravest battle for constitutional liberty and for the preservation of our institutions ever waged by an Executive" but was overwhelmed by the "poisonous propaganda" of the Radicals. Southern whites, as a result, "literally were put to the torture" by "emissaries of hate" who manipulated the "simple-minded" freedmen, "inflaming the negroes' egotism" and even inspiring "lustful assaults" by blacks upon white womanhood.

In a discipline that sometimes seems to pride itself on the rapid rise and fall of historical interpretations, this traditional portrait of Reconstruction enjoyed remarkable staying power. The long reign of the old interpretation is not difficult to explain. It presented a set of easily identifiable heroes and villains. It enjoyed the imprimatur of the nation's leading scholars. And it accorded with the political and social realities of the first half of this century. This image of Reconstruction helped freeze the mind of the white South in unalterable opposition to any movement for breaching the ascendancy of the Democratic party, eliminating segregation, or readmitting disfranchised blacks to the vote.

Nevertheless, the demise of the traditional interpretation was inevitable, for it ignored the testimony of the central participant in the drama of Reconstruction—the black freedman. Furthermore, it was grounded in the conviction that blacks were unfit to share in political power. As Dunning's Columbia colleague John W. Burgess put it, "A black skin means membership in a race of men which has never of itself succeeded in subjecting passion to reason, has never, therefore, created any civilization of any kind." Once objective scholarship and modern experience rendered that assumption untenable, the entire edifice was bound to fall.

The work of "revising" the history of Reconstruction began with the writings of a handful of survivors of the era, such as John R. Lynch, who had served as a black congressman from Mississippi after the Civil War. In the 1930s white scholars like Francis Simkins and Robert Woody carried the task forward. Then, in 1935, the black historian and activist W.E.B. Du Bois produced *Black Reconstruction* in America, a monumental reevaluation that closed with an irrefutable indictment of an historical profession that had sacrificed scholarly objectivity on the altar of racial bias. "One fact and one alone," he wrote, "explains the attitude of most recent writers toward Reconstruction; they cannot conceive of Negroes as men." Du Bois's work, however, was ignored by most historians.

It was not until the 1960s that the full force of the revisionist wave broke over the field. Then, in rapid succession, virtually every assumption of the traditional viewpoint was systematically dismantled. A drastically different portrait emerged to take its place. President Lincoln did not have a coherent "Plan" for Reconstruction, but at the time of his assassination he had been cautiously contemplating black suffrage. Andrew Johnson was a stubborn, racist politician who lacked the ability to compromise. By isolating himself from the broad currents of public opinion that had nourished Lincoln's career, Johnson created an impasse with Congress that Lincoln would certainly have avoided, thus throwing away his political power and destroying his own plans for reconstructing the South.

The Radicals in Congress were acquitted of both vindictive motives and the charge of serving as the stalking-horses of Northern capitalism. They emerged instead as idealists in the best nineteenth-century reform tradition. Radical leaders like Charles Sumner and Thaddeus Stevens had worked for the rights of blacks long before any conceivable political advantage flowed from such a commitment. Stevens refused to sign the Pennsylvania Constitution of 1838 because it disfranchised the state's black citizens; Sumner led a fight in the 1850s to integrate Boston's public schools. Their Reconstruction policies were based on principle, not petty political advantage, for the central issue dividing Johnson and these Radical Republicans was the civil rights of freedmen. Studies of congressional policy-making, such as Eric L. McKitrick's Andrew Johnson and Reconstruction, also revealed that Reconstruction legislation, ranging from the Civil Rights Act of 1866 to the Fourteenth and Fifteenth Amendments, enjoyed broad support from moderate and conservative Republicans. It was not simply the work of a narrow radical faction.

Even more startling was the revised portrait of Reconstruction in the South itself. Imbued with the spirit of the civil rights movement and rejecting entirely the racial assumptions that had underpinned the traditional interpretation, these historians evaluated Reconstruction from the black point of view. Works like Joel Williamson's *After Slavery* portrayed the period as a time of extraordinary political, social, and economic progress for blacks. The establishment of public school systems, the granting of equal citizenship to blacks, the effort to restore the devastated Southern economy, the attempt to construct an interracial political democracy from the ashes of slavery, all these were commendable achievements, not the elements of Bowers's "tragic era."

Unlike earlier writers, the revisionists stressed the active role of the freedmen in shaping Reconstruction. Black initiative established as many schools as did Northern religious societies and the Freedmen's Bureau. The right to vote was not simply thrust upon them by meddling outsiders, since blacks began agitating for the suffrage as soon as they were freed. In 1865 black conventions throughout the South issued eloquent, though unheeded, appeals for equal civil and political rights.

With the advent of Radical Reconstruction in 1867, the freedmen did enjoy a real measure of political power. But black supremacy never existed. In most states blacks held only a small fraction of political offices, and even in South Carolina, where they comprised a majority of the state legislature's lower house, effective power remained in white hands. As for corruption, moral standards in both government and private enterprise were at low ebb throughout the nation in the postwar years—the era of Boss Tweed, the Credit Mobilier scandal, and the Whiskey Ring. Southern corruption could hardly be blamed on former slaves.

Other actors in the Reconstruction drama also came in for reevaluation. Most carpetbaggers were former Union soldiers seeking economic opportunity in the postwar South, not unscrupulous adventurers. Their motives, a typically American amalgam of humanitarianism and the pursuit of profit, were no more insidious than those of Western pioneers. Scalawags, previously seen as traitors to the white race, now emerged as "Old Line" Whig Unionists who had opposed secession in the first place or as poor whites who had long resented planters' domination of Southern life and who saw in Reconstruction a chance to recast Southern society along more democratic lines. Strongholds of Southern white Republicanism like east Tennessee and western North Carolina had been the scene of resistance to Confederate rule throughout the Civil War; now, as one scalawag newspaper put it, the choice was "between salvation at the hand of the Negro or destruction at the hand of the rebels."

At the same time, the Ku Klux Klan and kindred groups, whose campaign of violence against black and white Republicans had been minimized or excused in older writings, were portrayed as they really were. Earlier scholars had conveyed the impression that the Klan intimidated blacks mainly by dressing as ghosts and playing on the freedmen's superstitions. In fact, black fears were all too real: the Klan was a terrorist organization that beat and killed its political opponents to deprive blacks of their newly won rights. The complicity of the Democratic party and the silence of prominent whites in the face of such outrages stood as an indictment of the moral code the South had inherited from the days of slavery.

By the end of the 1960s, then, the old interpretation had been completely reversed. Southern freedmen were the heroes, the "Redeemers" who overthrew Reconstruction were the villains, and if the era was "tragic," it was because change did not go far enough. Reconstruction had been a time of real progress and its failure a lost opportunity for the South and the nation. But the legacy of Reconstruction—the Fourteenth and Fifteenth Amendments—endured to inspire future efforts for civil rights. As Kenneth Stampp wrote in *The Era of Reconstruction,* a superb summary of revisionist findings published in 1965, "If it was worth four years of civil war to save the Union, it was worth a few years of radical reconstruction to give the American Negro the ultimate promise of equal civil and political rights."

As Stampp's statement suggests, the reevaluation of the first Reconstruction was inspired in large measure by the impact of the second—the modern civil rights movement. And with the waning of that movement in recent years, writing on Reconstruction has undergone still another transformation. Instead of seeing the Civil War and its aftermath as a second American Revolution (as Charles Beard had), a regression into barbarism (as Bowers argued), or a golden opportunity squandered (as the revisionists saw it), recent writers argue that Radical Reconstruction was not really very radical. Since land was not distributed to the former slaves, they remained economically dependent upon their former owners. The planter class survived both the war and Reconstruction with its property (apart from slaves) and prestige more or less intact.

Not only changing times but also the changing concerns of historians have contributed to this latest reassessment of Reconstruction. The hallmark of the past decade's historical writing has been an emphasis upon "social history"—the evocation of the past lives of ordinary Americans—and the downplaying of strictly political events. When applied to Reconstruction, this concern with the "social" suggested that black suffrage and officeholding, once seen as the most radical departures of the Reconstruction era, were relatively insignificant.

Recent historians have focused their investigations not upon the politics of Reconstruction but upon the social and economic aspects of the transition from slavery to freedom. Herbert Gutman's influential study of the black family during and after slavery found little change in family structure or relations between men and women resulting from emancipation. Under slavery most blacks had lived in nuclear family units, although they faced the constant threat of separation from loved ones by sale. Reconstruction provided the opportunity for blacks to solidify their preexisting family ties. Conflicts over whether black women should work in the cotton fields (planters said yes, many black families said no) and over white attempts to "apprentice" black children revealed that the autonomy of family life was a major preoccupation of the freedmen. Indeed, whether manifested in their withdrawal from churches controlled by whites, in the blossoming of black fraternal, benevolent, and self-improvement organizations, or in the demise of the slave quarters and their replacement by small tenant farms occupied by individual families, the quest for independence from white authority and control over their own day-to-day lives shaped the black response to emancipation.

In the post-Civil War South the surest guarantee of economic autonomy, blacks believed, was land. To the freedmen the justice of a claim to land based on their years of unrequited labor appeared self-evident. As an Alabama black convention put it, "The property which they [the planters] hold was nearly all earned by the sweat of *our* brows." As Leon Litwack showed in *Been in the Storm So Long,* a Pulitzer Prize-winning account of the black response to emancipation, many freedmen in 1865 and 1866 refused to sign labor contracts, expecting the federal government to give them land. In some localities, as one Alabama overseer reported, they "set up claims to the Plantation and all on it."

In the end, of course, the vast majority of Southern blacks remained propertyless and poor. But exactly why the South, and especially its black population, suffered from dire poverty and economic retardation in the decades following the Civil War is a matter of much dispute. In *One Kind of Freedom,* economists Roger Ransom and Richard Sutch indicted country merchants for monopolizing credit and charging usurious interest rates, forcing black tenants into debt and locking the South into a dependence on cotton production that impoverished the entire region. But Jonathan Wiener, in his study of postwar Alabama, argued that planters used their political power to compel blacks to remain on the plantations. Planters succeeded in stabilizing the plantation system, but only by blocking the growth of alternative enterprises, like factories, that might draw off black laborers, thus locking the region into a pattern of economic backwardness.

If the thrust of recent writing has emphasized the social and economic aspects of Reconstruction, politics has not been entirely neglected. But political studies have also reflected the postrevisionist mood summarized by C. Vann Woodward when he observed "how essentially nonrevolutionary and conservative Reconstruction really was." Recent writers, unlike their revisionist predecessors, have found little to praise in federal policy toward the emancipated blacks.

A new sensitivity to the strength of prejudice and laissez-faire ideas in the nineteenth-century North has led many historians to doubt whether the Republican party ever made a genuine commitment to racial justice in the South. The granting of black suffrage was an alternative to a long-term federal responsibility for protecting the rights of the former slaves. Once enfranchised, blacks could be left to fend for themselves. With the exception of a few Radicals like Thaddeus Stevens, nearly all Northern policy-makers and educators are criticized today for assuming that, so long as the unfettered operations of the marketplace afforded blacks the opportunity to advance through diligent labor, federal efforts to assist them in acquiring land were unnecessary.

Probably the most innovative recent writing on Reconstruction politics has centered on a broad reassessment of black Republicanism, largely undertaken by a new generation of black historians. Scholars like Thomas Holt and Nell Painter insist that Reconstruction was not simply a matter of black and white. Conflicts within the black community, no less than divisions among whites, shaped Reconstruction politics. Where revisionist scholars, both black and white, had celebrated the accomplishments of black political leaders, Holt, Painter, and others charge that they failed to address the economic plight of the black masses. Painter criticized "representative colored men," as national black leaders were called, for failing to provide ordinary freedmen with effective political leadership. Holt found that black officeholders in South Carolina mostly emerged from the old free mulatto class of Charleston, which shared many assumptions with prominent whites. "Basically bourgeois in their origins and orientation," he wrote, they "failed to act in the interest of black peasants."

In emphasizing the persistence from slavery of divisions between free blacks and slaves, these writers reflect the increasing concern with continuity and conservatism in Reconstruction. Their work reflects a startling extension of revisionist premises. If, as has been argued for the past twenty years, blacks were active agents rather than mere victims of manipulation, then they could not be absolved of blame for the ultimate failure of Reconstruction.

Despite the excellence of recent writing and the continual expansion of our knowledge of the period, historians of Reconstruction today face a unique dilemma. An old interpretation has been overthrown, but a coherent new synthesis has yet to take its place. The revisionists of the 1960s effectively established a series of negative points: the Reconstruction governments were not as bad as had been portrayed, black supremacy was a myth, the Radicals were not cynical manipulators of the freedmen. Yet no convincing overall portrait of the quality of political and social life emerged from their writings. More recent historians have rightly pointed to elements of continuity that spanned the nineteenth-century Southern experience, especially the survival, in modified form, of the plantation system. Nevertheless, by denying the real

changes that did occur, they have failed to provide a convincing portrait of an era characterized above all by drama, turmoil, and social change.

Building upon the findings of the past twenty years of scholarship, a new portrait of Reconstruction ought to begin by viewing it not as a specific time period, bounded by the years
1865 and 1877, but as an episode in a prolonged historical process—American society's ad-
justment to the consequences of the Civil War and emancipation. The Civil War, of course,
raised the decisive questions of America's national existence: the relations between local and
national authority, the definition of citizenship, the balance between force and consent in
generating obedience to authority. The war and Reconstruction, as Allan Nevins observed
over fifty years ago, marked the "emergence of modern America." This was the era of the com-
pletion of the national railroad network, the creation of the modern steel industry, the conquest of the West and final subduing of the Native Americans, and the expansion of the
mining frontier. Lincoln's America—the world of the small farm and artisan shop—gave way
to a rapidly industrializing economy. The issues that galvanized postwar Northern politics—
from the question of the greenback currency to the mode of paying holders of the national
debt—arose from the economic changes unleashed by the Civil War.

Above all, the war irrevocably abolished slavery. Since 1619, when "twenty negars" disem-
barked from a Dutch ship in Virginia, racial injustice had haunted American life, mocking its
professed ideals even as tobacco and cotton, the products of slave labor, helped finance the nation's economic development. Now the implications of the black presence could no longer be
ignored. The Civil War resolved the problem of slavery but, as the Philadelphia diarist Sydney
George Fisher observed in June 1865, it opened an even more intractable problem: "What
shall we do with the Negro?" Indeed, he went on, this was a problem "*incapable* of any solution that will satisfy both North and South."

As Fisher realized, the focal point of Reconstruction was the social revolution known as
emancipation. Plantation slavery was simultaneously a system of labor, a form of racial domination, and the foundation upon which arose a distinctive ruling class within the South. Its
demise threw open the most fundamental questions of economy, society, and politics. A new
system of labor, social, racial, and political relations had to be created to replace slavery.

The United States was not the only nation to experience emancipation in the nineteenth
century. Neither plantation slavery, nor abolition were unique to the United States. But Reconstruction was. In a comparative perspective Radical Reconstruction stands as a remarkable
experiment, the only effort of a society experiencing abolition to bring the former slaves within the umbrella of equal citizenship. Because the Radicals did not achieve everything they
wanted, historians have lately tended to play down the stunning departure represented by
black suffrage and officeholding. Former slaves, most fewer than two years removed from
bondage, debated the fundamental questions of the polity: What is a republican form of government? Should the state provide equal education for all? How could political equality be
reconciled with a society in which property was so unequally distributed? There was something inspiring in the way such men met the challenge of Reconstruction. "I knew nothing
more than to obey my master," James K. Greene, an Alabama black politician later recalled.
"But the tocsin of freedom sounded and knocked at the door and we walked out like free men
and we met the exigencies as they grew up, and shouldered the responsibilities."

"You never saw a people more excited on the subject of politics than are the negroes of the
south," one Planter observed in 1867. And there were more than a few Southern whites as
well who in these years shook off the prejudices of the past to embrace the vision of a new
South dedicated to the principles of equal citizenship and social justice. One ordinary South
Carolinian expressed the new sense of possibility in 1868 to the Republican governor of the

state: "I am sorry that I cannot write an elegant stiled letter to your excellency. But I rejoice to think that God almighty has given to the poor of S.C. a Gov. to hear to feel to protect the humble poor without distinction to race or color. . . . I am a native borned S.C. a poor man never owned a Negro in my life nor my father before me. . . . Remember the true and loyal are the poor of the whites and blacks, outside of these you can find none loyal."

Few modern scholars believe the Reconstruction governments established in the South in 1867 and 1868 fulfilled the aspirations of their humble constituents. While their achievements in such realms as education, civil rights, and the economic rebuilding of the South are now widely appreciated, historians today believe they failed to affect either the economic plight of the emancipated slave or the ongoing transformation of independent white farmers into cotton tenants. Yet their opponents did perceive the Reconstruction governments in precisely this way—as representatives of a revolution that had put the bottom rail, both racial and economic, on top. This perception helps explain the ferocity of the attacks leveled against them and the pervasiveness of violence in the postemancipation South.

The spectacle of black men voting and holding office was anathema to large numbers of Southern whites. Even more disturbing, at least in the view of those who still controlled the plantation regions of the South, was the emergence of local officials, black and white, who sympathized with the plight of the black laborer. Alabama's vagrancy law was a "dead letter" in 1870, "because those who are charged with its enforcement are indebted to the vagrant vote for their offices and emoluments." Political debates over the level and incidence of taxation, the control of crops, and the resolution of contract disputes revealed that a primary issue of Reconstruction was the role of government in a plantation society. During presidential Reconstruction, and after "Redemption," with planters and their allies in control of politics, the law emerged as a means of stabilizing and promoting the plantation system. If Radical Reconstruction failed to redistribute the land of the South, the ouster of the planter class from control of politics at least ensured that the sanctions of the criminal law would not be employed to discipline the black labor force.

An understanding of this fundamental conflict over the relation between government and society helps explain the pervasive complaints concerning corruption and "extravagance" during Radical Reconstruction. Corruption there was aplenty; tax rates did rise sharply. More significant than the rate of taxation, however, was the change in its incidence. For the first time, planters and white farmers had to pay a significant portion of their income to the government, while propertyless blacks often escaped scot-free. Several states, moreover, enacted heavy taxes on uncultivated land to discourage land speculation and force land onto the market, benefiting, it was hoped, the freedmen.

As time passed, complaints about the "extravagance" and corruption of Southern governments found a sympathetic audience among influential Northerners. The Democratic charge that universal suffrage in the South was responsible for high taxes and governmental extravagance coincided with a rising conviction among the urban middle classes of the North that city government had to be taken out of the hands of the immigrant poor and returned to the "best men"—the educated, professional, financially independent citizens unable to exert much political influence at a time of mass parties and machine politics. Increasingly the "respectable" middle classes began to retreat from the very notion of universal suffrage. The poor were no longer perceived as honest producers, the backbone of the social order; now they became the "dangerous classes," the "mob." As the historian Francis Parkman put it, too much power rested with "masses of imported ignorance and hereditary ineptitude." To Parkman the Irish of the Northern cities and the blacks of the South were equally incapable of utilizing the ballot: "Witness the municipal corruptions of New York, and the monstrosities of negro rule in South Carolina." Such attitudes helped to justify Northern inaction as, one by one, the Reconstruction regimes of the South were overthrown by political violence.

In the end, then, neither the abolition of slavery nor Reconstruction succeeded in resolving the debate over the meaning of freedom in American life. Twenty years before the American Civil War, writing about the prospect of abolition in France's colonies, Alexis de Tocqueville had written, "If the Negroes have the right to become free, the [planters] have the incontestable right not to be ruined by the Negroes' freedom." And in the United States, as in nearly every plantation society that experienced the end of slavery, a rigid social and political dichotomy between former master and former slave, an ideology of racism, and a dependent labor force with limited economic opportunities all survived abolition. Unless one means by freedom the simple fact of not being a slave, emancipation thrust blacks into a kind of no-man's land, a partial freedom that made a mockery of the American ideal of equal citizenship.

Yet by the same token the ultimate outcome underscores the uniqueness of Reconstruction itself. Alone among the societies that abolished slavery in the nineteenth century, the United States, for a moment, offered the freedmen a measure of political control over their own destinies. However brief its sway, Reconstruction allowed scope for a remarkable political and social mobilization of the black community. It opened doors of opportunity that could never be completely closed. Reconstruction transformed the lives of Southern blacks in ways unmeasurable by statistics and unreachable by law. It raised their expectations and aspirations, redefined their status in relation to the larger society, and allowed space for the creation of institutions that enabled them to survive the repression that followed. And it established constitutional principles of civil and political equality that, while flagrantly violated after Redemption, planted the seeds of future struggle.

Certainly, in terms of the sense of possibility with which it opened, Reconstruction failed. But as Du Bois observed, it was a "splendid failure." For its animating vision—a society in which social advancement would be open to all on the basis of individual merit, not inherited caste distinctions—is as old as America itself and remains relevant to a nation still grappling with the unresolved legacy of emancipation.

October 1983